NES

Health
Secrets Study Guide

DEAR FUTURE EXAM SUCCESS STORY

First of all, **THANK YOU** for purchasing Mometrix study materials!

Second, congratulations! You are one of the few determined test-takers who are committed to doing whatever it takes to excel on your exam. **You have come to the right place.** We developed these study materials with one goal in mind: to deliver you the information you need in a format that's concise and easy to use.

In addition to optimizing your guide for the content of the test, we've outlined our recommended steps for breaking down the preparation process into small, attainable goals so you can make sure you stay on track.

We've also analyzed the entire test-taking process, identifying the most common pitfalls and showing how you can overcome them and be ready for any curveball the test throws you.

Standardized testing is one of the biggest obstacles on your road to success, which only increases the importance of doing well in the high-pressure, high-stakes environment of test day. Your results on this test could have a significant impact on your future, and this guide provides the information and practical advice to help you achieve your full potential on test day.

Your success is our success

We would love to hear from you! If you would like to share the story of your exam success or if you have any questions or comments in regard to our products, please contact us at **800-673-8175** or **support@mometrix.com**.

Thanks again for your business and we wish you continued success!

Sincerely,
The Mometrix Test Preparation Team

Need more help? Check out our flashcards at:
http://MometrixFlashcards.com/NESINC

TABLE OF CONTENTS

Introduction

Thank you for purchasing this resource! You have made the choice to prepare yourself for a test that could have a huge impact on your future, and this guide is designed to help you be fully ready for test day. Obviously, it's important to have a solid understanding of the test material, but you also need to be prepared for the unique environment and stressors of the test, so that you can perform to the best of your abilities.

For this purpose, the first section that appears in this guide is the **Secret Keys**. We've devoted countless hours to meticulously researching what works and what doesn't, and we've boiled down our findings to the five most impactful steps you can take to improve your performance on the test. We start at the beginning with study planning and move through the preparation process, all the way to the testing strategies that will help you get the most out of what you know when you're finally sitting in front of the test.

We recommend that you start preparing for your test as far in advance as possible. However, if you've bought this guide as a last-minute study resource and only have a few days before your test, we recommend that you skip over the first two Secret Keys since they address a long-term study plan.

If you struggle with **test anxiety**, we strongly encourage you to check out our recommendations for how you can overcome it. Test anxiety is a formidable foe, but it can be beaten, and we want to make sure you have the tools you need to defeat it.

1

Secret Key #1 – Plan Big, Study Small

There's a lot riding on your performance. If you want to ace this test, you're going to need to keep your skills sharp and the material fresh in your mind. You need a plan that lets you review everything you need to know while still fitting in your schedule. We'll break this strategy down into three categories.

Information Organization

Start with the information you already have: the official test outline. From this, you can make a complete list of all the concepts you need to cover before the test. Organize these concepts into groups that can be studied together, and create a list of any related vocabulary you need to learn so you can brush up on any difficult terms. You'll want to keep this vocabulary list handy once you actually start studying since you may need to add to it along the way.

Time Management

Once you have your set of study concepts, decide how to spread them out over the time you have left before the test. Break your study plan into small, clear goals so you have a manageable task for each day and know exactly what you're doing. Then just focus on one small step at a time. When you manage your time this way, you don't need to spend hours at a time studying. Studying a small block of content for a short period each day helps you retain information better and avoid stressing over how much you have left to do. You can relax knowing that you have a plan to cover everything in time. In order for this strategy to be effective though, you have to start studying early and stick to your schedule. Avoid the exhaustion and futility that comes from last-minute cramming!

Study Environment

The environment you study in has a big impact on your learning. Studying in a coffee shop, while probably more enjoyable, is not likely to be as fruitful as studying in a quiet room. It's important to keep distractions to a minimum. You're only planning to study for a short block of time, so make the most of it. Don't pause to check your phone or get up to find a snack. It's also important to **avoid multitasking**. Research has consistently shown that multitasking will make your studying dramatically less effective. Your study area should also be comfortable and well-lit so you don't have the distraction of straining your eyes or sitting on an uncomfortable chair.

 The time of day you study is also important. You want to be rested and alert. Don't wait until just before bedtime. Study when you'll be most likely to comprehend and remember. Even better, if you know what time of day your test will be, set that time aside for study. That way your brain will be used to working on that subject at that specific time and you'll have a better chance of recalling information.

Finally, it can be helpful to team up with others who are studying for the same test. Your actual studying should be done in as isolated an environment as possible, but the work of organizing the information and setting up the study plan can be divided up. In between study sessions, you can discuss with your teammates the concepts that you're all studying and quiz each other on the details. Just be sure that your teammates are as serious about the test as you are. If you find that your study time is being replaced with social time, you might need to find a new team.

Secret Key #2 – Make Your Studying Count

You're devoting a lot of time and effort to preparing for this test, so you want to be absolutely certain it will pay off. This means doing more than just reading the content and hoping you can remember it on test day. It's important to make every minute of study count. There are two main areas you can focus on to make your studying count.

Retention

It doesn't matter how much time you study if you can't remember the material. You need to make sure you are retaining the concepts. To check your retention of the information you're learning, try recalling it at later times with minimal prompting. Try carrying around flashcards and glance at one or two from time to time or ask a friend who's also studying for the test to quiz you.

To enhance your retention, look for ways to put the information into practice so that you can apply it rather than simply recalling it. If you're using the information in practical ways, it will be much easier to remember. Similarly, it helps to solidify a concept in your mind if you're not only reading it to yourself but also explaining it to someone else. Ask a friend to let you teach them about a concept you're a little shaky on (or speak aloud to an imaginary audience if necessary). As you try to summarize, define, give examples, and answer your friend's questions, you'll understand the concepts better and they will stay with you longer. Finally, step back for a big picture view and ask yourself how each piece of information fits with the whole subject. When you link the different concepts together and see them working together as a whole, it's easier to remember the individual components.

Finally, practice showing your work on any multi-step problems, even if you're just studying. Writing out each step you take to solve a problem will help solidify the process in your mind, and you'll be more likely to remember it during the test.

Modality

Modality simply refers to the means or method by which you study. Choosing a study modality that fits your own individual learning style is crucial. No two people learn best in exactly the same way, so it's important to know your strengths and use them to your advantage.

For example, if you learn best by visualization, focus on visualizing a concept in your mind and draw an image or a diagram. Try color-coding your notes, illustrating them, or creating symbols that will trigger your mind to recall a learned concept. If you learn best by hearing or discussing information, find a study partner who learns the same way or read aloud to yourself. Think about how to put the information in your own words. Imagine that you are giving a lecture on the topic and record yourself so you can listen to it later.

For any learning style, flashcards can be helpful. Organize the information so you can take advantage of spare moments to review. Underline key words or phrases. Use different colors for different categories. Mnemonic devices (such as creating a short list in which every item starts with the same letter) can also help with retention. Find what works best for you and use it to store the information in your mind most effectively and easily.

3

Secret Key #3 – Practice the Right Way

Your success on test day depends not only on how many hours you put into preparing, but also on whether you prepared the right way. It's good to check along the way to see if your studying is paying off. One of the most effective ways to do this is by taking practice tests to evaluate your progress. Practice tests are useful because they show exactly where you need to improve. Every time you take a practice test, pay special attention to these three groups of questions:

- The questions you got wrong
- The questions you had to guess on, even if you guessed right
- The questions you found difficult or slow to work through

This will show you exactly what your weak areas are, and where you need to devote more study time. Ask yourself why each of these questions gave you trouble. Was it because you didn't understand the material? Was it because you didn't remember the vocabulary? Do you need more repetitions on this type of question to build speed and confidence? Dig into those questions and figure out how you can strengthen your weak areas as you go back to review the material.

 Additionally, many practice tests have a section explaining the answer choices. It can be tempting to read the explanation and think that you now have a good understanding of the concept. However, an explanation likely only covers part of the question's broader context. Even if the explanation makes perfect sense, **go back and investigate** every concept related to the question until you're positive you have a thorough understanding.

As you go along, keep in mind that the practice test is just that: practice. Memorizing these questions and answers will not be very helpful on the actual test because it is unlikely to have any of the same exact questions. If you only know the right answers to the sample questions, you won't be prepared for the real thing. **Study the concepts** until you understand them fully, and then you'll be able to answer any question that shows up on the test.

It's important to wait on the practice tests until you're ready. If you take a test on your first day of study, you may be overwhelmed by the amount of material covered and how much you need to learn. Work up to it gradually.

On test day, you'll need to be prepared for answering questions, managing your time, and using the test-taking strategies you've learned. It's a lot to balance, like a mental marathon that will have a big impact on your future. Like training for a marathon, you'll need to start slowly and work your way up. When test day arrives, you'll be ready.

Start with the strategies you've read in the first two Secret Keys—plan your course and study in the way that works best for you. If you have time, consider using multiple study resources to get different approaches to the same concepts. It can be helpful to see difficult concepts from more than one angle. Then find a good source for practice tests. Many times, the test website will suggest potential study resources or provide sample tests.

Practice Test Strategy

If you're able to find at least three practice tests, we recommend this strategy:

UNTIMED AND OPEN-BOOK PRACTICE

Take the first test with no time constraints and with your notes and study guide handy. Take your time and focus on applying the strategies you've learned.

TIMED AND OPEN-BOOK PRACTICE

Take the second practice test open-book as well, but set a timer and practice pacing yourself to finish in time.

TIMED AND CLOSED-BOOK PRACTICE

Take any other practice tests as if it were test day. Set a timer and put away your study materials. Sit at a table or desk in a quiet room, imagine yourself at the testing center, and answer questions as quickly and accurately as possible.

Keep repeating timed and closed-book tests on a regular basis until you run out of practice tests or it's time for the actual test. Your mind will be ready for the schedule and stress of test day, and you'll be able to focus on recalling the material you've learned.

Secret Key #4 – Pace Yourself

Once you're fully prepared for the material on the test, your biggest challenge on test day will be managing your time. Just knowing that the clock is ticking can make you panic even if you have plenty of time left. Work on pacing yourself so you can build confidence against the time constraints of the exam. Pacing is a difficult skill to master, especially in a high-pressure environment, so **practice is vital**.

Set time expectations for your pace based on how much time is available. For example, if a section has 60 questions and the time limit is 30 minutes, you know you have to average 30 seconds or less per question in order to answer them all. Although 30 seconds is the hard limit, set 25 seconds per question as your goal, so you reserve extra time to spend on harder questions. When you budget extra time for the harder questions, you no longer have any reason to stress when those questions take longer to answer.

Don't let this time expectation distract you from working through the test at a calm, steady pace, but keep it in mind so you don't spend too much time on any one question. Recognize that taking extra time on one question you don't understand may keep you from answering two that you do understand later in the test. If your time limit for a question is up and you're still not sure of the answer, mark it and move on, and come back to it later if the time and the test format allow. If the testing format doesn't allow you to return to earlier questions, just make an educated guess; then put it out of your mind and move on.

On the easier questions, be careful not to rush. It may seem wise to hurry through them so you have more time for the challenging ones, but it's not worth missing one if you know the concept and just didn't take the time to read the question fully. Work efficiently but make sure you understand the question and have looked at all of the answer choices, since more than one may seem right at first.

Even if you're paying attention to the time, you may find yourself a little behind at some point. You should speed up to get back on track, but do so wisely. Don't panic; just take a few seconds less on each question until you're caught up. Don't guess without thinking, but do look through the answer choices and eliminate any you know are wrong. If you can get down to two choices, it is often worthwhile to guess from those. Once you've chosen an answer, move on and don't dwell on any that you skipped or had to hurry through. If a question was taking too long, chances are it was one of the harder ones, so you weren't as likely to get it right anyway.

On the other hand, if you find yourself getting ahead of schedule, it may be beneficial to slow down a little. The more quickly you work, the more likely you are to make a careless mistake that will affect your score. You've budgeted time for each question, so don't be afraid to spend that time. Practice an efficient but careful pace to get the most out of the time you have.

Secret Key #5 – Have a Plan for Guessing

When you're taking the test, you may find yourself stuck on a question. Some of the answer choices seem better than others, but you don't see the one answer choice that is obviously correct. What do you do?

The scenario described above is very common, yet most test takers have not effectively prepared for it. Developing and practicing a plan for guessing may be one of the single most effective uses of your time as you get ready for the exam.

In developing your plan for guessing, there are three questions to address:

- When should you start the guessing process?
- How should you narrow down the choices?
- Which answer should you choose?

When to Start the Guessing Process

Unless your plan for guessing is to select C every time (which, despite its merits, is not what we recommend), you need to leave yourself enough time to apply your answer elimination strategies. Since you have a limited amount of time for each question, that means that if you're going to give yourself the best shot at guessing correctly, you have to decide quickly whether or not you will guess.

Of course, the best-case scenario is that you don't have to guess at all, so first, see if you can answer the question based on your knowledge of the subject and basic reasoning skills. Focus on the key words in the question and try to jog your memory of related topics. Give yourself a chance to bring the knowledge to mind, but once you realize that you don't have (or you can't access) the knowledge you need to answer the question, it's time to start the guessing process.

It's almost always better to start the guessing process too early than too late. It only takes a few seconds to remember something and answer the question from knowledge. Carefully eliminating wrong answer choices takes longer. Plus, going through the process of eliminating answer choices can actually help jog your memory.

Summary: Start the guessing process as soon as you decide that you can't answer the question based on your knowledge.

How to Narrow Down the Choices

The next chapter in this book (**Test-Taking Strategies**) includes a wide range of strategies for how to approach questions and how to look for answer choices to eliminate. You will definitely want to read those carefully, practice them, and figure out which ones work best for you. Here though, we're going to address a mindset rather than a particular strategy.

Your odds of guessing an answer correctly depend on how many options you are choosing from.

Number of options left	5	4	3	2	1
Odds of guessing correctly	20%	25%	33%	50%	100%

You can see from this chart just how valuable it is to be able to eliminate incorrect answers and make an educated guess, but there are two things that many test takers do that cause them to miss out on the benefits of guessing:

- Accidentally eliminating the correct answer
- Selecting an answer based on an impression

We'll look at the first one here, and the second one in the next section.

To avoid accidentally eliminating the correct answer, we recommend a thought exercise called **the $5 challenge**. In this challenge, you only eliminate an answer choice from contention if you are willing to bet $5 on it being wrong. Why $5? Five dollars is a small but not insignificant amount of money. It's an amount you could afford to lose but wouldn't want to throw away. And while losing

$5 once might not hurt too much, doing it twenty times will set you back $100. In the same way, each small decision you make—eliminating a choice here, guessing on a question there—won't by itself impact your score very much, but when you put them all together, they can make a big difference. By holding each answer choice elimination decision to a higher standard, you can reduce the risk of accidentally eliminating the correct answer.

The $5 challenge can also be applied in a positive sense: If you are willing to bet $5 that an answer choice *is* correct, go ahead and mark it as correct.

Summary: Only eliminate an answer choice if you are willing to bet $5 that it is wrong.

Which Answer to Choose

You're taking the test. You've run into a hard question and decided you'll have to guess. You've eliminated all the answer choices you're willing to bet $5 on. Now you have to pick an answer. Why do we even need to talk about this? Why can't you just pick whichever one you feel like when the time comes?

The answer to these questions is that if you don't come into the test with a plan, you'll rely on your impression to select an answer choice, and if you do that, you risk falling into a trap. The test writers know that everyone who takes their test will be guessing on some of the questions, so they intentionally write wrong answer choices to seem plausible. You still have to pick an answer though, and if the wrong answer choices are designed to look right, how can you ever be sure that you're not falling for their trap? The best solution we've found to this dilemma is to take the decision out of your hands entirely. Here is the process we recommend:

Once you've eliminated any choices that you are confident (willing to bet $5) are wrong, select the first remaining choice as your answer.

Whether you choose to select the first remaining choice, the second, or the last, the important thing is that you use some preselected standard. Using this approach guarantees that you will not be enticed into selecting an answer choice that looks right, because you are not basing your decision on how the answer choices look.

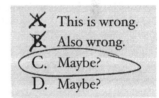

This is not meant to make you question your knowledge. Instead, it is to help you recognize the difference between your knowledge and your impressions. There's a huge difference between thinking an answer is right because of what you know, and thinking an answer is right because it looks or sounds like it should be right.

Summary: To ensure that your selection is appropriately random, make a predetermined selection from among all answer choices you have not eliminated.

Test-Taking Strategies

This section contains a list of test-taking strategies that you may find helpful as you work through the test. By taking what you know and applying logical thought, you can maximize your chances of answering any question correctly!

It is very important to realize that every question is different and every person is different: no single strategy will work on every question, and no single strategy will work for every person. That's why we've included all of them here, so you can try them out and determine which ones work best for different types of questions and which ones work best for you.

Question Strategies

⊘ READ CAREFULLY

Read the question and the answer choices carefully. Don't miss the question because you misread the terms. You have plenty of time to read each question thoroughly and make sure you understand what is being asked. Yet a happy medium must be attained, so don't waste too much time. You must read carefully and efficiently.

⊘ CONTEXTUAL CLUES

Look for contextual clues. If the question includes a word you are not familiar with, look at the immediate context for some indication of what the word might mean. Contextual clues can often give you all the information you need to decipher the meaning of an unfamiliar word. Even if you can't determine the meaning, you may be able to narrow down the possibilities enough to make a solid guess at the answer to the question.

⊘ PREFIXES

If you're having trouble with a word in the question or answer choices, try dissecting it. Take advantage of every clue that the word might include. Prefixes can be a huge help. Usually, they allow you to determine a basic meaning. *Pre-* means before, *post-* means after, *pro-* is positive, *de-* is negative. From prefixes, you can get an idea of the general meaning of the word and try to put it into context.

⊘ HEDGE WORDS

Watch out for critical hedge words, such as *likely, may, can, sometimes, often, almost, mostly, usually, generally, rarely,* and *sometimes.* Question writers insert these hedge phrases to cover every possibility. Often an answer choice will be wrong simply because it leaves no room for exception. Be on guard for answer choices that have definitive words such as *exactly* and *always.*

⊘ SWITCHBACK WORDS

Stay alert for *switchbacks.* These are the words and phrases frequently used to alert you to shifts in thought. The most common switchback words are *but, although,* and *however.* Others include *nevertheless, on the other hand, even though, while, in spite of, despite,* and *regardless of.* Switchback words are important to catch because they can change the direction of the question or an answer choice.

10

⊘ Face Value

When in doubt, use common sense. Accept the situation in the problem at face value. Don't read too much into it. These problems will not require you to make wild assumptions. If you have to go beyond creativity and warp time or space in order to have an answer choice fit the question, then you should move on and consider the other answer choices. These are normal problems rooted in reality. The applicable relationship or explanation may not be readily apparent, but it is there for you to figure out. Use your common sense to interpret anything that isn't clear.

Answer Choice Strategies

⊘ Answer Selection

The most thorough way to pick an answer choice is to identify and eliminate wrong answers until only one is left, then confirm it is the correct answer. Sometimes an answer choice may immediately seem right, but be careful. The test writers will usually put more than one reasonable answer choice on each question, so take a second to read all of them and make sure that the other choices are not equally obvious. As long as you have time left, it is better to read every answer choice than to pick the first one that looks right without checking the others.

⊘ Answer Choice Families

An answer choice family consists of two (in rare cases, three) answer choices that are very similar in construction and cannot all be true at the same time. If you see two answer choices that are direct opposites or parallels, one of them is usually the correct answer. For instance, if one answer choice says that quantity x increases and another either says that quantity x decreases (opposite) or says that quantity y increases (parallel), then those answer choices would fall into the same family. An answer choice that doesn't match the construction of the answer choice family is more likely to be incorrect. Most questions will not have answer choice families, but when they do appear, you should be prepared to recognize them.

⊘ Eliminate Answers

Eliminate answer choices as soon as you realize they are wrong, but make sure you consider all possibilities. If you are eliminating answer choices and realize that the last one you are left with is also wrong, don't panic. Start over and consider each choice again. There may be something you missed the first time that you will realize on the second pass.

⊘ Avoid Fact Traps

Don't be distracted by an answer choice that is factually true but doesn't answer the question. You are looking for the choice that answers the question. Stay focused on what the question is asking for so you don't accidentally pick an answer that is true but incorrect. Always go back to the question and make sure the answer choice you've selected actually answers the question and is not merely a true statement.

⊘ Extreme Statements

In general, you should avoid answers that put forth extreme actions as standard practice or proclaim controversial ideas as established fact. An answer choice that states the "process should be used in certain situations, if..." is much more likely to be correct than one that states the "process should be discontinued completely." The first is a calm rational statement and doesn't even make a definitive, uncompromising stance, using a hedge word *if* to provide wiggle room, whereas the second choice is far more extreme.

11

⊘ BENCHMARK

As you read through the answer choices and you come across one that seems to answer the question well, mentally select that answer choice. This is not your final answer, but it's the one that will help you evaluate the other answer choices. The one that you selected is your benchmark or standard for judging each of the other answer choices. Every other answer choice must be compared to your benchmark. That choice is correct until proven otherwise by another answer choice beating it. If you find a better answer, then that one becomes your new benchmark. Once you've decided that no other choice answers the question as well as your benchmark, you have your final answer.

⊘ PREDICT THE ANSWER

Before you even start looking at the answer choices, it is often best to try to predict the answer. When you come up with the answer on your own, it is easier to avoid distractions and traps because you will know exactly what to look for. The right answer choice is unlikely to be word-for-word what you came up with, but it should be a close match. Even if you are confident that you have the right answer, you should still take the time to read each option before moving on.

General Strategies

⊘ TOUGH QUESTIONS

If you are stumped on a problem or it appears too hard or too difficult, don't waste time. Move on! Remember though, if you can quickly check for obviously incorrect answer choices, your chances of guessing correctly are greatly improved. Before you completely give up, at least try to knock out a couple of possible answers. Eliminate what you can and then guess at the remaining answer choices before moving on.

⊘ CHECK YOUR WORK

Since you will probably not know every term listed and the answer to every question, it is important that you get credit for the ones that you do know. Don't miss any questions through careless mistakes. If at all possible, try to take a second to look back over your answer selection and make sure you've selected the correct answer choice and haven't made a costly careless mistake (such as marking an answer choice that you didn't mean to mark). This quick double check should more than pay for itself in caught mistakes for the time it costs.

⊘ PACE YOURSELF

It's easy to be overwhelmed when you're looking at a page full of questions; your mind is confused and full of random thoughts, and the clock is ticking down faster than you would like. Calm down and maintain the pace that you have set for yourself. Especially as you get down to the last few minutes of the test, don't let the small numbers on the clock make you panic. As long as you are on track by monitoring your pace, you are guaranteed to have time for each question.

⊘ DON'T RUSH

It is very easy to make errors when you are in a hurry. Maintaining a fast pace in answering questions is pointless if it makes you miss questions that you would have gotten right otherwise. Test writers like to include distracting information and wrong answers that seem right. Taking a little extra time to avoid careless mistakes can make all the difference in your test score. Find a pace that allows you to be confident in the answers that you select.

⊘ Keep Moving

Panicking will not help you pass the test, so do your best to stay calm and keep moving. Taking deep breaths and going through the answer elimination steps you practiced can help to break through a stress barrier and keep your pace.

Final Notes

The combination of a solid foundation of content knowledge and the confidence that comes from practicing your plan for applying that knowledge is the key to maximizing your performance on test day. As your foundation of content knowledge is built up and strengthened, you'll find that the strategies included in this chapter become more and more effective in helping you quickly sift through the distractions and traps of the test to isolate the correct answer.

Now that you're preparing to move forward into the test content chapters of this book, be sure to keep your goal in mind. As you read, think about how you will be able to apply this information on the test. If you've already seen sample questions for the test and you have an idea of the question format and style, try to come up with questions of your own that you can answer based on what you're reading. This will give you valuable practice applying your knowledge in the same ways you can expect to on test day.

Good luck and good studying!

14

Health Promotion and Disease Prevention

Anatomy and Physiology

BODY SYSTEMS

Functions of the human body can be divided into the following body systems:

- **Cardiovascular**: Pumps blood throughout the body via the heart and blood vessels
- **Digestive**: Transforms food into energy and eliminates solid waste
- **Endocrine**: Releases hormones into the bloodstream to control metabolism, growth, and reproduction
- **Immune**: Defends against all foreign substances
- **Integumentary**: Skin prevents moisture loss, regulates temperature, protects from sunburn, and senses pain, pressure, touch, hot and cold
- **Musculoskeletal**: Skeletal muscles move the body, smooth muscles control the physical functioning of internal organs, and cardiac muscle pumps blood. The skeleton supports and shapes, protects internal organs, stores minerals, and produces blood cells
- **Nervous**: Controls movement, memory, and senses and communicates with the outside world
- **Reproductive**: Allows continuation of the human species through reproduction and childbearing and differentiates the sexes
- **Respiratory**: Regulates gas exchange (oxygen intake and carbon dioxide expulsion)
- **Urinary**: Removes waste and toxins from the blood and expels them from the body through urine

CARDIOVASCULAR SYSTEM

The cardiovascular system controls blood flow throughout the body and to the tissues, controls gas exchange (carbon dioxide and oxygen) by transporting oxygenated blood from the lungs, serves as a reservoir for blood, maintains blood pH through a buffer system, responds to infections, and facilitates coagulation (blood clotting). The cardiovascular system has the following components:

- **Heart**: The heart has four chambers, two upper (right atrium, left atrium) and two lower (right ventricle and left ventricle). The heart muscle receives blood from four major coronary arteries (right, left main, left anterior descending, and left circumflex) and their branches, and then distributes blood via the aorta and pulmonary arteries.
- **Vessels**: The venous system includes veins, venules, and venous capillaries and returns blood back to the heart via the inferior and superior vena cava. The arterial system, (including the coronary arteries) branches from the aorta after it leaves the heart and includes arteries, arterioles, and arterial capillaries.
- **Blood**: Blood consists of red blood cells (erythrocytes), white blood cells (leukocytes including monocytes, lymphocytes, basophils, neutrophils, and eosinophils), platelets (thrombocytes), and plasma, the liquid portion of the blood (which contains clotting factors). Blood carries oxygen from the lungs and distributes it to the rest of the body.

The cardiovascular system is responsible for oxygenation of cells, perfusion (carrying of blood with oxygen, glucose, and nutrients to cells) and removing waste products, such as carbon dioxide.

ANATOMY OF THE HEART

The human heart is about the size of a fist and weighs 7–15 ounces. It is located in the middle of the chest, behind the sternum, and leans slightly left. The heart is covered by a double-layered membrane called the **pericardium**. The outer layer, called the parietal pericardium, is fibrous and surrounds the roots of the major blood vessels of the heart. The inner layer, called the visceral pericardium, is attached to and covers the heart muscle. The two layers of membrane are separated by fluid. The heart itself has **four connecting chambers**. The two upper chambers are the **right atria and left atria**; the lower chambers are the **left ventricle and right ventricle**. The left and right atria and the left and right ventricle are separated by a muscular structure called the septum.

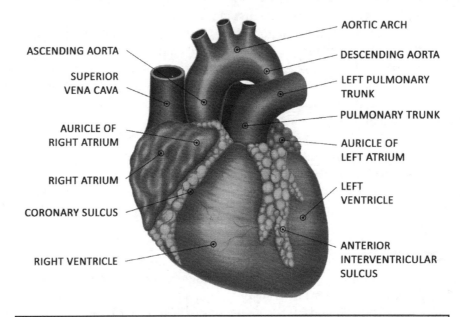

HEART'S CONDUCTION SYSTEM

The **sinoatrial node (SA)** is referred to as the pacemaker of the heart because electrical impulses normally originate in the SA, within the wall of the right atrium. The SA produces electrical impulses that are transmitted to the **atrioventricular node (AV)** by specialized conducting tissue. The AV node is found between the atria and ventricles. From here, the electrical impulse is relayed down the conducting tissue called the Bundle of His. The **Bundle of His** splits into a right bundle branch (RBB) and a left bundle branch (LBB), which serve the right and left ventricles, respectively, through both sides of the intraventricular septum. The bundle branches then split to form the **Purkinje fibers**, which transmit electrical impulses to the myocardium.

A **normal sinus rhythm** on an EKG (the expected result in a healthy individual) denotes that the electrical impulses start in the sinoatrial node (SA) first. The intrinsic rate of the SA node is 60–100 beats per minute (bpm), which reflects the normal range for an adult's pulse rate. If the SA node does not initiate the electrical impulse, the atrioventricular node (AV) can do so. However, the AV node is not as capable of increasing the heart rate, with an intrinsic rate of only 40-60 beats per minute. The patient may require a pacemaker to address the slow heart rate. All of the cells of the heart are capable of generating the electrical impulses necessary to trigger a heartbeat (automaticity). Signal conduction problems (block) can occur at any site along the conduction pathway, causing alterations in the normal rhythm (arrhythmia).

HEART VALVES AND BLOOD FLOW

Four heart valves regulate the flow of blood through the heart.

- The **tricuspid valve** controls the flow of deoxygenated blood from the right atrium to the right ventricle.
- The **pulmonary semilunar valve** controls the flow of blood from the right ventricle to the pulmonary artery. The pulmonary artery carries the blood into the lungs where it is oxygenated.
- The blood then flows through the pulmonary vein back to the heart, and the **mitral valve** controls the flow of the now oxygenated blood from the left atrium to the left ventricle.
- The **aortic semilunar valve** regulates blood flow from the left ventricle to the aorta. From the aorta, the oxygenated blood is conducted to the rest of the body. The deoxygenated blood travels through the venules, then the veins, and then the inferior vena cava and superior vena cava back to the right atrium.

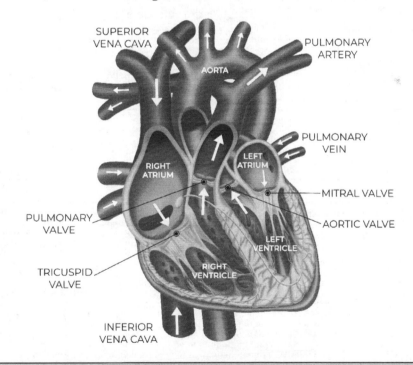

Review Video: **Heart Blood Flow**
Visit mometrix.com/academy and enter code: 783139

ENDOCRINE SYSTEM

The major glands that comprise the endocrine system, the hormones they secrete, and diseases resulting from their dysfunction include the following:

Gland	Hormones	Disease
Adrenal Cortex	Aldosterone Cortisol Androgens	Addison's Disease Cushing's Disease
Adrenal Medulla	Epinephrine Norepinephrine	Anxiety Attacks Depression
Anterior Pituitary	Adrenocorticotropic hormone (ACTH) Follicle-stimulating hormone (FSH) Gonadotropic hormones Growth hormone (GH) Luteinizing hormone (LH) Prolactin Thyroid Stimulating Hormone (TSH)	Dwarfism Gigantism
Hypothalamus/ Posterior Pituitary	Inhibiting hormones (stop the release of other hormones) Antidiuretic hormone (ADH) Oxytocin Releasing hormones (trigger the release of other hormones)	Diabetes Insipidus
Kidneys	Calcitriol Erythropoietin	Hypertension
Ovaries	Estrogen Progesterone	Endometriosis Menometrorrhagia
Pancreas	Insulin Glucagon	Diabetes Mellitus
Parathyroid	Parathyroid hormone	Tetany Renal calculi
Pineal	Melatonin	Alzheimer's Disease
Testes	Testosterone	Gynecomastia Klinefelter Syndrome
Thymus	Thymic factor (TF) Thymosin Thymic humoral factor (THF) Thymopoietin	DiGeorge Syndrome
Thyroid	Calcitonin Thyroxine (T4) Triiodothyronine (T3)	Cretinism Hypo/Hyperthyroidism Goiter Myxedema
Digestive tract	Gastrin Cholecystokinin Secretin Ghrelin Motilin	Gastritis Gastroesophageal reflux

MAJOR ENDOCRINE GLANDS

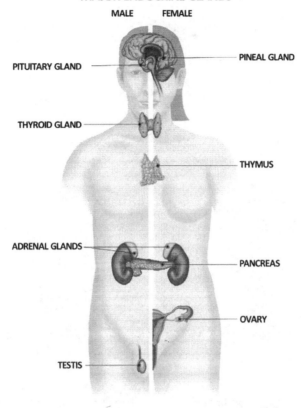

MALE   FEMALE

PITUITARY GLAND

PINEAL GLAND

THYROID GLAND

THYMUS

ADRENAL GLANDS

PANCREAS

OVARY

TESTIS

GASTROINTESTINAL SYSTEM

DIGESTIVE TRACT

The gastrointestinal tract (GI tract) is divided into upper and lower sections:

- The **upper GI tract** consists of the mouth (buccal mucosa, tongue, and teeth), pharynx, esophagus, and stomach.
- The **lower GI tract** is comprised of the small intestine (duodenum, jejunum, ileum, and ileocecal valve) and the large intestine (ascending, transverse, and descending colon, sigmoid flexure, rectum, and anus).

The vermiform appendix is attached to the cecum, the first section of the ascending colon, closest to the ileocecal valve. The sigmoid flexure leads into the rectum, which terminates in the anus. An internal and external sphincter control the anus. The liver, gall bladder, and pancreas secrete digestive enzymes into the GI tract through various ducts that aide in the breaking down of food and absorption of nutrients.

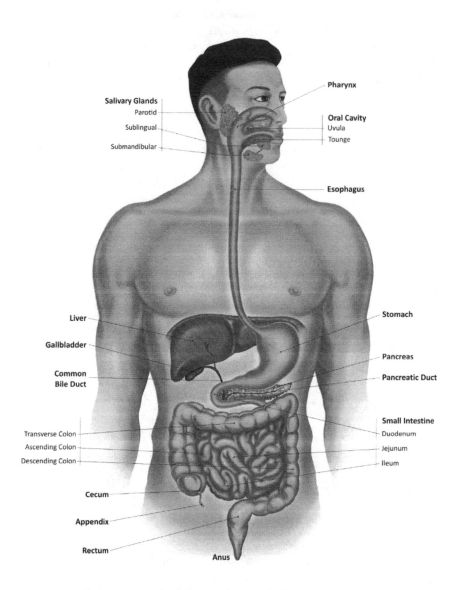

FUNCTIONS

The gastrointestinal tract is a system of organs responsible for the:

- Ingestion of food
- Digestion of food
- Absorption of nutrients and medications
- Production of Vitamins B_{12} and K
- Elimination of waste products

The process begins at the mouth with ingestion and ends at the anus with excretion. The GI tract breaks down and reabsorbs nutrients using ptyalin in the mouth, hydrochloric acid in the stomach,

20

bile from the gall bladder, and insulin, glucagon, amylase, lipase, and other chemicals from the pancreas. Food is digested into slurry in the stomach, where B_{12} is manufactured to prevent anemia. The small intestine absorbs nutrients. The large intestine (colon) reabsorbs water and salts and turns semi-liquid waste matter into firm, formed stools. Bacteria, normally found in the large intestine, produce Vitamin K, necessary for blood clotting. Fecal waste matter is held temporarily in the rectum and expelled by the anus.

ACCESSORY ORGANS OF DIGESTION

The accessory organs of digestion include the liver, the gallbladder, and the pancreas. The liver produces bile as a by-product of breaking down old red blood cells. The liver excretes bile into the small intestine to break up fatty foods by way of the biliary system. The gallbladder's only function is to store and concentrate bile, so if painful stones form in it, the gallbladder can be safely removed. The pancreas secretes hormones and excretes digestive enzymes, so it is both an endocrine and an exocrine gland. As an exocrine gland, the pancreas releases an isosmotic fluid into the small intestine containing the enzymes trypsin, chymotrypsin, lipase, pancreatic amylase, deoxyribonuclease, and ribonuclease. These enzymes break down proteins, fats, and starches. The pancreatic duct makes bicarbonate to decrease the acidity of the food slurry (chyle and chyme). As an endocrine gland, the pancreas regulates blood sugar with the hormone insulin, and the pancreas and liver regulate blood sugar with glucagon. The liver also metabolizes most drugs.

PASSAGE OF FOOD

The main parts of the digestive system in order of how food passes through them are as follows:

1. Digestion starts in the **mouth** with the action of saliva containing amylase to start starch digestion. The mouth also contains the hard and the soft palates.
2. The 20 primary or 32 permanent **teeth** are used for mastication of food.
3. The **tongue** holds the taste buds and moves the food towards the esophagus.
4. The **pharynx** connects the mouth to the esophagus. The **epiglottis** keeps food from entering the trachea. The pharynx is about 5" long.
5. The **esophagus** is a 12" tube leading to the stomach. Peristaltic waves start here and move food into the stomach.
6. The **stomach** sac is controlled by the lower esophageal sphincter (at the top) and the pyloric sphincter (at the bottom). Food mixes with hydrochloric acid in the stomach to make chyme. Food stays in the stomach for 2–4 hours.
7. The **small intestine** contains the duodenum (10"), jejunum (8'), and ileum (12'). The majority of digestion takes place in the duodenum. The small intestine receives bile, produced by the liver and stored in the gall bladder, to digest fats, and amylase and insulin from the pancreas to break down starches and sugars. Digestion in the small intestine can take between 3 and 10 hours.
8. The **large intestine** absorbs water and salts. The large intestine consists of the cecum (with vermiform appendix), ascending, transverse, descending, and sigmoid colon, the rectum, and anus for defecation. The ileocecal valve prevents food from reentering the small intestine.

Total digestion can take between 24 hours and 3 days.

HEMATOLOGIC SYSTEM

COMPONENTS

Blood is the liquid that moves through the circulatory system. The average adult has about 5 liters of blood. Bone marrow produces red blood cells (RBC or erythrocytes), white blood cells (WBC or leukocytes), and platelets (thrombocytes).

- **Red blood cells** transport oxygen and carbon dioxide, **white blood cells** fight infection, and **platelets** clot blood after an injury. These blood cells travel through the circulatory system suspended in plasma: 55% of blood is yellow, liquid plasma, and 45% is cells. **Blood plasma** carries nutrients, proteins, hormones, and waste products.
- White blood cells that absorb Wright stain are classified as **granulocytes**, because there are granules in the cytoplasm, and agranulocytes, with no granules present. There are three different kinds of granulocytes: neutrophils, basophils, and eosinophils. The **agranulocytes** include lymphocytes (T and B cells) and monocytes. Each type of WBC proliferates to combat a different type of pathogen. For example, increased eosinophils (eosinophilia) can indicate allergies, whereas increased monocytes (monocytosis) can indicate tuberculosis (TB).

RED BLOOD CELLS

A red blood cell **(erythrocyte, RBC)** is a doughnut-shaped raft that transports oxygen to cells through hemoglobin. The RBC offloads its oxygen, takes on carbon dioxide from the cells, and changes color, turning a bluish-purple. The RBC then returns to the lungs, where it takes on oxygen again during gas exchange. Red blood cells typically have a life span of 120 days and require the nutrients iron, protein, B_{12}, and folate. If a patient has too few erythrocytes from heavy bleeding or lacks the nutrients, then he or she is considered anemic.

PLATELETS

Platelets **(thrombocytes)** clot the blood when a vessel is damaged by converging on the area to seal the leak. Platelets have a life span of nine days and work in conjunction with clotting factors in the blood, the proteins that work with platelets to produce a clot. If a patient lacks a clotting factor, then the platelets alone are unable to seal an injury adequately. This occurs in hemophiliacs, who lack Factor VIII. This disease and others that lead to decreased platelets put individuals at high risk for bleeding. Bone marrow produces red blood cells and platelets daily to replace dead or lost circulating cells.

IMMUNE SYSTEM

The immune system is the body's main defender against disease. The immune system is comprised of the spleen, thymus, bone marrow, and a series of transparent tubes that run throughout the body, parallel to the blood vessels. The tubes are lymph vessels, and carry 4 liters of clear lymphatic fluid, or lymph. Lymph circulates throughout the body in the same manner as blood, with valves opening and closing to move the liquid along. There are hundreds of small glands, called lymph nodes, stationed at intervals along the lymphatic vessels. The lymphatic fluid carries invaders to the nodes to be destroyed by lymphocytes, a type of white blood cell. Antibodies are also found in lymphatic fluid. Nodes swell during infections. Plasma from the blood vessels seeps out of the capillaries, immerses body tissues, and then drains off into the lymph vessels. Once in the lymphatic system, the plasma is called lymph. Lymph travels through the lymphatic vessels until it reaches the thoracic duct, the largest lymph vessel, extending from L2 to the neck. The lymph drains from the thoracic duct into the blood and is then carried to the kidneys and liver by the cardiovascular system where the waste is removed.

THE COMPLEMENT SYSTEM

The complement system consists of proteins produced by the liver that work with an individual's antibodies to clear the body of pathogens. Complement proteins are a part of the immune system that burst (lyze) pathogens and alert the phagocytes that the dead pathogen must be removed. If the patient is hypersensitive, the complement system may work against its own body. An exaggerated inflammatory response may occur, called a cytokine storm. Young people are most prone to cytokine storm if they have pandemic influenza, rheumatoid arthritis, sepsis, bronchitis, bird flu, or pneumonia. Complications from the COVID-19 pandemic also included the overreaction of the immune system, leading to excessive fluid accumulation in the lungs and excessive clotting. In a cytokine storm, the complement system calls too many immune cells to defend the site of infection, which can cause the blockage of small arteries with clumped white cells (aggregate). The inflammatory response may be so extreme that gangrene develops in the fingers and toes or the patient dies from the cytokine storm.

WHITE BLOOD CELLS

The white blood cells of the immune system include the following:

WBC	Type	% of WBCs	Causes of Increase	Causes of Decrease
Basophils (black or purple)	Granulocyte	1%	Asthma, chronic myelocytic leukemia, Crohn's disease, dermatitis, estrogen, hemolytic anemia, Hodgkin's disease, hypothyroidism, polycythemia vera, and viruses	Allergies, corticosteroids, hyperthyroidism, pregnancy, and stress.
Eosinophils (orange-red, double-lobed nucleus)	Granulocyte	1-3%	Allergy, asthma, or parasitic infestation	Cushing's disease or glucocorticoids use
Lymphocytes (dark, large nucleus surrounded by thin cytoplasm rim)	Agranulocyte	15-40%	Antigens or chronic irritation	AIDS
Monocytes (lavender)	Agranulocyte	2-8%	Myeloproliferative process, like an inflammatory response or chronic myelomonocytic leukemia (CMML)	Hairy cell leukemia
Neutrophils (pink cytoplasm, dark nucleus)	Granulocyte	50-70%	Burns, kidney failure, heart attack, cancer, hemolytic anemia	Leukemia and abscess

Lymphocytes make proteins for immunoglobulins and cytokine production. Small B and T cells secrete antibodies and regulate the immune system. Large Natural Killer cells lyze tumors and virus-infected cells. Children, aged four months to four years, normally have inverted differential (relative neutropenia and increased lymphocytes). **Neutrophils** are phagocytic. A segmented nucleus (seg) indicates a mature cell. A banded nucleus (band) indicates an immature cell.

INTEGUMENTARY SYSTEM

The largest organ of the body is the skin, which forms the **integumentary system**, along with cutaneous glands, hair, and nails. It has three layers: epidermis, dermis, and hypodermis (subcutaneous or superficial fascia). The functions of the integumentary system are to:

- Excrete salts and nitrogenous wastes
- Metabolize vitamin D
- Prevent bacteria, parasites, and other invaders from entering the body
- Protect the body from chemicals
- Produce melanin as sunscreen
- Protect the body from water loss
- Regulate body temperature through perspiration, fat storage, and radiating heat from capillaries
- Serve as a sensory communication tool through temperature, touch, pain, and pressure receptors

Skin can be damaged by chemicals, sharp or blunt instruments, heat, friction, pressure and radiation. Among the injuries that can happen to the skin are abrasions, burns, contusions, crushing injuries, decubitus ulcers (bedsores), gunshots, hematomas, incisions, lacerations, and punctures.

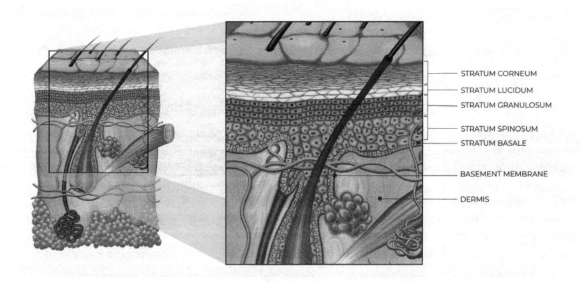

Review Video: Integumentary System
Visit mometrix.com/academy and enter code: 655980

MUSCULOSKELETAL SYSTEM

BONES AND JOINTS

The bones of the musculoskeletal system include the following:

- **Head**: The cranium includes frontal (forehead), parietal (back), temporal (side), mandibular (lower jaw), maxillary (upper jaw), nasal conchae and septum (nose), and zygomatic (cheek) bones; the ear includes the malleus (hammer), incus (anvil) and stapes (stirrup) bones.
- **Spine**: Comprised of seven cervical (neck), 12 thoracic (upper back), and five lumbar (lower back) vertebrae, the sacrum, and the coccyx (tail bone).

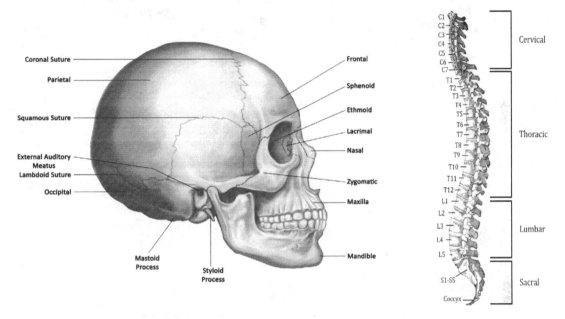

- **Chest**: Ribs, scapula (shoulder blade), and clavicle (collar bone).
- **Pelvis**: Ilium (upper), ischium (lower), and pubis (front).
- **Arms**: Humerus (upper), radius and ulna (forearm), carpals (wrist), metacarpals (hand), and phalanges (fingers).
- **Legs**: Femur (thigh), patella (knee), tibia and fibula (calf), tarsals (ankle), metatarsals (front foot), calcaneus (heel), and phalanges (toes).
- **Diarthrotic articulations**: Moveable joints with synovial fluid and cartilage cushions that are held together by ligaments, like the limbs.
- **Synarthrotic articulations**: Immovable joints, such as the spine and skull.

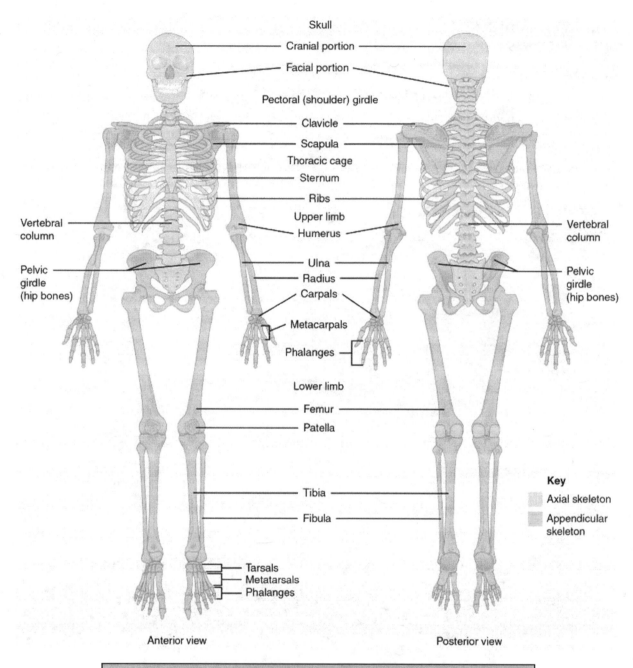

Anterior view   Posterior view

Key
Axial skeleton
Appendicular skeleton

Review Video: Skeletal System
Visit mometrix.com/academy and enter code: 256447

CARTILAGE AND LIGAMENTS

Cartilage is a dense connective tissue composed of collagen and/or elastin fibers on the end of bones, which provides a smooth surface for articulation by reducing friction.

- **Hyaline cartilage** contains chondrocytes that make it look glassy and is found in the nose, larynx, trachea, ribs, and sternum. Hyaline cartilage makes an embryo's skeleton.
- **Elastic cartilage** contains elastin, which makes it yellow, and is found in the outer ear (pinna) and epiglottis.

- **Fibrocartilage** is composed of strands of fibers that function to help limit movement and prevent bones from rubbing together. Fibrocartilage is found in the knee, the pubic bones in the pelvic region and between the vertebrae in the spine.

A **ligament** is a fibrous band composed of connective tissue stretching from one bone to another in a joint to provide lateral stability. Ligaments also connect cartilages and other structures. Injuries to ligaments are sprains, which are slow to heal and may require physiotherapy and surgery.

TENDONS

A tendon is also called a **sinew**, and connects muscle to bone. Tendons grow into the bone and make mineralized connections with the bone. Tendons transform muscle contraction into joint movement. Tendons can withstand great pressure, but tendons that tear do not heal well. A complete tear requires surgical repair. Damage to a tendon and its muscle in a joint is a strain. Tendonitis is inflammation of the tendon.

> **Review Video: Muscular System**
> Visit mometrix.com/academy and enter code: 967216

NERVOUS SYSTEM

The human nervous system is divided into the central nervous system (CNS) and the peripheral nervous system (PNS).

- The **CNS** is composed of the brain and spinal cord and is located in the dorsal cavity. The brain is protected by the skull, while the spinal cord is protected by the vertebrae.
- The **PNS** is made of those structures of the nervous system not contained in the dorsal cavity, such as long nerves (neuron axons). The PNS is divided into the somatic nervous system and the autonomic nervous system. The autonomic nervous system is further divided into the sympathetic nervous system and the parasympathetic nervous system.

> **Review Video: Nervous System**
> Visit mometrix.com/academy and enter code: 708428

SOMATIC NERVOUS SYSTEM

The somatic division of the peripheral nervous system is involved in the coordination of body movements. It is comprised of peripheral nerve fibers that receive sensory information and carry this information into the spinal cord. It also contains motor nerve fibers that connect to skeletal muscle. The somatic system employs an afferent nerve network to carry sensory information to the brain and an efferent nerve network with motor nerves that transmit information from the brain to the skeletal muscles. The somatic nervous system regulates activities that are under the individual's conscious control, processes sensory information, and executes voluntary movements. The somatic nervous system does not control reflex arcs.

AUTONOMIC NERVOUS SYSTEM

The **sympathetic division** of the peripheral nervous system is involved in the "fight-or-flight" response and is activated in times of danger or stress. Signs and symptoms of sympathetic stimulation are an increased heart rate (tachycardia), vasoconstriction and rise in blood pressure, dilation of the pupils (mydriasis), goose bumps on the skin (piloerection or cutis anserine), increased sweat secretion (diaphoresis), and feelings of excitement. These reactions are due to the release of adrenaline (epinephrine).

The **parasympathetic nervous system** is in charge when the individual feels relaxed or is resting. The parasympathetic system is responsible for constriction of the pupil, slowing of the heart rate, dilation of blood vessels, and stimulation of the digestive tract and genitourinary system. The neurotransmitter at work is acetylcholine.

DORSAL CAVITY

The dorsal cavity contains the brain and spinal cord, which are the organs of the central nervous system (CNS). Like the ventral cavity, the dorsal cavity is divided into two smaller cavities: the cranial cavity and the spinal cavity. The cranial cavity contains the brain, eyes, and ears, while the spinal cavity holds the spinal cord. The brain and spinal cord are covered by three layers of connective tissue called the meninges. The outermost layer is the dura mater; the middle layer is the arachnoid mater; and the innermost layer is the pia mater. The space between the arachnoid mater and the pia mater is filled with cerebrospinal fluid (CSF), which flows throughout the CNS. If an injured patient has clear yellow fluid leaking from the ears, nose, eyes, or mouth, it is probably CSF and indicates a skull fracture.

NEURONS

Neurons are nerve cells that transmit nerve impulses throughout the central and peripheral nervous systems. The basic structure of a neuron includes the cell body, the dendrites, and the axons. The **cell body**, also called the soma, contains the nucleus. The nucleus contains the chromosomes. The **dendrite** of the neuron extends from the cell body and resembles the branches of a tree. The dendrite receives chemical messages from other cells across the synapse, a small gap. The **axon** is a thread-like extension of the cell body, which varies in length, up to 3 feet in the case of spinal nerves. The axon transmits an electro-chemical message along its length to another cell. Peripheral nervous system (PNS) neurons that deal with muscles are myelinated with fatty Schwann cell insulation to speed up the transmission of messages. Gaps between the Schwann cells that expose the axon are **nodes of Ranvier** and increase the speed of the transmission of nerve impulses along the axon. Neurons in the PNS that deal with pain are unmyelinated because transmission does not have to be as fast. Some neurons in the central nervous system (CNS) are myelinated by oligodendrocytes. If the myelin in the CNS oligodendrocytes breaks down, the patient develops multiple sclerosis (MS).

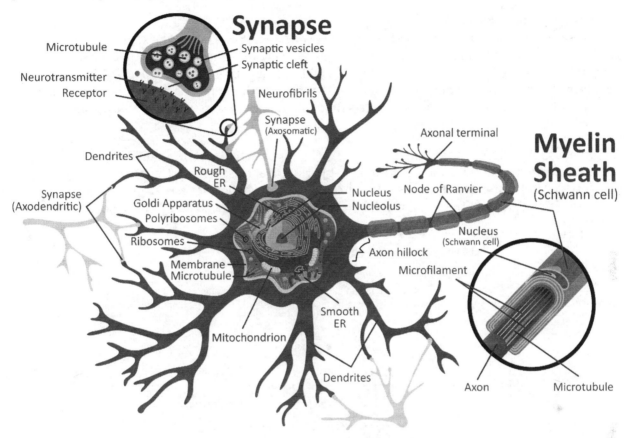

The three **categories of neurons** are as follows:

- **Afferent neurons** carry sensory impulses from the environment to the brain and spinal cord and are also called sensory neurons or receptor neurons. Afferent neurons are found in the skin, muscles, joints, and sensory organs. They permit the perception of pressure, pain, temperature, taste, odor, sound, and visual stimuli.
- **Efferent neurons** transmit motor impulses from the brain and spinal cord to effectors, such as muscles and glands. Efferent neurons are involved in motor control and stimulate movement throughout the body.
- **Interneurons** connect sensory and motor neurons. Also called connection neurons or relay neurons, interneurons are located in the CNS; sensory and motor neurons are found in both the CNS and PNS.

REPRODUCTIVE SYSTEM
MALE REPRODUCTIVE SYSTEM

The functions of the male reproductive system are to produce, maintain, and transfer **sperm** and **semen** into the female reproductive tract and to produce and secrete **male hormones**.

The external structure includes the penis, scrotum, and testes. The **penis**, which contains the **urethra**, can fill with blood and become erect, enabling the deposition of semen and sperm into the female reproductive tract during sexual intercourse. The **scrotum** is a sack of skin and smooth muscle that houses the testes and keeps the testes outside the body wall at a cooler, proper

29

temperature for **spermatogenesis**. The **testes**, or testicles, are the male gonads, which produce sperm and testosterone.

The internal structure includes the epididymis, vas deferens, ejaculatory ducts, urethra, seminal vesicles, prostate gland, and bulbourethral glands. The **epididymis** stores the sperm as it matures. Mature sperm moves from the epididymis through the **vas deferens** to the **ejaculatory duct**. The **seminal vesicles** secrete alkaline fluids with proteins and mucus into the ejaculatory duct also. The **prostate gland** secretes a milky white fluid with proteins and enzymes as part of the semen. The **bulbourethral**, or Cowper's, glands secrete a fluid into the urethra to neutralize the acidity in the urethra, which would damage sperm.

Additionally, the hormones associated with the male reproductive system include **follicle-stimulating hormone (FSH)**, which stimulates spermatogenesis; **luteinizing hormone (LH)**, which stimulates testosterone production; and **testosterone**, which is responsible for the male sex characteristics. FSH and LH are gonadotropins, which stimulate the gonads (male testes and female ovaries).

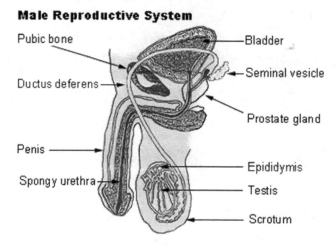

Male Reproductive System

FEMALE REPRODUCTIVE SYSTEM

The functions of the female reproductive system are to produce **ova** (oocytes or egg cells), transfer the ova to the **fallopian tubes** for fertilization, receive the sperm from the male, and provide a protective, nourishing environment for the developing **embryo**.

The external portion of the female reproductive system includes the labia majora, labia minora, Bartholin's glands, and clitoris. The **labia majora** and the **labia minora** enclose and protect the vagina. The **Bartholin's glands** secrete a lubricating fluid. The **clitoris** contains erectile tissue and nerve endings for sensual pleasure.

The internal portion of the female reproductive system includes the ovaries, fallopian tubes, uterus, and vagina. The **ovaries**, which are the female gonads, produce the ova and secrete **estrogen** and **progesterone**. The **fallopian tubes** carry the mature egg toward the uterus. Fertilization typically occurs in the fallopian tubes. If fertilized, the egg travels to the **uterus**, where it implants in the uterine wall. The uterus protects and nourishes the developing embryo until birth. The **vagina** is a muscular tube that extends from the **cervix** of the uterus to the outside of the body. The vagina receives the semen and sperm during sexual intercourse and provides a birth canal when needed.

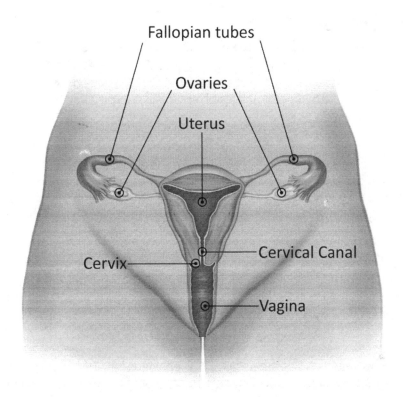

Fallopian tubes

Ovaries

Uterus

Cervical Canal

Cervix

Vagina

Review Video: Reproductive Systems
Visit mometrix.com/academy and enter code: 505450

FEMALE REPRODUCTIVE CYCLE

The female reproductive cycle is characterized by changes in both the ovaries and the uterine lining (endometrium).

The ovarian cycle has three phases: the follicular phase, ovulation, and the luteal phase. During the **follicular phase**, FSH stimulates the maturation of the follicle, which then secretes estrogen. Estrogen helps to regenerate the uterine lining that was shed during menstruation. **Ovulation**, the release of a secondary oocyte from the ovary, is induced by a surge in LH. The **luteal phase** begins with the formation of the corpus luteum from the remnants of the follicle. The corpus luteum secretes progesterone and estrogen, which inhibit FSH and LH. Progesterone also maintains the thickness of the endometrium. Without the implantation of a fertilized egg, the corpus luteum begins to regress, and the levels of estrogen and progesterone drop. FSH and LH are no longer inhibited, and the cycle renews.

The uterine cycle also consists of three phases: the proliferative phase, secretory phase, and menstrual phase. The **proliferative phase** is characterized by the regeneration of the uterine lining. During the **secretory phase**, the endometrium becomes increasingly vascular, and nutrients are secreted to prepare for implantation. Without implantation, the endometrium is shed during **menstruation**.

PREGNANCY, PARTURITION, LACTATION

Pregnancy: When a blastocyst implants in the uterine lining, it releases hCG. This hormone prevents the corpus luteum from degrading, and it continues to produce estrogen and progesterone. These hormones are necessary to maintain the uterine lining. By the second trimester, the placenta secretes enough of its own estrogen and progesterone to sustain pregnancy and the levels continue to increase throughout pregnancy, while hCG hormone levels decrease.

Parturition: The precise mechanism for the initiation of parturition (birth) is unclear. Birth is preceded by increased levels of fetal glucocorticoids, which act on the placenta to increase estrogen and decrease progesterone. Stretching of the cervix stimulates the release of oxytocin from the posterior pituitary gland. Oxytocin and estrogen stimulate the release of prostaglandins, and prostaglandins and oxytocin increase uterine contractions. This positive feedback mechanism results in the birth of the fetus.

Lactation: During pregnancy, levels of the hormone prolactin increase, but its effect on the mammary glands is inhibited by estrogen and progesterone. After parturition, the levels of these hormones decrease, and prolactin is able to stimulate the production of milk. Suckling stimulates the release of oxytocin, which results in the ejection of milk.

RESPIRATORY SYSTEM

The respiratory system is made up of the nasal cavity, pharynx, larynx, trachea, right and left bronchi, and lungs, which branch into bronchioles and alveoli. The respiratory system has two divisions. The upper respiratory tract is comprised of the nasal cavity and pharynx and their associated structures. The lower respiratory tract consists of the larynx, trachea, bronchi, and lungs.

The diaphragm and muscles of the thoracic wall are responsible for the bellows movements necessary for breathing. The process of external respiration (breathing) involves the inspiration of oxygen and the exhalation of carbon dioxide. Normally, respiration occurs through the nasal cavity.

Patients who are congested or under exertion breathe through their mouths. Those with airway blockages are neck-breathers with stomas.

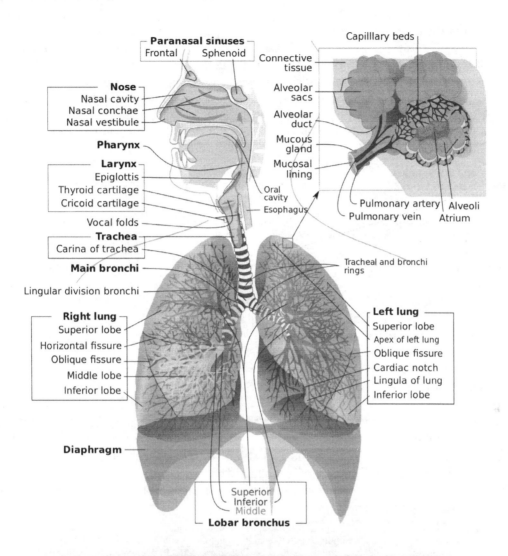

CONTROL OF RESPIRATION

Respiratory neurons in the medulla, pons, and brainstem control the speed and depth of respiration and are responsible for maintaining its normal rhythm. The normal respiration rate in adults is 12-20 breaths per minute. Infants breathe faster; the newborn rate is 44 breaths per minute. The respiratory neurons stimulate motor neurons in the spinal cord to cause the contraction of the muscular diaphragm and intercostal muscles. The respiratory neurons also receive information from receptors about the levels of carbon dioxide (CO_2), oxygen (O_2), and hydrogen (H) in the body, as well as the degree of stretch present in the lungs and chest. Chemoreceptors in the carotid arteries inform the respiratory neurons when the concentration of oxygen falls; chemoreceptors located in the medulla, carotid arteries, and aorta keep track of the levels of carbon dioxide and hydrogen. Breathing can be controlled consciously to a certain extent but is basically an autonomic function.

MECHANICS OF RESPIRATION

Respiration occurs when the air pressure within the alveoli differs from the air pressure external to the body. The air pressure in the lungs is altered by changes in the size of the thoracic cavity, which occur as a result of the contraction and relaxation of the muscular diaphragm and intercostal muscles. The muscular diaphragm is primarily responsible for allowing respiration. Inhalation is brought about by two actions that increase the size of the thoracic cavity. The contraction of the diaphragm causes it to flatten, lengthening the thoracic cavity, and the contraction of the intercostal muscles pulls the rib cage upward, widening it. With the enlargement of the thoracic cavity, the pressure within decreases and air enters the lungs. Air is then pushed out of the lungs as the muscular diaphragm and intercostal muscles relax and the volume of the thoracic cavity decreases.

INTERNAL AND EXTERNAL RESPIRATION

Internal respiration refers to the exchange of oxygen, carbon dioxide, and trace gases at the cellular level. **External respiration** refers to the exchange of oxygen, carbon dioxide, and other gases between the lungs and blood, commonly known as breathing. The passage of gases through the respiratory system can be traced as follows:

1. **Inspiratory neurons** in the respiratory center of the medulla oblongata (brain stem) tell the body to inhale.
2. **Nostrils** and **mouth** warm inhaled air by moving it over nasal conchae and sinuses.
3. Air passes through the **pharynx** to the **larynx** (voice box).
4. The **epiglottis** flips to cover the esophagus.
5. Air passes into the **trachea** (windpipe).
6. **Diaphragm** contracts and flattens to raise the ribs as breathing occurs.
7. **Intercostal muscles** between the ribs pull the ribs up enabling the chest to expand and air to pull inward.
8. Trachea splits into the left and right **bronchi** that connect to the **lungs**. The bronchi split into fine branches called **bronchioles**.
9. Bronchioles end in thin-walled, grape-like **alveoli** where the red blood cells absorb oxygen (O_2) from the inhaled air and give off carbon dioxide (CO_2).
10. **Expiratory neurons** in the brain stem tell the diaphragm and ribs to relax and exhale carbon dioxide into the atmosphere.

> **Review Video: Pulmonary Circuit**
> Visit mometrix.com/academy and enter code: 955608

NASAL CAVITY

The inside of the nose is the nasal cavity. The external nares (nostrils) are its outside openings; the internal nares (conchae) are its posterior openings; and the vestibule refers to the front (anterior) portion. Air is taken in through the external nares, warmed, humidified, and filtered by the conchae. The posterior part of the septum is made of bone, and the anterior part is cartilage. The nasal cavity is divided into left and right halves by the nasal septum (vomer). The hard palate forms the cavity floor. The nasal cavity is lined with mucous membrane. The goblet cells of the mucous membrane secrete mucus to trap particles of dust and debris. Ciliated cells wave hairs to stop large particles from advancing any further into the respiratory tract.

PHARYNX

The internal nares lead to the pharynx. Mucous is swept back in the nasal cavity to the pharynx, where it is swallowed and excreted through the digestive tract. Air is humidified and warmed in the nasal cavity before passing into the pharynx to prevent damage to the lining of the deeper respiratory passages. The pharynx is the common opening from the nasal cavity to the rest of the respiratory tract, as well as the digestive tract. It is split into three regions: the nasopharynx, oropharynx, and laryngopharynx. The nasopharynx is the upper (superior) part of the pharynx; it extends from the internal nares down to the uvula and contains the pharyngeal tonsil. The oropharynx runs between the uvula and epiglottis. The laryngopharynx lies below the upper edge of the epiglottis and opens to the esophagus.

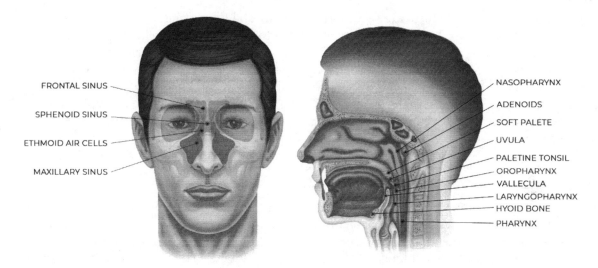

LARYNX

The larynx is comprised of a cartilaginous skeleton, muscles, ligaments, and mucosal lining. The cartilages making up the larynx are the thyroid, cricoid, and arytenoid. The largest and most superior of these is the thyroid cartilage, or Adam's apple. The cricoid cartilage is the most inferior of the cartilages. If the patient's airway is closed by trauma, foreign body obstruction, or edema from anaphylaxis, the cricoid can be punctured to permit breathing (cricothyrotomy). The arytenoid cartilage lies between the cricoid and thyroid cartilages. The thyroid cartilage is attached to the epiglottis. It covers the opening of the larynx during swallowing to prevent food and fluid from entering the larynx. The vallecula is a depression that lies anterior to the epiglottis. The larynx contains the vocal folds (vocal cords) for speech and provides an entrance to the lower respiratory passages. The movement of the intrinsic muscles of the larynx alters the shape and tension of the vocal cords, adjusting voice pitch.

TRACHEA

Also called the windpipe, the trachea is a tube comprised of connective tissue, cartilage, and smooth muscle. Its lateral sides are made of cartilage, which protects the trachea and keeps the structure open for the passage of air. The posterior position of the trachea consists of ligamentous membrane and smooth muscle. The smooth muscle can alter the trachea's shape. The esophagus is positioned posterior to the trachea's back wall. Cilia in the trachea push mucus and particles of foreign matter toward the larynx. Their movement allows the mucus and foreign matter to enter the esophagus, where it can be swallowed. The trachea splits into the right and left mainstream bronchi at the carina.

PRIMARY BRONCHI

The primary bronchi (extrapulmonary bronchi) are large passageways that conduct air into the lungs; no gas exchange takes place. They form where the trachea splits at the carina and run from the mediastinum down into the lungs. The two primary bronchi are different shapes. The right bronchus is shorter, wider, and positioned more vertically than the left bronchus. If a patient has an obstructed bronchus, it is more likely the right one. The primary bronchi are supported by C-shaped cartilage rings and split into the secondary bronchi as they enter the lungs. This site, where the bronchi, vessels, and nerves enter the lungs, is called the hilus.

BRONCHIAL TREE

The primary bronchi split to form the **secondary bronchi**, and the secondary bronchi divide to form the **tertiary bronchi**. The tertiary bronchi reach into the lobules of the lungs and continue to branch into the bronchioles. The bronchioles divide many times to form the terminal bronchioles, which split into respiratory bronchioles. Each individual respiratory bronchiole also divides and becomes an alveolar duct. The alveolar ducts terminate in the alveoli, clusters of air sacs that resemble clusters of grapes. A single alveolus is 0.1-0.2 mm in diameter. Each one is surrounded by capillaries. It is here in the alveoli where the exchange of respiratory gases (oxygen for carbon dioxide) occurs.

LUNGS

The lungs (pulmones) are the main organs of respiration. They are light enough to float in water, elastic, smooth, shiny, and spongy. When touched, the tiny, grape-like alveoli crackle. The lungs are covered in a double-walled sac called the pleura. The base of each lung rests on the diaphragm, which raises and lowers the lungs. The right lung is the larger of the two lungs, comprised of three lobes, versus two lobes in the left lung. The lung's lobes are separated by fissures on the surface of the organs. Each lobe of the lung is split into lobules that are separated by connective tissue. Major blood vessels and bronchi do not pass through the connective tissue, so surgeons can remove diseased lobules fairly easily. The right lung contains 10 lobules, and the left lung holds nine. As the primary bronchi enter the lungs, they split into secondary bronchi.

> **Review Video: Lung Sounds**
> Visit mometrix.com/academy and enter code: 765616

PLEURA

The pleura is the thin membrane that protects the lungs. The parietal pleura lines the inside of the chest cavity; the visceral pleura covers the lungs. The space between the two is called the pleural space. The visceral pleura lubricates the surfaces of the lungs by secreting small amounts of fluid. The lungs expand and contract during respiration, and pleural fluid allows the different lung surfaces to glide smoothly across each other. Pleurisy is a painful condition in which the pleura become inflamed as a result of fluid collecting in the pleural space (wet pleurisy) or the two membranes rubbing together (dry pleurisy). A pleural rub may be audible with a stethoscope (auscultation) if the patient has pleurisy, pleural effusion, pneumonia, pulmonary infarction, neoplasm, lupus, or asbestosis.

URINARY SYSTEM

The urinary system is comprised of two kidneys (which are located in the right and left flank areas), which filter the blood of toxins and excess fluid, creating urine. Ureters carry the urine to the bladder, and a urethra carries the urine to the external meatus (opening) during urination. The urethra of the female is about 0.5-1.5 cm long, and the male urethra is about 15-29 cm long, so the female is more at risk for ascending infections.

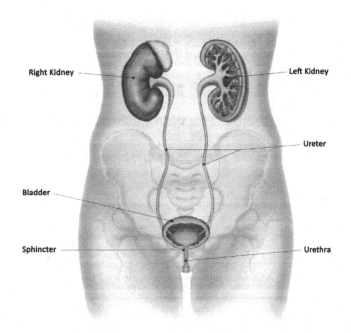

Review Video: Urinary System
Visit mometrix.com/academy and enter code: 601053

KIDNEYS

Two kidneys are located in the retroperitoneal space, in the posterior abdomen, one on each side of the spinal column. They are bean-shaped and concave on their medial aspects. The concave area contains an opening called the hilum, the point of entrance for the renal artery, renal vein, nerves, and ureter. The kidney controls blood pressure through the renal artery with the hormone renin.

The kidney is surrounded by a capsule of fibrous and connective tissue. The renal cortex is the outer part of the organ, lying underneath this capsule. Inside the cortex is the renal medulla, split into 10–20 renal pyramids. A renal pyramid and the overlying cortex associated with it form a renal lobe. The tip of a renal pyramid is called a papilla. Each papilla drains into a minor calyx. A number of minor calyces act together to drain into a major calyx. The major calyces, in turn, drain into the renal pelvis, from which urine then drains from through the ureter into the urinary bladder.

PATH OF BLOOD AND URINE

The path of blood through the kidney and the subsequent path of urine is as follows:

1. Unfiltered blood enters the **nephron** through the afferent arteriole and flows into the **renal corpuscle.**
2. Minerals and some fluid filter out of the blood in the **glomerulus**, a tuft of blood vessels.
3. Filtrate enters **Bowman's capsule**, a shell around the glomerulus, where the majority of filtration takes place.

4. Blood leaves the glomerulus through the efferent tubule and enters the **peritubular network**.
5. Water and salt get reabsorbed in the **proximal convoluted tubule** (PCT), and return to the bloodstream.
6. Filtrate flows into the **descending loop of Henle**.
7. Blood continues through the peritubular network and out of the nephron through a venule.
8. Filtrate flows into the **ascending loop of Henle**, and into the **distal convoluted tubule (DCT)** in the cortex.
9. Hormones fine tune the filtrate to reabsorb only what amino acids, glucose, and salts the body needs.
10. **Filtrate** is now urine, and flows into the **collecting duct**, where ADH controls its concentration.
11. Urine passes from the kidney to the **ureters, bladder, urethra, and meatus** for micturition (urination).

KIDNEY FUNCTION

The kidneys produce 2-3 liters of urine daily. Waste products excreted in the urine include urea from protein catabolism, uric acid from nucleic acid metabolism, creatinine, excess water, and some drugs and toxins. Necessary minerals are reabsorbed. The kidneys maintain the acid-base balance, regulate electrolyte concentrations, control the volume of blood, and govern blood pressure. The entire blood supply is filtered 20-25 times per day through the 1.4 million nephrons of a healthy kidney cortex. If the number of nephrons decreases to 700,000, the patient develops hypertension. The kidneys help maintain the body's homeostasis (balance) by communicating with other organs using three hormones: erythropoietin (EPO), renin, and calcitriol. EPO signals the bone marrow to produce red blood cells while the lack of it causes anemia, renin regulates blood pressure, and calcitriol is the active form of Vitamin D. Calcitriol aids in the maintenance of calcium, needed for bones, teeth, and normal chemical balance, particularly in the heart.

REGULATION OF PH

The pH of the blood is determined by the blood levels of carbon dioxide and bicarbonate. The kidneys work in conjunction with the lungs to modify these levels and regulate acid-base homeostasis. Acid-base balance is achieved by controlling the blood levels of carbon dioxide and bicarbonate. The lungs help to regulate carbon dioxide balance, while the kidneys control the levels of bicarbonate through the secretion and reabsorption of bicarbonate and hydrogen ions. The kidneys prevent and respond to acidosis by secreting hydrogen ions and reabsorbing bicarbonate ions. They correct alkalosis in the opposite way, releasing bicarbonate ions and reabsorbing hydrogen ions. Because the body normally contains 20 times more bicarbonate than carbonic acid, it is better able to correct acidosis than alkalosis.

THE EYES

The main **parts of the eye** and their functions are as follows:

- **Aqueous humor** is watery fluid that maintains eye pressure.
- The **bony orbit** is the socket protecting the eye.
- **Cranial nerves** that help with the function of the eye such as movement or vision include the optic nerve (cranial nerve II), oculomotor (III), trochlear (IV), trigeminal (V), abducens (VI), and vagus (X) nerves.
- **Eyelashes and lids** protect the eye and sweep out particles.
- **Extrinsic muscles** focus the eye.
- The **lacrimal glands** are tear ducts to moisten the eye.

38

- The **lens** refracts light.
- The **optic disc** is the blind spot.
- The **pupil** regulates light entry.
- The **retina** has rods for black and white imaging and cones for color imaging, and helps trigger the optic nerve to send impulses to the brain.
- The **macula** is at the retinal center that is very sensitive to light. The black spot in the center is called the fovea which provides the sharpest vision.
- The **choroid** is a black layer behind the retina that absorbs light and nourishes the retina.
- The **cornea** is the window at the front of the eye that helps with focus.
- The **iris** regulates light entry.
- The **sclera** is tough, white fibrous connective tissue holding nerves and vessels that acts as protection for the eye.
- The **suspensory ligament** connects the lens to the ciliary muscles of the iris.
- The **vitreous humor** is jelly that maintains the eye's shape and refracts images.

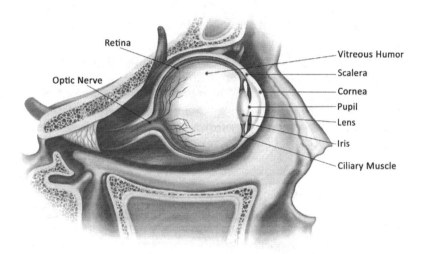

Growth and Development

JEAN PIAGET'S THEORY OF COGNITIVE DEVELOPMENT

SENSORIMOTOR STAGE

From birth to around 2 years, infants are in what psychologist **Jean Piaget** termed the **sensorimotor stage** because they learn about the world through sensory input and motor output. They see, hear, smell, taste, and feel; and they move their body parts in response to these sensory perceptions. They learn about the environment through looking, listening, sucking, and grasping things around them. During this stage, babies develop object permanence: the realization that things out of sight still exist. Piaget divided the sensorimotor stage into six substages.

1. **Reflexes** (0-1 month): inborn reflexive actions like sucking and looking
2. **Primary circular reactions** (1-4 months): babies form new schemas (concepts), intentionally repeating accidental actions they find rewarding, e.g., thumb-sucking
3. **Secondary circular reactions** (4-8 months): babies purposefully repeat actions to cause environmental effects, e.g., picking objects up to suck them
4. **Coordination of reactions** (8-12 months): children combine schemas to accomplish goals; imitate others' behaviors; act intentionally; and understand objects, e.g., that rattles make sounds if shaken
5. **Tertiary circular reactions** (12-18 months): children perform trial-and-error experiments, e.g., sounds and movements to get parental attention
6. **Early representational thought** (18-24 months): children use symbols to represent other things, e.g., make-believe and pretend play, developing understanding not just via actions but mental operations.

PREOPERATIONAL STAGE

Jean Piaget called the stage from around 2-7 years **preoperational** because children cannot yet perform logical, formal mental operations. Children extend the symbolic representation they began to develop in the previous sensorimotor stage, playing adult roles, using toys as animals, etc. They develop language. Piaget defined preoperational children as **egocentric**, i.e., they cannot see others' points of view—literally and physically as well as abstractly. Piaget found children could easily select the picture among three showing a scene they had observed; but asked to select the picture of what people sitting in a different location saw, they would still select the picture of what they themselves saw. They neither manipulate ideas or information mentally nor comprehend logic concerning concrete objects. Piaget's experiments with conservation of volume, quantity, number, length, weight, and mass showed preoperational children who did not understand these properties were conserved regardless of changes in shape, arrangement, or appearance—e.g., objects numbered the same whether clustered together or spread out; or liquid was the same amount despite container shapes. Piaget also characterized preoperational thinking as **intuitive** (non-logical), **magical** (believing their thoughts cause events), and **animistic** (ascribing human emotions and motivations to inanimate objects).

CONCRETE OPERATIONS STAGE

Jean Piaget described concrete operations in children aged 7-11 as developing logical thought, but only about concrete events and objects; he found they still had difficulty understanding hypothetical and/or abstract ideas. **Concrete operational children** are better at inductive logic (i.e., moving from a specific event to a general principle) than deductive logic (i.e., moving from a general principle to predict a specific outcome). A milestone of this stage is developing **reversibility**, i.e., that actions and categories can be reversed. Whereas preoperational children focused on only one aspect of a problem at a time, which Piaget termed **centration** (e.g., they thought more liquid was in a taller, thinner container than a shorter, wider container even though it was the same amount because they focused only on container height), in concrete operations, Piaget found children **decentrate**, considering multiple components of a problem simultaneously. The egocentrism of preoperational thinking gives way to **sociocentrism**, i.e., children now realize others have different viewpoints from their own. However, they may not yet know what is included in others' perspectives, though they know they exist. Children can think logically in this stage if they have concrete objects and events to observe and manipulate.

FORMAL OPERATIONS STAGE

What Jean Piaget called formal operations occurs around ages 11-12 and continues into adulthood. Piaget found that pre-adolescents and adolescents develop the ability to think logically without needing concrete objects as they did in the previous concrete operations stage; perform deductive reasoning; plan systematically; and understand abstract concepts like justice, morality, democracy, etc. In **formal operations**, people can manipulate information mentally, reason through hypothetical situations, and determine specific outcomes from general principles (deductive reasoning), which mathematics and sciences often require. Whereas concrete operational children rely on their actual experiences, in formal operations they develop the ability to consider **potential consequences** of actions and possible outcomes, which is necessary for long-term planning. Rather than solving problems through trial-and-error, they use logic to develop organized, **methodical approaches**. Considering and rejecting ineffective solutions without attempting them enhances their efficiency. Thinking abstractly without objects and imagining hypothetical outcomes enables adolescents to engage in the systematic decision-making and future planning required of them at their ages.

HOWARD GARDNER'S MULTIPLE INTELLIGENCES AS DIFFERENT LEARNING STYLES

Students with strong **visual-spatial intelligence** are very aware of their environments. They conceptualize in terms of physical space, as sailors and architects do. They enjoy reading maps, drawing, completing jigsaw puzzles, and visually daydreaming. Good teaching materials and methods for them include models, drawings, charts, graphics, photos, physical and verbal imagery, 3-D models, videos, videoconferencing, multimedia, TV, and texts with many illustrations, diagrams, and graphs. Students with strong **bodily-kinesthetic intelligence** are highly aware of their bodies and effectively use them, like surgeons and dancers. They like moving, touching things, and making things. They communicate effectively via body language. They learn well through hands-on learning, acting out concepts, physical activity, role-playing, and being taught using real objects and equipment. Students with strong **musical intelligence** are sensitive to sound and rhythm. In addition to loving music, they respond to all environmental sounds. Playing music in the background may help them study. They learn well by learning verbal information as song lyrics, using rhythmic speech, and beating or tapping out rhythms. Compatible teaching uses audio recordings, live music, musical instruments, radios, and multimedia presentations.

Students with high **logical-mathematical intelligence** excel at calculations and reasoning, thinking abstractly and conceptually. They detect and explore patterns and relationships, ask cosmic questions, enjoy solving puzzles, and conducting experiments. Before addressing details of a problem, they must learn and formulate concepts. Compatible teaching strategies include offering mysteries, investigations, and logic games. Students with strong **linguistic intelligence** are effective with words. Their auditory skills are highly developed. They often think in words, not pictures, feelings, sounds, etc. They enjoy reading, writing, and playing word games. Teaching methods and tools include reading books with them, encouraging them to see and pronounce words, lectures, books, computers, multimedia materials, voice recorders, and spoken-word recordings. Students with high **intrapersonal intelligence** tune into their own feelings and are "loners," avoiding social interaction. They are independent, confident, strong-willed, motivated, opinionated, intuitive, and wise. Introspective reflection and independent study, journals, diaries, books, creative materials, time, and privacy are useful instructional methods and materials. Students with strong **interpersonal intelligence** are social, interactive, empathetic, and "street-smart." Group activities, dialogues, seminars, telephones, audio- and video-conferencing or Skyping, and email are good teaching methods and tools.

EARLY CHILDHOOD PHYSICAL GROWTH AND DEVELOPMENT

From birth to 3 years, children typically grow to twice their height and gain four times their weight. Whereas infants' heads are nearly one-fourth of their full body length, toddlers develop more balanced proportions similar to those of adults. They overcome the disequilibrium of changing so rapidly: generally, children usually start walking around 1 year, climb stairs holding banisters around 18 months, and master running around 2 years. Three-year-olds have normally mastered sitting, walking, toilet training, eating with spoons, scribbling, and demonstrating enough eye-hand coordination to throw and catch a ball. Most children develop sufficient gross motor skills for balancing on one foot and skipping; fine motor skills for controlling scissors, crayons, and pencils; and further refinement of their body proportions between 5 and 8 years old. Implications of the period from birth to 8 years include its being a critical time for developing many **fundamental skills**; hence it is also a critical time for **developmental delays** to be identified and to receive early intervention, which has proven more effective than later intervention.

PHYSICAL GROWTH AND DEVELOPMENT DURING MIDDLE CHILDHOOD

When contrasted with the rapid, obvious, and dramatic changes of early childhood, **middle childhood** is a period of slower physical growth and development. Children continue to grow, but at a slower and steadier rate than when they were younger. In middle childhood, muscle mass develops and children grow stronger. Their **strength** and **coordination in motor skills** advance, evidenced by gradually improving skills for tasks like accurately throwing baseballs; walking on tiptoes; broad-jumping; skipping; lacing and tying shoes; cutting and pasting paper; and drawing people including heads, bodies, arms, and legs. Children can typically dress themselves unassisted, skip using both feet, ride bicycles, skate, and bounce a ball four to six times by the time they are 6. By the time they are around 9, children usually can learn to sew and build models; by age 10, children are capable of catching fly balls. Their hair darkens slightly, and their skin appearance and texture more closely approximate those of adults. Girls and boys in middle childhood are usually similar in height until **puberty**, which frequently begins near the end of middle childhood, averaging around 10 years in girls and 11 years in boys.

PHYSICAL GROWTH AND DEVELOPMENT IN ADOLESCENCE

The most salient physical growth and development aspects of adolescence undoubtedly involve **puberty**. Girls today develop the first signs of puberty, breast buds, before adolescence in late middle childhood, at an average of 10 years within a range between 8 and 13 years; peak growth in height, weight, muscle mass, etc. is around a year after puberty's onset and menarche about two years after, averaging before age 13. Boys begin puberty around a year later than girls, averaging around 11 years within a range of 9-14 years, with peak growth around two years after onset. The first signs are testicular enlargement and scrotal reddening and thinning. Both girls and boys go through a series of **stages** that make up puberty. These stages incorporate changes to almost all of their body systems, including most notably the **skeletal, muscular, and reproductive systems**. Voices deepen, and body hair and other secondary sex characteristics develop. Acne often plagues adolescents. Whereas girls and boys are about the same heights in middle childhood, girls frequently become taller in their early teens. However, boys catch up within one or two years, typically growing taller than girls. Puberty accounts for around 25 percent of individual growth in height.

BASIC PRINCIPLES OF GENETICS

Humans have 23 pairs of **chromosomes** (bundles of DNA and genes) in the nucleus of body cells, with half of each pair coming from each parent. The chromosomes in each cell contain 35,000 or more **genes**, which carry instructions for producing proteins. Chromosomes carry the blueprint for the individual, including traits inherited from the parents. There are two types of chromosomes:

- **Autosomal**: Pairs 1 to 22, ranked in size according to the number of base pairs they each contain with 1 being the largest and 22 being the smallest.
- **Allosomal** (Sex): Pair 23. XX for female and XY for male.

Genetic disorders occur when there is a **mutation** (spontaneous or transmitted) in one or more genes. Diseases are classified as **autosomal recessive** if both parents must carry the defective autosomal gene in order to pass it on to offspring, and they are classified as **autosomal dominant** if only one parent must carry the defective gene. Genetic disorders may also be X-linked recessive or dominant and Y-linked.

> **Review Video: Chromosomes**
> Visit mometrix.com/academy and enter code: 132083

FACTORS THAT CAN AFFECT HEREDITY

Inheritance is complex. In some cases, a disorder is directly inherited through transmission of defective **genes**, such as with sickle cell disease; however, in other cases, people may inherit a defective gene that increases risk but does not necessarily result in disease. These include the BRCA1 and BRCA2 gene mutations that increase risk of breast and ovarian cancer as well as the HER2 gene mutation associated with estrogen-progesterone-positive breast cancers. Many **environmental factors** may spur the development of diseases with a genetic component or may cause genetic mutations. Most **sporadic genetic mutations** are harmless, but some result in disease. Environmental factors that may affect outcomes include stress, smoking, poor diet, exposure to second-hand smoke, exposure to ultraviolet (UV) radiation, excessive drinking, poor air quality, some viruses, and exposure to toxic substances. Researchers have theorized that there may be a genetic component to many common disorders.

> **Review Video: Gene Mutation**
> Visit mometrix.com/academy and enter code: 955485

HEREDITARY DISORDERS AND THEIR CHARACTERISTICS
AUTOSOMAL RECESSIVE

If a disease is inherited in the autosomal recessive pattern, each parent must be a carrier and pass on the defective gene to the offspring, resulting in a 25% chance that an offspring will develop the disease (two defective copies) and a 50% chance that the offspring will be a carrier (one defective copy). Common autosomal recessive disorders include the following:

- **Cystic fibrosis** - Chronic progressive disease of the mucous glands, causing blockage in the respiratory system and gastrointestinal system and affecting most body systems. Blockage in the pancreatic ducts results in impaired digestion of fats and proteins and malabsorption. Respiratory infections, pneumonia, constipation, and bowel obstructions are common.

- **Sickle cell disease (SCD)** - Disease that results in sickle-shaped red blood cells, which clump together and occlude vessels, causing severely painful occlusive crises. Patients are chronically anemic and often require routine transfusions and medications. Onset within six months of birth. SCD affects primarily African Americans and people of South American descent.

AUTOSOMAL DOMINANT

If a disease is inherited in the autosomal dominant pattern, only one parent must pass on the defective gene and each pregnancy carries a 50% risk that the child will inherit the disease. There is no carrier state. Common autosomal dominant disorders include the following:

- **Achondroplasia (dwarfism)** - Disorder in which the body can't respond normally to growth factors, resulting in short stature; large, prominent forehead; and short arms, legs, and fingers. Some may develop hydrocephalus. Chronic otitis media, lordosis (swayback), and orthopedic problems are common.
- **Huntington disease** - This is a progressive fatal neurodegenerative disorder characterized by motor, cognitive, and psychiatric disturbances. Onset is usually between ages 35 and 45, but the juvenile-onset variety has onset before age 20.
- **Marfan syndrome** - Disorder of the connective tissue characterized by elongated head; long arms and legs; scoliosis; crowded teeth; unusual stretch marks; and cardiac abnormalities including aortic enlargement, which can result in rupture and sudden death.
- **Otosclerosis** - Disorder with abnormal bone growth in the middle ear, resulting in hearing loss.

X-LINKED RECESSIVE

Because males have only one X chromosome, X-linked recessive disorders usually affect only males because females have one healthy X chromosome that can compensate for the defective one, although daughters of a mother with the recessive gene have a 50% chance of being carriers. If the father carries the defective gene, sons are unaffected, but all daughters are carriers.

- **Duchenne muscular dystrophy (MD)** - This progressive fatal disease of boys is characterized by degeneration of muscle fibers; muscle wasting; and, frequently, intellectual disabilities. Onset is at age 3 to 4, and most are not ambulatory by age 12 with death occurring during adolescence. Boys tire easily and exhibit lordosis (swayback) and a waddling gait. Other MD varieties are less common and may be milder or have some different clinical symptoms.
- **Fragile X** - Most common inheritable cause of intellectual disabilities. Condition includes macrocephaly (large head), macroorchidism (large testicles), and low IQ.
- **Hemophilia (A, B, and von Willebrand)** - Disorder is characterized by deficiency of blood-clotting proteins causing bruising and excessive bleeding.

X-LINKED DOMINANT AND Y-LINKED

X-linked disorders can be inherited by males and females, but they are more common in females. A father with a defective gene on the X-chromosome gives the disorder to all daughters but no sons (who inherit their X chromosome from their mother). A positive mother, however, has a chance of passing the trait to 50% of female and male children.

- **Rett syndrome** - This disorder affects only females and becomes evident at about age 6 to 18 months because of a gene defect that impairs brain development, so the head fails to grow properly, resulting in progress microcephaly and cognitive impairment. Hands and feet are small, and the child often exhibits repetitive hand movements. Autistic-like behavior is common.
- **Incontinentia pigmenti** - This rare disorder, which affects males more than females, is characterized by excessive deposits of melanin in the skin, resulting in unusual patterns of skin discoloration.

Y-linked disorders affect only males and are much less common because they result in male infertility and impaired development of male secondary sexual characteristics, so those affected are rarely able to procreate.

AGING PROCESS
INFANCY TO EARLY CHILDHOOD

The stages of aging in infancy, toddlerhood, and early childhood include the following:

- **Infancy** (0–1): The infant is almost completely dependent on adults for his or her needs. The child grows rapidly and begins to develop both fine and gross motor skills as well as an understanding of simple words. The infant begins to display some distinct personality traits.
- **Toddlerhood** (1–3): Growth slows but cognitive ability increases as the child begins to use words and shows beginning problem-solving skills. The toddler begins to enjoy playing side by side with others and has improved fine and gross motor skills. The toddler shows increasing independence and may react negatively if thwarted.
- **Early childhood** (3 to 6): The preschool years are characterized by steady physical growth, increased fine and gross motor skills, and increased visual acuity. The child begins to engage in associative play and interactions with other children. Language skills improve markedly. Personality traits of infancy persist and may be at odds with learning environments.

MID-CHILDHOOD TO ADOLESCENCE

The stages of aging in mid-childhood to adolescence include the following:

- **Mid-childhood** (6–8): The child loses baby teeth and begins to mature physically. The child relies on concrete experiences but makes improvements at problem solving. The child begins to enjoy cooperating with others and team sports. The child's temperament remains relatively unchanged, but communication skills improve.
- **Late childhood** (8–12): Girls undergo a growth spurt at about age 9, and boys start a year or so later with the maturing of internal organs and lengthening of the long bones. The child understands the concept of conservation (matter remains unchanged when its form changes) and continues to enjoy group activities and sports. The child may become interested in sexuality and gender differences.
- **Adolescence** (12–18): Sexual maturation occurs, and the adolescent is concerned with identity. The adolescent can reason abstractly and may begin to act independently and to rebel. Peer interactions are especially important. The adolescent may undergo a period of stress before developing a strong identity.

45

ADULTHOOD

The stages of aging in adulthood include the following:

- **Early adulthood** (18–35): Physical and social changes emerge slowly as the adult makes choices about a career and sets goals. The person may experiment with lifestyle and sexuality and expands social circles. Problem-solving skills improve, and moral development continues.
- **Middle adulthood** (35–50): This is a period of relative stability and good health, although bad habits such as smoking may begin to cause impairment. The person has many obligations and responsibilities, including family and job, and may experience increased stress. Social relationships are often stable and rewarding.
- **Maturity** (50–80): The person experiences gradual physical decline and may have serious illnesses. Some may show cognitive decline and increased incidence of chronic and acute illnesses. The person may have an improved sense of well-being, self-confidence, and emotional stability.
- **Late adulthood** (80+): The person may have chronic illness and increased dependency on others, such as adult children. Cognition varies, with short-term memory loss being common. Many live alone or in assisted living.

METHODS OF CARE FOR THE TERMINALLY ILL

Because of advances in the treatment of disease and longer life expectancies, the process of dying for the terminally ill is often prolonged. Methods of care for the terminally ill include the following:

- **Aggressive treatment**: This includes life support, such as tube feedings, transfusions, IVs, and ventilators, and it often involves hospitalization in an effort to prolong life as much as possible, often regardless of the quality of life.
- **Comfort care**: This approach provides only measures that promote comfort, such as adequate pain management and emotional support, with avoidance of life support and extraordinary measures to prolong life, although curative treatments may be used.
- **Hospice care**: This is one model of comfort care in which the person stops curative treatment and remains in the home environment with the assistance of home health hospice caregivers to support the person and family members. Some people may opt for this if their condition is advanced or after aggressive treatment has failed.

ASPECTS OF DEATH, DYING, AND GRIEVING AMONG VARIOUS CULTURES AND TRADITIONS IN SOCIETY

ASIANS AND HISPANICS

- **Asians (Buddhists)** - Asians often believe that people should not hear bad news about their health, and the family may shield a person from knowledge that he or she is dying. People may be stoic in the face of pain. Buddhists believe in rebirth and may want monks to chant during the dying process to ensure a happy rebirth. The spirit is believed to linger around the body after death, so the body must be treated respectfully. Grieving is usually done privately.
- **Hispanics** - Most are Christian and Catholic and may want a priest present to administer the Sacraments of Reconciliation and Holy Communion (last rites). Males, especially, often believe that admitting to pain is a sign of weakness. Care is often provided by female family members. Family members commonly grieve openly and hold a wake after death to celebrate the person's life and to talk about memories. The funeral usually includes a processional and a Mass.

MIDDLE EASTERNERS

- **Middle Easterners (Muslims)** - The sick and dying are usually cared for by a female family member in the home, although some may be hospitalized. The person's bed should be facing Mecca, and the person should be assisted with washing prior to prayers as long as the he or she is able. Pain management is acceptable. A Koran should be at the bedside so visitors (often many) can read from it. On death, the eyes are closed and the arms and legs straightened. The family will wash and wrap the body. Muslims are never cremated, and postmortem exams are usually not allowed. Burial should take place within 24 hours. Females are usually prohibited from attending a burial, and demonstrations of grief should not be excessive. The family has three days of mourning after the burial during which they greet visitors. The grave is visited daily or weekly, and prayers are said for 40 days. Grief counseling is often considered to be intrusive.

ERIKSON'S THEORY OF PSYCHOSOCIAL DEVELOPMENT

FIRST STAGE

Each stage of Erik Erikson's theory of psychosocial development involves a **nuclear conflict**. When this conflict is successfully resolved, Erikson proposed a positive outcome that the individual would realize. Erikson called the stage from birth to around 18 months **basic trust vs. mistrust**. The key event during this stage is **nursing**. When an infant's needs are met fully, consistently, reliably, and with affection and care, the baby develops a basic sense of trust in the world and feels secure and safe. On the other hand, if the baby's needs are not adequately met, met only inconsistently, or the parent or caregiver does not give the infant a sense of love, caring, and affection, then the baby develops a sense of basic mistrust in the world, finds it unpredictable and inconsistent, and feels fearful and insecure. Erikson said the positive outcome of the infant stage of basic trust vs. mistrust is **hope**. Babies nurtured properly develop confidence and optimism through feeling secure and trusting. Those not well cared for develop feelings of worthlessness through feeling insecure and mistrustful.

SECOND STAGE

Erik Erikson named the nuclear conflict of the toddlerhood (ages 18-36 months) stage as **autonomy vs. shame and self-doubt**. The positive outcome of successfully resolving this conflict, Erikson found, is **will**. The significant event during this stage is **toilet training**. Toddlers, in learning to control their bladders and bowels and to control their bodies for walking, develop autonomy (independence) through developing this self-control. They develop fine motor skills for manipulating small objects as well as gross motor skills. Concurrently with physical skills, they learn right vs. wrong. Developing independence helps develop self-esteem. Properly nurtured children display confidence and pride. Those not well cared for, and/or who may be unable to learn the requisite skills, feel ashamed and doubt themselves. This stage includes the "terrible twos," when children naturally display stubbornness, defiance, and temper tantrums in the process of asserting their individual will. Children who do not develop appropriate autonomy in this stage lack self-confidence, are afraid to try new things, and may be overly dependent on parents.

THIRD STAGE

Erik Erikson named the preschool (ages 3-5) stage for the nuclear conflict **initiative vs. guilt**. He identified the positive outcome of successfully resolving this conflict as **purpose**. Children in this stage engage in pretend and make-believe play, imitating their parents. They also explore the environment, wanting to know why things are as they are and happen as they do. They display initiative by taking action, exerting power and control over their environments. Successful children realize a sense of purpose. Those who exert too much power, causing damage to the environment and incurring parental disapproval, develop guilt feelings. Instead of purpose, they feel frustration about not being able to attain their desires or accomplish their goals. Children's most significant relationships during this stage are with their **immediate family**. Erikson was influenced by Freud, but unlike Freud's psychosexual orientation, Erikson's was **psychosocial**. Freud described the Oedipal conflict: unconsciously desiring the opposite-sex parent and wanting to eliminate the rival same-sex parent, the child resolves this through "identification with the aggressor"—wanting to be like the same-sex parent. Erikson saw this psychosocially as a **child-parent struggle**, resolved via "**social role identification**."

FOURTH STAGE

Erik Erikson characterized school-aged (6-12 years old) children as being in the stage centered on the nuclear conflict of **industry vs. inferiority**. He found that children who successfully resolved this conflict experienced the positive outcome of **competence**. At this time, children's focus shifts away from being exclusively on the parents, outward to the wider world of the **neighborhood** and the **school**, as they make new friends and learn new academic skills. While parents are still very important to school-age children, they are no longer the ultimate authorities they were in early childhood. As they acquire many types of new knowledge and skills, and create new products, successful children develop a sense of industry. Those who fail academically and/or socially develop feelings of inferiority, comparing themselves unfavorably to their peers. They feel incompetent and their self-esteem suffers. Children who succeed enjoy enhanced self-esteem and feel competent to handle the increased demands of their expanding environments.

ADOLESCENCE

Adolescents begin developing a sense of personal identity. In his theory, Erik Erikson named this stage of psychosocial development **identity vs. role confusion**. In the stages previous to this one, Erikson portrayed development in terms of how the parents cared for the child, and how the child reacted to that care or lack thereof. A key change in adolescence is that Erikson depicted this stage in terms of what the child does instead. The nuclear conflict in this stage revolves around the adolescent's efforts to discover his or her own **individual identity**. At the same time, the teenager is learning how to negotiate social interactions, how to fit in with peer groups, and developing an abstract concept of morality beyond the concrete ideas of right and wrong in earlier childhood. Some teens, unready for the responsibilities, withdraw into what Erikson termed **moratorium** to delay entering adulthood. In experimenting with and developing identity, adolescents experience strong ties and dedication to friends, ideals, and causes. Successful resolution of this stage's conflict has the positive outcome of **fidelity**; unsuccessful teens are confused about their roles and identities.

YOUNG ADULTHOOD

Erik Erikson described the stage of young adulthood (18-35 years) as centering on the nuclear conflict of **intimacy vs. isolation**. Young adults are primarily occupied with finding love and companionship through the development of **intimate relationships** with others. Erikson identified the positive outcome of successfully resolving this conflict as **love**. Young adults who do not succeed in finding another individual with whom they can form a satisfying relationship in which they can develop deep intimacy suffer the consequence of isolation. They feel isolated and lonely. At the time when Erikson was formulating his theory, it was more common for young adults also to marry, have children, and start their own families. In recent years, though, this often occurs later in life as many young adults defer domestic matters to pursue advanced educations and/or build and further their careers. Some young adults also spend longer times experimenting socially through dating multiple partners without settling on one; having series of less serious relationships; or a series of serious, intimate relationships which do not ultimately progress to lifetime commitments.

Another influence on this stage is that more people are living much longer now, extending the duration of lifetime commitments.

MIDDLE ADULTHOOD

Erik Erikson called the nuclear conflict of middle adulthood (35-55/65 years) **generativity vs. stagnation**. He called the positive outcome of this conflict **care**. The focus in this stage is on work, career, and family. As they mature into increased control and responsibility, middle adults endeavor to create stability, and to produce something of value to society, i.e., **generativity**—they want to establish a legacy that will live beyond them. This can include raising successful children and seeing them have grandchildren; establishing successful businesses or organizations; making creative and industrial products; and discoveries, inventions, scholarships, research, etc. that give meaningful contributions to society and will exist even after they die. Significant relationships are in families, workplaces, local religious institutions, and other community entities. Successful adults feel they are caring for others and generating valuable products. Unsuccessful ones feel self-absorbed and/or stagnant, fearing their lives lack meaning and purposeful activity. Empty nests, career changes, and other major shifts in life are characteristic of this stage.

EIGHTH STAGE AND PROPOSED NINTH STAGE

Erik Erikson described late adulthood (55-65 years to death) as involving the nuclear conflict of **ego integrity vs. despair**. Older adults review their lives, reflecting on what they have and/or have not accomplished. The positive outcome of resolving this conflict is **wisdom**. Older adults feeling they contributed value to society and lived meaningful lives experience fulfillment and contentment, i.e., **integrity of self**. They have learned and gained insight and perspective from their life experiences, attaining wisdom. They can accept impending death peacefully. Those feeling they failed to attain their goals, did not accomplish anything significant, had no clear purpose, and/or did not realize meaning in life instead experience regret, bitterness, fear of death, and despair. Erikson, who died just before his 92nd birthday, made notes about a ninth stage, **old age**, which his widow Joan completed. She wrote that the very old revisit all eight previous stages simultaneously, but with negative outcomes dominating positive ones (mistrust vs. trust, etc.) as life presents daily new challenges. The elderly can lose autonomy as abilities and roles diminish. They no longer have the "luxury" of retrospective despair. However, the positive outcome is "**gerotranscendence**"—peaceful readiness to progress to another stage of being.

Nutrition

ENTERTAINING PRESENTATIONS TO TEACH NUTRITION EDUCATION AT SCHOOL ASSEMBLIES

Jump with Jill, an interactive instructional program designed by Jill Jayne, MS, RD, a registered dietitian and professional musician, is "the world's only rock and roll nutrition show." Research proves its effectiveness: a 2013 study found 92.4 percent of students very excited and happy, 75 percent of students surveyed reported trying to be more active, 81 percent of 4th-graders trying to drink more water afterward, and teachers found student engagement and entertainment value excellent. With live original music, a professional sound system and lighting and "hip" costumes, songs help students remember healthy messages; structured dance breaks enable singing and dancing along with performers, providing kinesthetic learning and exercise. Students learn to value healthy eating and b as fun ways of expressing individuality, recall healthy behaviors through song and dance, describe energizing healthy choices, and recognize their personal health impacts. Studies show results of measurable positive emotional affect and self-reported behavior improvements. Recommended for grades K-6 in groups of 300-600, the 1-hour show is adaptable to preschool, middle school, and professionals. The follow-up CD and website resources inform future and continuing lessons. Faculty and staff participate for modeling. By inviting parents and community members, educators can shape not only individual health habits, but also health culture.

DEVELOPMENTALLY APPROPRIATE INSTRUCTION IN NUTRITION

PIAGET'S PREOPERATIONAL COGNITIVE STAGE

Preoperational children "**centrate**" on one property at a time: if you say, "Eating many different vegetables like peas, carrots, and corn is healthy," they only hear, "Eating peas is healthy." Inability to **categorize** means not differentiating "food" from "snacks," or including "peas" among "vegetables." Lacking **reversibility** means they cannot reverse "Overeating makes you fat" to "Not overeating keeps you from getting fat." They can repeat certain words, phrases, and sentences without understanding their meanings; e.g., "Vegetables are good for us," but they cannot explain how, or name specific vegetables. If told foods contain vitamins, they may object by saying, "Vitamins are pills, not things in food." They think **intuitively**, not logically, not understanding cause-and-effect relationships or changes and transformations. Asked how foods give our bodies nutrients, they might respond, "Little pieces of broccoli go into your arms and legs." For this age group, focus on one simple concept or subject at a time. Postpone trying to explain logical sequences. Animistic and intuitive ideas, like certain foods making a happy, smiling tummy or Popeye's biceps popping out when he eats spinach, are understandable and appealing. Sorting concrete food-group members may help and can be fun.

PIAGET'S CONCRETE OPERATIONS AND FORMAL OPERATIONS STAGES

Concrete operational children can follow **concrete** cause-and-effect; reversibility, e.g., being well, getting sick, and recovering; event chains, e.g., growing crops, harvesting, selling, shipping, processing, and selling in stores; classification, e.g., beef, chicken, and pork are all meats, food vs. snacks, and good vs. bad foods. However, they are still **present-oriented**, not considering future health effects of nutrition. Educators can now teach digestion and energy processes, weight gain and loss, cycles of the food chain, and the food groups, all using concrete objects and illustrations. They should emphasize current, not future, benefits of healthy eating, e.g., feeling better now, running faster today, etc. **Formal operational** students start understanding **abstract** concepts, e.g., dietary fat contributes to heart disease; formulating hypotheses, e.g., "If I stop eating so much junk food, then I'll lose weight"; taking others' perspectives, e.g., "Other kids teasing him about his weight must make him feel bad"; considering multiple consequences, e.g., "Eating healthy foods may or may not make me better at sports"; and informing decisions with their values, e.g., choosing foods and behaviors relative to independence, appearance, and peers. Educators can now discuss protein, vitamins, and minerals; classification of foods by nutrients; processes whereby foods affect health; and chronic disease risks.

CHOOSEMYPLATE.GOV

ChooseMyPlate.gov is the current federal healthy eating guide, formerly the Food Pyramid. Since replacing the Food Pyramid with MyPlate, the US Department of Agriculture (USDA) eliminated oils and sugars. The **five food groups** are: fruits, vegetables, grains, proteins, and dairy. USDA advises that in a meal, half the plate should be fruits and vegetables. **Vegetables** are categorized as dark green, red and orange, legumes (beans and peas), starchy, and other, according to nutrient content. **Whole grains** include whole wheat and whole-wheat flour; cracked or bulgur wheat; oatmeal; whole rye; whole barley; cornmeal; brown rice; amaranth; millet; quinoa; sorghum; triticale, etc. White flour and bread, white rice, and de-germed cornmeal are refined grains. USDA advises at least half the grains we eat be whole grains, not processed or refined, which have beneficial fiber removed. **Proteins** include meats, poultry, seafood, eggs, soy, nuts, seeds, and legumes (also in the vegetables group). USDA recommends eating a variety of lean proteins. **Dairy** includes milk and milk products and calcium-fortified soymilk. Recommended dairy foods are fat-free or low-fat. Milk products retaining calcium content (cheeses, yogurt, etc.) are in the dairy group; cream, butter, cream cheese and others having little or no calcium are not. Oils are not a USDA food group, but included for essential nutrients.

HISTORY OF AMERICAN DIETARY GUIDELINES FROM 1977-1980

Early in 1977, the US Senate Select Committee on Nutrition and Human Needs, then chaired by Senator George McGovern, following extensive reviews of science and discussions, recommended dietary goals consisting of recommendations concerning food and nutrients. The first goal recommended Americans only eat as much energy from food—i.e., calories—as they expended. This goal addressed obesity through **balanced consumption**. Regarding nutrients, the committee recommended eating more complex carbohydrates and fewer simple (i.e., processed or refined) carbohydrates and decreasing total fat, saturated fat, cholesterol, and sodium. Food goals also included eating more vegetables, fruits, and whole grains and replacing more saturated fats with unsaturated fats. Due to controversy and skepticism from industrial and scientific groups, the US Departments of Agriculture and Health and Human Services (formerly Health, Education, and Welfare) jointly issued a nutrition and health brochure in 1980, partly based on the Surgeon General's 1979 report on health promotion and disease prevention and reflecting research findings about relationships between diet and health. However, this too met with debate.

AMERICA'S FEDERAL HISTORY OF DIETARY GUIDELINES AFTER 1980 INTO 2010

Despite their straightforward, scientific basis, **US Dietary Guidelines** issued in 1980 encountered arguments from various industrial and scientific quarters. In response, Congress directed the Departments of Agriculture (USDA) and Health and Human Services (HHS, formerly HEW) to form an advisory committee to solicit formal and informal outside and private-sector advice for subsequent editions. Though the 1985 edition of the Guidelines did not incorporate extensive changes, adding non-federal scientists' input resulted in far less controversy and wider adoption. HHS and USDA formed a second scientific advisory committee in 1989 to review and revise the Guidelines. The 1990 edition reinforced earlier editions' principles, but additionally suggested **numerical targets** for saturated and total fat amounts—emphasizing these did not apply to a single food or meal, but to eating choices over multiple days. While these first three editions were voluntarily issued, the 1990 National Nutrition Monitoring and related Research Act first legally mandated the **Dietary Guidelines report**, required a new report every five years, and established a **Dietary Guidelines Advisory Committee** for that purpose. The 2005 committee adopted systematic methods to review scientific evidence and literature. The 2010 committee extended these, also establishing the **Nutrition Evidence Library** to support its work with a comprehensive, evidence-based review process.

CARBOHYDRATES, FATS, PROTEIN, VITAMINS, AND MINERALS FOUND IN FOODS

Carbohydrates are starches, fibers, and sugars in foods from which the body manufactures glucose, the blood sugar used to fuel all activities of the body, including the brain. Glucose is accessed immediately, or stored in the muscles and liver for future use. **Fats** are necessary to normal bodily functions, but only 20-35 percent of the human diet need be from fats—preferably oils, not solid fats; and unsaturated, not saturated or trans fats. USDA recommends eating below 10 percent of calories in saturated fats, and avoiding trans fats. (Trans fats are found in partially hydrogenated oils.) We need to eat foods with protein, which our bodies digest into amino acids to rebuild all organs, tissues, and cells, which contain protein that is continually broken down and replaced. **Animal proteins** are complete protein sources with all essential amino acids. **Vegetable proteins** are incomplete sources, but combining complementary vegetable proteins can yield complete protein. Ten to 35 percent of daily calories should be protein; Americans typically eat enough. **Vitamins and minerals** are important to health; for instance, vitamin D aids calcium absorption, and calcium promotes strong bone formation. Supplements are available, but eating a nutritious and varied diet usually provides enough vitamins and minerals.

RELATIONSHIP BETWEEN DIET AND EXERCISE

Diet and exercise are **interdependent**. For example, it can be difficult to achieve optimal energy, effort, or results from exercising after eating nothing but junk food. Alternatively, people who do eat healthy diets but never exercise may find it hard to maintain optimal weights. According to the American Council on Exercise, only about five percent of people losing weight exclusively through diet maintain the loss. Weight loss requires a **negative balance of calories**, attained by either burning more calories from exercising, eating fewer calories, or a combination of the two. The individuals most successful in losing weight and maintaining weight loss both **exercise more** and **eat fewer calories** than people who cannot lose weight or who lose it and then regain it. Snacks containing complex carbohydrates and some protein afford energy before exercising. Afterward, water, milk and juice rehydrate; carbohydrates replenish energy; and protein supports muscle repair and growth. Nutritional experts recommend eating 15 percent of calories from protein, 55 percent from carbohydrates, and 30 percent from fat for optimal exercising.

FAD DIETS

Fad diets are extreme, unbalanced, and ultimately **unhealthy**. Some **fad diets** fail to provide all necessary nutrients. Some contain insufficient calories to support normal life functions. Some eliminate certain food groups, causing unbalanced nutrition. Some may cause weight loss initially; however, this typically does not last, and because these diets are impossible to maintain long-term, any weight lost is usually regained soon after ending the diet. Many people not only regain what they lost, but also gain beyond their starting weights as their bodies rebound from nutritional deprivation. Moreover, fad diets do not establish healthy eating habits for **maintaining** ongoing healthy weight and nutrition. Nine common characteristics of many fad diets include:

- sounding "too good to be true"
- promising "quick fix" results
- banning certain regimens and/or products
- oversimplifying complex science
- making dramatic claims rejected by science
- basing claims on isolated testimonials and/or a single research study

- basing claims on studies lacking independent expert reviews
- promoting product sales
- eliminating food groups. Moderate portions of varied, whole or unprocessed foods and regular, moderate exercise are better for losing and controlling weight

Exercise and Physical Fitness

HEALTH BENEFITS OF REGULAR PHYSICAL ACTIVITY

According to the US Department of Health and Human Services Office of Disease Prevention and Health Promotion, regular **physical activity (PA)** affords a myriad of benefits to cardiorespiratory health, musculoskeletal health, mental health, metabolic health, weight control, and life expectancy. It helps prevent high blood pressure, high cholesterol, heart disease, strokes, osteoporosis, falls and fractures, some cancers, cognitive decline, depression, anxiety, type 2 diabetes, obesity, and premature death. PA promotes **functional capacity** for activities of daily living. Some of these benefits, like greater muscle strength, cardiorespiratory fitness, lowered blood pressure and less depression can appear after only a few weeks. Moreover, only modest amounts and moderate intensity of PA, e.g., 150 minutes weekly of brisk walking, are needed to realize most health benefits. For children and adolescents, research finds strong evidence of better bone health, muscular and cardiorespiratory fitness, body composition, and cardiovascular and metabolic health biomarkers through regular PA. Studies also show moderate evidence that PA reduces child and teen **anxiety and depression** symptoms. Not only does PA help control weight, but even obese and overweight people who are physically active have lower premature death rates than those who are inactive.

Across numerous research studies, consensus has been established about the health benefits of regular physical activity (PA) for all people. As reported by the US Department of Health and Human Services Office of Disease Prevention and Health Promotion, regular PA lowers risks of many health problems. Although added benefits accrue as individuals increase the intensity, frequency, and/or duration of their PA, scientists also find even some PA is superior to inactivity. A person can spend as little as 30 minutes, five days a week, doing something simple like walking briskly, to obtain the majority of health benefits available. More PA realizes more benefits. Studies find both **aerobic activity** to increase endurance and **resistance activity** to increase strength beneficial. Research shows health benefits from PA to every racial and ethnic group studied, and every age group—children, teens; young, middle-aged, and older adults—including people with disabilities. Though some people fear injuries, researchers have determined the benefits of PA are far superior to its risks. Engaging in moderate PA regularly also achieves conditioning, lowering injury risk compared to sudden or unaccustomed, excessive exertion.

SERIES OF NATIONAL HEALTH INITIATIVES

The US Department of Health and Human Services (HHS) has launched a series of **Healthy People initiatives** in support of prevention endeavors across its divisions for making the national population healthier. More information is available on the website healthypeople.gov, including the latest news and events, health indicators, progress updates, and webinars. The **Healthy People 2010 initiative**, managed by HHS' Office of Disease Prevention and Health Promotion, had the primary goals of increasing life expectancy and quality, and eliminating demographic health disparities in the US population. The **Healthy People 2020 initiative**, launched in 2010 and addressing 42 areas of public health, has targeted the main goals of achieving longer, high-quality lives without premature death, preventable injury, disease, and disability; eliminating health disparities, attaining health equity, and improving all population groups' health; creating physical and social environments promoting good health for everybody; and furthering healthy development, behaviors, and quality of life across all ages and life stages.

PRIMARY HEALTH INDICATORS INVESTIGATED BY US RESEARCHERS

Scientists have studied 10 leading **health indicators** from 2000-2010, and have continued to assess these since 2010. These health behaviors have strong influences on American health:

- **Physical activity**: a goal is getting more teenagers to engage in vigorous physical activity.
- **Obesity and overweight**: a goal is to decrease numbers of obese and overweight teens and children.
- **Tobacco use**: the goal is to decrease teen cigarette smoking.
- **Substance abuse**: the goal is to augment the number of teenagers not using alcohol and other drugs.
- **Responsible sexual behavior**: the goal is to encourage more adolescents to abstain from engaging in sexual intercourse.
- **Mental health**: among adults with diagnoses of depression, the goal is to raise the proportion of people who receive treatment for it.
- **Injury and violence**: the goal is to decrease the number of motor vehicle deaths and homicides in the population.
- **Environmental quality**: the goal is to decrease non-smoker exposure to secondhand tobacco smoke.
- **Immunization**: a goal is to raise the percentage of young children receiving all recommended vaccinations for a minimum of five years.
- **Healthcare access**: the goal is to raise the percentage of people covered by health insurance.

BODY COMPOSITION

Body composition equals the proportions of fatty and muscular tissue that make up a person's body weight. The percentage of body fat an individual has is significant to health and fitness because people with excessive body fat have higher risks of many chronic diseases, including type 2 diabetes, hypertension, coronary artery disease, osteoarthritis, and many kinds of cancer. Recommended **body fat levels** differ by age and sex. Men are generally advised to have a maximum of 25 percent body fat, and women 30 percent. Somewhat higher levels are often allowed at older ages, because muscle mass decreases with aging. Women naturally have higher levels of essential body fat for reproductive purposes. One method of measuring body fat is by using calipers to measure skinfold thickness at the triceps, suprailiac (above the hip), male chest, thigh, abdomen, subscapular (below shoulder blade) and calf sites. The sum of these measurements can yield an estimate of body fat percentage.

CARDIORESPIRATORY ENDURANCE

"**Cardio**" refers to heart and "**respiratory**" to breathing. One definition of **cardiorespiratory endurance** is the ability to perform dynamic exercise using large muscles over long times. Cardiorespiratory endurance is determined by functioning of the cardiovascular (heart and blood vessel), pulmonary (lungs), and skeletal muscle systems. Higher risk of dying prematurely from all causes is associated with low cardiorespiratory endurance levels. Moreover, the leading cause of death in America is **coronary artery disease**, and high cardiorespiratory endurance levels protect strongly against this. To evaluate cardiorespiratory endurance, a stress test uses an electrocardiogram (ECG) and metabolic cart. First, resting blood pressure and heart rate are measured to obtain baselines and compare with normal values. Then the individual ambulates on a treadmill, pedals on a stationary bicycle, or repeatedly steps onto and off a step, with an ergometer measuring energy output. The ECG has 12 leads attached to the individual to measure heart function. The metabolic cart measures how much oxygen the person's body can consume during exercise—labeled **VO₂ max**, maximal oxygen consumption. Higher VO_2 max indicates higher cardiorespiratory endurance. This assesses cardiovascular fitness and informs planning safe, effective exercise programs.

BENEFITS OF ENHANCING FLEXIBILITY

Having or developing a good range of motion and **flexibility** can greatly improve an individual's **functional abilities** for many everyday living tasks. For example, when driving, turning to see the blind spot before changing lanes is highly difficult when one has poor upper-back and neck flexibility. But with improved range of motion, this common movement becomes simple. The same applies to everyday activities like getting out of bed, picking something up off the floor, or even fastening a seat belt. However, the benefits of flexibility are not only functional. Flexibility **prevents injuries** to joints and muscles, both in daily life and in sports. Stretching following exercise can decrease short-term muscular stiffness and soreness. Flexibility **improves performance** in sports and other exercise. Stretching relieves both general muscular tightness and specific muscle tightness from repetitive motions, ergonomic and/or occupational issues, and even sleeping in bad positions. Two main sources of **lower-back pain**, tightness and muscle spasms, can be treated by stretching; and its long-term benefits decrease future episodes. Neck and upper-back stretching can relieve **muscle-tension headaches**. Stretching can rehabilitate many soft tissue injuries and conditions.

SARCOMERE HYPERTROPHY

Sarcomere hypertrophy builds muscular strength. It apparently requires breaking down muscle fibers to build them up. When tension accumulates in muscle fibers during exercise, connections between actin and myosin protein filaments are damaged, and muscle cell plasma membranes (sarcolemma) rupture, leaking calcium between cells. Increased levels of **intracellular calcium ions** activate **calpains**, enzymes that remove damaged tissue. This activates monocytes, neutrophils, macrophages, and other immune system cells to remove and break down damaged fibers. Also, muscle cells near the damage site are stimulated by ruptured sarcolemma to make and release growth factors. **Satellite cells**, a type of myogenic stem cells activated by the damaged fiber cells' removal and the released growth factors, repair damaged muscle fibers and stimulate muscular growth. Satellite cells activated by muscle damage differentiate into myoblasts and then skeletal muscle cells, which fuse with existing muscle fibers in damaged areas. The fusion adds satellite cell nuclei to skeletal cell nuclei; the larger total number of nuclei then enables muscle fibers to make larger amounts of actin and myosin important to muscular contraction, enhancing muscle contractile ability and strength. Lifting heavier weights with fewer repetitions stimulates **sarcomere hypertrophy**, increasing muscular strength.

PRINCIPLES IN EXERCISE SCIENCE
DIMINISHING RETURN, VARIATION PRINCIPLE, AND ADAPTATION AND SPECIFICITY

In exercise science, the **principle of diminishing returns** means that, when unconditioned individuals start training, their fitness levels improve quickly because they have so far to progress. However, as their fitness increases, they improve less as they near their genetic limits and their fitness levels have plateaued. A corollary to this is that, as people's fitness levels grow, they must train harder to achieve equal gains. Both athletes and trainers designing training programs should remember fitness levels will not continue improving at constant rates as fitness progresses. The **variation principle** means that athletes should alternate hard with light training every several days. Light days enable bodies to recover. Varying training volume and intensity enables attaining peak fitness levels for competing, prevents overstressing or injuring body parts, and sustains athlete interest and motivation for training. Variation relates to **adaptation** because routines must be varied because the body adjusts and adapts to the same routines, stopping challenge and progress. Variation and **specificity** appear to conflict—sport and activity improvement requires more sport- and activity-specific training, while variation dictates training variety—but these can be balanced between enough sport- and activity-specific training for improvement, and some variety using the same muscle groups.

FITT

FITT is a good mnemonic device, homonymous with "fit." It makes it easier to remember exercise variables, which we can manipulate to keep our bodies from adapting and ceasing to progress, and also keep our minds from becoming bored. "FITT" stands for frequency, intensity, time, and type. **Frequency** represents how often we exercise; **intensity** how hard; **time** how long; and **type** the kind of exercise, e.g., walking, running, bicycling, etc. When we work out often enough, hard enough, long enough, and using exercise types appropriate for our individual physiological makeup, body composition, fitness levels, skill levels, mental and psychological dispositions, and preferences, we begin seeing changes in our aerobic capacity, cardiovascular endurance, strength, body fat percentage, and weight. When our bodies adapt to current FITT levels, we can manipulate one or more variables every four to six weeks for ongoing training effects. For example, if someone stops seeing improvement after walking for 20 minutes three times a week, they can: add another day each week; add short bursts of speed-walking, jogging, or hill training; add 10-15 minutes to the duration; or switch to swimming, cycling, or aerobics.

Personal Health and Wellness

Personal Hygiene

Good personal hygiene promotes good health by preventing and limiting exposure to bacterial and viral microorganisms. In addition to **physical benefits**, good bodily hygiene also supports good **mental health** by promoting psychological well-being and feeling good about oneself. When people neglect their personal hygiene, they develop body odors, bad breath, damaged and lost teeth, and unkempt hair and clothing. Other people then view them as unhealthy; as a result, they can encounter social and employment discrimination. Some components of good personal hygiene include bathing, nail care, and foot care. Not everybody needs to bathe or shower daily; for some people, this can remove too many body oils, exacerbating dry skin. However, individuals should wash their bodies and hair regularly as often as they find necessary. The skin is continually shedding dead cells, which must be removed. If it accumulates, it can cause health problems. Trimming the fingernails and toenails regularly averts problems like hangnails and infected nailbeds. Keeping the feet clean and dry, and wearing clean flip-flops at public facilities, gyms, health clubs, spas, and around swimming pools prevents contracting athlete's foot and other fungal infections.

Oral Hygiene, Hand Washing, and Sleep

Ideally, we should brush our teeth after every time we eat. Health professionals recommend brushing and flossing the teeth twice a day at a minimum. **Brushing teeth** removes plaque and reduces mouth bacteria, inhibiting tooth decay. This prevents not only tooth cavities, but also gum disease. **Flossing and gum massage** keep gums healthy and strong. If oral bacteria build up, it can cause gum disease. Gum disease not only causes irreversible bone loss in the jaw; the bacteria can travel from the gums directly to the heart, causing serious heart valve disorders. Unhealthy gums can loosen teeth, causing difficulty chewing, eating, and tooth loss. Most people need dental cleanings and checkups twice yearly, some more often. **Hand washing** prevents bacteria and viruses from spreading. We should wash our hands after using the bathroom; before preparing food and eating; after sneezing or coughing; and after handling garbage. Having alcohol-based hand sanitizing gels on hand is recommended when water is inaccessible. **Sleeping** enough and well must not be overlooked as a component of personal hygiene: insufficient or inadequate sleep impairs the immune system, inviting illness.

Relationship Between Personal Hygiene and Mental and Emotional Status

Physicians and other experts advise that if a friend or acquaintance is neglecting his or her **personal hygiene**, especially if this is unaccustomed, or has an unkempt appearance, this can be a sign of underlying **depression**. When people are depressed or feeling sad, they tend to neglect taking care of themselves and their bodies. This has multiple sources: depression commonly causes low energy and fatigue, making even routine hygiene practices seem to require too much effort. Depression also lowers self-esteem; people do not feel good enough about themselves to show their bodies and health the self-respect or attention they deserve. Additional depression symptoms are feelings of helplessness, inhibiting motivation to control personal care and health; and hopelessness, removing motivation to take any positive action for self-care. Preoccupation with other concerns can also make people forget hygiene. One should not always assume depression is the cause, however; some people simply lack awareness, particularly if poor hygiene is habitual. Honest yet sensitive conversations about hygiene's importance in disease prevention can help some friends and acquaintances. If not, it is best to encourage their seeing a physician, therapist, or counselor.

Decreasing Tobacco Use

WHO recognizes tobacco as "the most widely available harmful product on the market." Therefore, it negotiated the first international, legally binding treaty, the **WHO Framework Convention on Tobacco Control (FCTC)**, providing protocols and guidelines for evidence-based interventions to decrease tobacco supply and consumption. Raising tobacco prices and taxes is a documented cost-effective method that substantially increases quitting and decreases starting smoking, particularly among poor and young people. With proper implementation, enforcing smoke-free public place and workplace laws obtains high compliance levels: fewer youths start smoking; smokers are supported in quitting or reducing smoking; and smoke-free policies prevent perpetuating addiction at earlier stages, especially in youth. Informing and educating the public is another cost-effective measure. Studies in multiple countries find graphic health warnings on cigarette and tobacco packaging and creative media campaigns succeed in powerfully decreasing consumer demand, despite opposition from wealthy tobacco companies and health officials' comparatively limited resources. Another cost-effective measure is providing smoking cessation assistance, combining pharmaceutical and behavioral therapies, through primary medical care and public health providers. Though a minority of the global population has received these measures, research finds them affordable in all world nations.

Role of Physical Activity in Preventing and Reducing Health Risks

Studies demonstrate regular **physical activity (PA)** lowers risks of heart disease, strokes, diabetes, colon cancer, and breast cancer. Thirty to 60 minutes daily of PA decreases breast and colon cancer risks significantly; 150 minutes weekly of PA commonly reduces cardiovascular disease and diabetes risks. The World Health Organization (WHO) finds media promotion of combined PA and healthy diet very cost-effective, inexpensive, and feasible. **Schools** should include physical education with trained teachers and parental involvement in supportive environments. Successful **workplace** strategies include furnishing fitness spaces and signs encouraging staircase use; engaging employees in planning and implementing fitness programs; engaging families via festivals, newsletters, self-learning programs, etc.; and supplying self-monitoring and individual behavior change strategies. Effective **community** interventions include group PA classes and programs; community development campaigns concentrating on shared goals like reducing cardiovascular disease risk; and lifestyle modification advice regarding diet and physical activity, which research has proven to prevent diabetes with effectiveness similar to pharmacological therapy in people with impaired glucose tolerance.

Measures Found Globally to Decrease Harmful Alcohol Consumption

To be effective, strategies for prevention of cardiovascular disease, cirrhosis of the liver, and certain cancers secondary to **harmful alcohol consumption** must change both amounts and patterns of use. Based on evidence from research in Brazil, China, Mexico, Russia, Vietnam, and other countries, the World Health Organization (WHO) recommends these interventions to reduce harmful alcohol use: raising alcoholic beverage taxes; government monopolies of retail alcohol sales where applicable; restricting sales times and outlet density; regulating alcoholic beverage availability and minimum legal purchasing age; comprehensive advertising bans and/or effective marketing regulations limiting exposure to alcoholic drink advertising and marketing; measures to counter drinking and driving including lower (a half-gram per liter) driver blood alcohol concentration limits, zero tolerance or limits lowered further for younger drivers, sobriety checkpoints, and random breath testing; brief interventions for harmful and hazardous drinking, and treatment for alcohol abuse disorders. Isolated classroom and public education, mass media campaigns, and consumer warning messages and labels have not been found effective by research; however, informational and educational campaigns supporting the aforementioned effective measures can enhance their public acceptance.

HEALTHY DIET COMPONENTS FOR PREVENTING AND REDUCING HEALTH RISKS

To prevent and reduce risks of cardiovascular disease, diabetes, and some cancers, healthy diets should balance calorie intake and expenditure for healthy weight maintenance; limit intake from total fats to 30 percent; eliminate trans fats, and substitute unsaturated fats for saturated; limit consumption of free sugars; increase consumption of vegetables, legumes, fruits, whole grains, and nuts; make all salt iodized; and limit sodium intake from all sources. Although studies find multiple nutritional interventions more cost-effective with greater potential health gains than individual interventions, the World Health Organization (WHO) also identifies **salt reduction** for preventing noncommunicable diseases. A major cause of death is high blood pressure, frequently caused or exacerbated by excess dietary sodium. About 75 percent of salt intake in North America and Europe comes from sodium added to manufactured meals and foods. Most sodium consumed in many Asian and African countries is from soy sauce and salt added at home during cooking and eating. WHO estimates decreasing salt to recommended levels could prevent up to 2.5 million deaths annually. Finland, France, Ireland, Japan, and the United Kingdom have successfully implemented salt reduction initiatives, preventing thousands of premature deaths and saving billions in healthcare and other expenses annually.

Chronic and Communicable Diseases

LIFE CHOICES TO PREVENT CHRONIC DISEASES AND HEALTH CONDITIONS, AND CONTRASTING HEALTH RISK BEHAVIORS

Regular **aerobic exercise** or **physical activity** can prevent cardiovascular disease. Weight-bearing exercise strengthens bones, preventing osteoporosis which leads to fractures. Exercising, limiting sodium intake, not smoking, eating diets low in saturated and trans fats and high in fiber, and losing or controlling weight all reduce risks for strokes and heart disease by strengthening the heart and blood vessels and reducing blood pressure, cholesterol and arterial plaque. **Not smoking** also prevents lung cancer and other respiratory, oral, and digestive system cancers. **Eating vegetables and fruits** accesses antioxidants protecting against many cancers, and fibers protecting against colorectal cancers, as does eating whole grains. Binge drinking kills many Americans, most of whom are not alcohol-dependent; hence **avoiding binge drinking** prevents deaths. According to the CDC, more than half of adults do not get recommended levels of aerobic or muscle-strengthening exercise or physical activity. Most Americans consume **excessive sodium**, risking hypertension. Almost half have other major heart-disease risk factors, i.e., uncontrolled hypertension and/or high LDL cholesterol. Over one-third of adults reported (2011) eating fruit less than once daily, almost one-fourth vegetables less than once daily; over one-third of teens ate fruit and vegetables less than once daily. Nearly 20 percent of adults smoked in 2012.

TREATMENT FOR MANY TYPES OF CANCER

Whether they involve localized solid tumors or diffuse conditions like leukemia and other cancers of the blood, all **cancer** is, by definition, an uncontrolled growth of abnormal cells. Therefore, treatment typically involves removing and/or killing the cancerous cells, growths, or masses. One treatment is **surgically removing** cancerous tissue. Some inoperable cancers would require removing needed healthy tissue, as with sarcoidosis wrapped around the spinal cord, or aggressive tumors having invaded too much of vital organs. In some cases, an entire organ may be surgically replaced by **donor transplantation**. Surgical removal of a cancerous growth is often followed by **radiation treatment**—exposure to radioactive elements—to eliminate any remaining cancer cells and/or prevent new regrowth. Side-effects include burns or other damages to the treatment site. Another treatment method to kill cancer cells is **chemotherapy**. Various drugs, administered orally or intravenously, are toxic to cancer growths. Unfortunately, most treatments toxic enough to kill cancer cells are also toxic to the patient. Chemotherapy side effects include severe nausea, vomiting, debilitating fatigue, hair loss, skin damage, and osteoporosis. Some treatment protocols combine methods, e.g., surgery followed by radiation and chemotherapy, radiation to shrink a tumor followed by surgery, etc.

HEALTH EDUCATION PROGRAM FOR MANAGING CHRONIC DISEASES AND HEALTH CONDITIONS

Stanford University's School of Medicine Patient Education Research Center offers a chronic disease self-management program called the **Better Choices, Better Health® Workshop**. Facilitated by two trained leaders, one or both non-health professionals with their own chronic diseases, this workshop is held in hospitals, libraries, senior centers, churches, and other community settings. Weekly classes are two-and-a-half hours each for six weeks. The workshop covers subjects including techniques for coping with pain, fatigue, frustration, and isolation; exercises appropriate for preserving and enhancing endurance, strength, and flexibility; using medications appropriately; nutrition; decision-making; effective communication with health professionals, family, and friends; and how to evaluate new treatments. Participants are given the accompanying *Relaxation for Mind and Body* audio CD and *Living a Healthy Life with Chronic Conditions, 4th edition* book. Sessions involve high participation levels, mutual success, and support. This course was developed based on federally- and state-funded research. Researchers included Stanford psychologist Albert Bandura, originator of self-efficacy, i.e., self-confidence for mastering new skills or influencing one's health. Bandura and colleagues deemed **self-management skills instruction** instrumental in managing chronic disease; program evaluation yielded positive outcomes. Stanford offers healthcare organization representatives program training four to five times yearly.

HIV/AIDS

The **human immunodeficiency virus** (HIV) impairs or destroys an infected individual's immune system, raising infection risk and ruining infection defenses. As HIV advances, its final stage is **AIDS**, acquired immune deficiency syndrome. The World Health Organization (WHO) estimated that by the end of 2013, 35 million humans were living with HIV. Of these, 23.4-26.2 million lived in sub-Saharan Africa. Global health community efforts include research and development of new medications to address symptoms for people already infected, as well as preventing new infections; outreach and education to stop HIV spread; and supporting children and families who have lost parents to AIDS deaths. **Anti-retroviral therapy (ART) drugs** have enabled many HIV patients to survive 15+ years before developing AIDS symptoms. WHO estimated 12.9 million people were receiving these by the end of 2013, 11.7 million of them in low-income and middle-income nations. The most successful global health effort, this program has been significantly helped by the **President's Emergency Plan for AIDS Relief (PEPFAR)**. Additionally, the US Department of Health and Human Services (HHS), National Institutes of Health (NIH) offices, Gates Foundation, and Centers for Disease Control and Prevention (CDC) are all actively involved in global HIV/AIDS research, researcher training, coordination, and vaccine development.

CYSTIC FIBROSIS

In cystic fibrosis (**CF**), a defective gene produces a protein causing the body to secrete mucus that is much thicker and stickier than normal. This mucus clogs up the lungs, resulting in infections that can cause or threaten death. It also blocks the pancreas from delivering enzymes that help break down and absorb necessary nutrients from foods. Over 75 percent of CF patients are diagnosed by age 2. Today, almost half of CF patients are aged 18 or more. Around 1,000 new CF cases are diagnosed annually. Symptoms include shortness of breath; wheezing; chronic persistent coughing, including phlegm-productive coughs; slow weight gain and inadequate growth despite good appetite; frequently developing lung infections; difficult, bulky, greasy, and/or frequent bowel movements; and skin with an extremely salty taste. Most children with CF died before entering elementary school during the 1950s. Today, significant progress in the understanding and treatment of CF has dramatically improved longevity and life quality in CF patients. Many now live into middle adulthood or older; life expectancy has doubled in the past three decades. The **Cystic Fibrosis Foundation**, whose support has enabled almost all available CF treatment medications, views research for a cure as "promising."

SICKLE CELL ANEMIA

Anemia means the blood has fewer **red blood cells (RBC)** than normal. RBCs, which transport oxygen in **hemoglobin** (an iron-rich protein) through the bloodstream and remove the waste product carbon dioxide, are produced in the bone marrow, normally living about four months. **Sickle cell** is one genetic type of anemia, inherited when both parents have the gene. When one parent has this gene but the other's is normal, children inherit sickle cell trait; they do not have the disease, but pass the sickle hemoglobin gene to their children. In America, sickle cell anemia is commonest in African-Americans (around one in 500). It also affects Hispanic-Americans (around one in 36,000); and people of Caribbean, Mediterranean, Indian, and Saudi Arabian descent. Normal RBCs are disc-shaped and travel easily through blood vessels. Sickle cells are crescent-shaped, sticky, and stiff, impeding blood flow. This causes organ damage, pain, and increased risk of infections. Some patients have chronic fatigue and/or pain. A few patients may receive future cures through stem cell transplants, but no widespread cure currently exists. Symptoms and complications are managed through treatments. Improved care and treatments enable some patients to live into their 40s, 50s, or older.

TAY-SACHS DISEASE

Tay-Sachs disease is a rare genetic disorder, inherited through an **autosomal recessive pattern**; i.e., both parents carry copies of a mutated gene and are usually asymptomatic, but pass these to their children. **Tay-Sachs** is rare overall, and more common among Eastern/Central European Jewish, certain Quebec French-Canadian, Old-Order Pennsylvania Dutch/Amish, and Louisiana Cajun populations. The genetic defect prevents an enzyme from breaking down a toxic substance, which builds up in the brain and spinal cord, progressively destroying neurons. The commonest form appears in infancy, typically around 3-6 months. A typical sign is a "cherry-red spot" eye abnormality, detectable through eye examination. Babies' motor muscles weaken; development slows; they lose motor skills like turning over, sitting up, and crawling; and develop exaggerated startle reactions to loud sounds. As it progresses, this disease causes seizures, loss of vision and hearing, intellectual impairment, and paralysis. Most children with the commoner infantile form of Tay-Sachs disease typically only survive until early childhood. Later-onset forms of the disease are extremely rare, typically with milder, highly variable symptoms including muscular weakness, poor coordination, other motor symptoms, speech difficulties, and mental illness.

TYPE 2 DIABETES

Historically, type 1 diabetes, which has a greater genetic component, was called "juvenile diabetes" because symptoms appeared during childhood, contrasting with type 2 "adult-onset diabetes." However, these terms were abandoned as more cases of **type 2 diabetes** are occurring in childhood and adolescence—evidence of the contributions of **lifestyle factors** including obesity, poor nutrition, and physical inactivity. When people consume large amounts of refined carbohydrates (simple sugars and starches processed to remove all fibers) with no fiber slowing digestion, these enter the bloodstream rapidly, causing a sudden spike in blood sugar, experienced by some as an energy rush. However, with quick metabolism and the pancreas' secretion of extra insulin to neutralize excessive blood sugar, sugars exit as fast as they entered, causing a precipitous blood-sugar drop, or "crash," with fatigue, sleepiness, irritability, depression and cycle-perpetuating cravings for more sugar or starch. Moreover, **metabolic syndrome** eventually develops—insulin resistance to the pancreas' attempts to neutralize repeated artificial blood sugar elevation. In type 1 diabetes, the pancreas fails to produce insulin; in type 2, the body becomes immune to insulin, causing chronically high, unstable blood sugar. Blindness, limb loss, shock, coma, and death are a few of many sequelae from uncontrolled diabetes.

CHRONIC, NONCOMMUNICABLE DISEASES

According to the World Health Organization (WHO, 2013), over 36 million people die annually from **noncommunicable diseases (NCDs)**, with almost 80 percent (29 million) in low-income and middle-income nations. Of these, over 9 million are before age 60. Of these premature deaths, 90 percent are in low-income and middle-income nations. Roughly 80 percent of all NCD deaths are due to four disease types: **cardiovascular diseases**, e.g., strokes and heart attacks, which cause the majority (17.3 million yearly); **cancers** (7.6 million yearly); **respiratory diseases** like asthma and chronic obstructive pulmonary disease (COPD) (4.2 million yearly); and **diabetes** (1.3 million yearly). These four disease groups have four **risk factors** in common: tobacco use, physical inactivity, harmful alcohol use, and poor nutrition. WHO projects the greatest increases in NCD mortality by 2020 will be in African countries, where NCDs are also predicted to surpass maternal and infant mortality from childbirth and nutritional and communicable diseases combined as the most common killers by 2030. Behavioral risk factors for NCDs that can be modified are tobacco use, physical inactivity, unhealthy diets, and harmful alcohol consumption.

MEASURES TAKEN BY WHO TO PREVENT NCDS

WHO's *Action Plan of the global strategy for the prevention and control of noncommunicable diseases* gives member states and international partners steps for preventing and addressing NCDs in world nations. WHO is also working to reduce **NCD risk factors**, including: implementing anti-tobacco measures identified in the WHO Framework Convention on Tobacco Control in world nations to decrease public tobacco exposure; helping world communities lower rates of death and disease from physical inactivity and unhealthy diets through the WHO *Global strategy on diet, physical activity and health aims to promote and protect health;* identifying action areas with priority and recommending measures of protection against the harmful consumption of alcohol through the WHO *Global strategy to reduce the harmful use of alcohol;* responding to the United Nations Political Declaration on NCDs by developing a comprehensive framework for global NCD prevention, monitoring, and control, which includes a group of global voluntary targets and a list of indicators; and responding to the World Health Assembly's resolution (WHA 64.11) by developing a 2013-2020 **Global NCD Action Plan** with comprehensive guidance for implementing the United Nations High-Level Meeting's political commitments. WHA endorsed this plan, urging member state, Director-General and Secretariat implementation and future WHA progress reports.

DISEASE ETIOLOGY

Etiology is defined in medicine as the study of origins or causes of diseases or pathological conditions. Early writings attributed diseases to various unproven "causes" including spells, curses, and imbalances in bodily humors. Ancient Greek physicians Galen and Hippocrates often associated disease with unidentified components in the air, influencing miasmatic perspectives on disease etiology of Medieval European physicians. Ancient Roman scholar Marcus Terentius Varro suggested **microorganisms** caused diseases in his book *On Agriculture* in the 1st century BC. German physician Robert Koch (1843-1910), modern bacteriology founder, discovered scientific evidence of microorganisms causing the infectious diseases anthrax, cholera, and tuberculosis. As in all experimental science, in **epidemiology**, statistical correlation between/among variables does not prove causation. Sir Austin Bradford-Hill, the epidemiologist who proved causal relationship between tobacco smoking and lung cancer, defined criteria for showing causation. American epidemiologist Alfred Evans proposed the **Unified Concept of Causation**, synthesizing previous thinking. **Etiology** can contribute to causal chains including independent co-factors and promoters. For example, stress, once believed to cause peptic ulcer disease, was belatedly identified as a promoter, with excess stomach acid a prerequisite and *Helicobacter pylori* infection the primary etiology.

RELATIONSHIPS AMONG AND WITHIN DISEASE ETIOLOGIES

Certain diseases, e.g., hepatitis or diabetes, can be diagnosed according to their symptoms. However, these diseases can also develop from **different etiologies**, and can co-exist with, result from, or result in various other conditions. For instance, type 1 diabetes includes a strong genetic component in its etiology, though it also appears to involve complex interactions of genetic and environmental influences; whereas type 2 diabetes more often appears to result from environmental (i.e., lifestyle) influences to a greater extent. Hepatitis (liver inflammation) has separate etiologies: hepatitis A, B, and C are each caused by distinct viruses; autoimmune hepatitis is not infectious, but caused by the patient's own immune system attacking the liver. On the other hand, several different diseases can also result from one **single etiology**. For example, the Epstein-Barr virus can cause the infectious disease mononucleosis, or either of two types of cancer—Burkitt's lymphoma or nasopharyngeal carcinoma—under different conditions.

INFLUENZA

Influenza (flu) is an infectious viral respiratory illness. Its symptoms can range from mild to fatal. Young children, seniors, and people with some health conditions have greatest risk for serious complications. Annual **vaccination** is the best way to prevent it. The US Department of Health and Human Services' (HHS) Office of Global Affairs, International Influenza Unit (IIU) is an international partnership to enhance global flu identification and response, coordinated by HHS personnel and Operation Divisions including National Institutes of Health (NIH); Centers for Disease Control and Infection (CDC); Food and Drug Administration (FDA); Office of the Assistant Secretary for Preparedness and Response, Biomedical Advanced Research and Development Authority (ASPR/BARDA); the US Departments of State (DOS), Defense (DOD), Agriculture (USDA), Commerce, and Treasury; the US Agency for International Development (USAID); foreign governments; the international World Health Organization (WHO), World Bank, International Partnership on Avian and Pandemic Influenza (IPAPI), Global Health Security Action Group (GHSAG), UN System Influenza Coordination (UNSIC), Pan-American Health Organization (PAHO); and nonprofits like PATH and the Gates Foundation. **Influenza pandemics**—world outbreaks— occur when a new virus with little or no human immunity emerges. There were three in the 20th century and one so far in the 21st.

RELATIONSHIP BETWEEN COMMUNICABLE DISEASES AND EMERGENCY AND DISASTER CONDITIONS

According to the World Health Organization (WHO), **natural disasters** and **war conditions** can break water and sewer pipes and sewage treatment mechanisms, and disrupt electricity for pumping water. This can lead to **waterborne** and **vector-borne diseases**. When disaster or war survivors live in crowded temporary arrangements with inadequate personal hygiene and laundry facilities and poor ventilation, personal contact can spread highly contagious diseases into **epidemics**. Disaster victims are also more susceptible to communicable diseases as unsanitary living conditions, stress, fatigue, and malnutrition lower their resistance. An additional disease transmission factor is how long refugees live in temporary shelters: mass settlement for extended times can cause epidemic outbreaks. Famine relief camps particularly involve many people already weakened, potentially ill, and staying there for long durations. Storms, floods, earthquakes, mudslides, etc. can both contaminate water supplies with sewage and waste and create standing water where insect disease vectors breed. **Communicable disease control** requires adequate shelter, sanitation, clean water, vector control, health workers trained in early diagnosis and treatment, and immunization which combine to produce healthy environments.

PREPARING FOR AND PREVENTING COMMUNICABLE DISEASE OUTBREAKS

Research by the World Health Organization (WHO) has identified the five commonest **causes of mortality** related to emergency and disaster conditions: malaria (in certain areas), malnutrition, diarrhea, measles, and acute respiratory infections. While not a communicable disease, **malnutrition** is made significantly worse by communicable diseases; the others, all communicable diseases, are related directly to environmental health conditions. When conditions preceding disasters are **unsanitary**, as in large cities with dense populations in developing nations, disease problems following disasters are more likely. Therefore, advance measures to alleviate poverty, raise awareness, improve organization, and establish sanitary and health services offer greater community protection in the event of disaster. **Preparedness** includes training outreach and health personnel to identify and manage specific disease threats; stocking equipment and supplies locally for environmental health; diagnosis and treatment for potential disease outbreaks; applying protocols for information management practices regarding particular diseases; raising local awareness of communicable diseases and the importance of early health facility referral;

Copyright © Mometrix Media. You have been licensed one copy of this document for personal use only. Any other reproduction or redistribution is strictly prohibited. All rights reserved.
This content is provided for test preparation purposes only and does not imply an endorsement by Mometrix of any particular political, scientific, or religious point of view.

strengthening health-surveillance systems; promoting hygiene; and providing adequate clean water supplies, suitable shelter, sanitation facilities, and advance vaccination campaigns.

PUBLIC HEALTH SURVEILLANCE

Public health surveillance involves collecting, analyzing, and distributing health information for the purpose of taking prompt and appropriate action. As reported by Doctors Without Borders, during emergency and disaster situations, affected populations are more susceptible to diseases; the instability of the circumstances causes sudden changes in health; and to take effective action quickly, health workers must share quantitative data with a variety of partners. The World Health Organization (WHO) emphasizes the importance of designating certain health personnel to conduct public health surveillance. Hospital staff, temporary relief center workers, and community and neighborhood health personnel must be vigilant for unusual numbers of malaria cases, food poisoning, other toxicity, encephalitis, meningitis, cholera, plague, typhus, typhoid fever, paratyphoid fever, and other ailments or diseases. Workers should take patient histories, identify contacts, and isolate disease sources. **Public health surveillance** can be conducted to some degree even in large-scale population movement's worst circumstances. Health workers can extend existing reporting systems to area-wide surveillance systems addressing sanitation- and water-related epidemics and other high-priority diseases. **Active population movement pattern surveillance** affords data for predicting future settlement patterns, general disease surveillance, and emergency intervention planning.

Skills for Enhancing Health and Reducing Risks

Mental and Emotional Health

EQ

COMPONENTS, ASPECTS OF LIFE EFFECTED, AND DEVELOPMENT SKILLS

Emotional intelligence (EQ) includes self-awareness, self-regulation (self-management), social awareness, and relationship management. EQ affects physical health, mental health, school and work performance, and relationships. Five **skills to develop EQ** are:

- ability to reduce stress quickly in various contexts
- ability to recognize our emotions and prevent their overwhelming us
- ability to relate to others emotionally through nonverbal communication
- ability to maintain connections during challenging circumstances through playfulness and humor
- ability for confident, positive conflict resolution

To function well under stress, identify your **physiological responses to stress** (e.g., shallow/rapid breathing, tight stomach, muscle tension/pain, clenched hands). Recognition enables **regulation**. Identify your individual stress response: those who become agitated or angry can relieve stress with calming, quieting activities. Those who become withdrawn or depressed can relieve stress through stimulating activities. Those who slow down in some ways and speed up in others, causing paralysis, need activities combining stimulation and comfort. Sensory engagement rapidly decreases stress. Individuals should discover which sense(s) (vision, hearing, touch, smell, taste) and technique(s) are most energizing and/or soothing personally.

To recognize your emotions and stay focused and calm during stressful interactions, ask yourself about the quality of your **relationship with your emotions**. Do your emotions flow from one to another along with your changing momentary experiences? Do you feel physical sensations in your body associated with your emotions? Do you feel distinct emotions, e.g., joy, sadness, anger, and fear; and do your subtle facial expressions show each of these? Are you able to feel intense emotions, strong enough to capture both your and others' attention? Do you attend to your emotions? Do they affect your decision-making? If any of these are unfamiliar, you may have shut your emotions off. Many people do this in reaction to negative childhood experiences. Reconnecting with, becoming comfortable with, and accessing **core emotions** are necessary to emotional intelligence and health. Mindful meditation can facilitate these.

To interact well with others, **nonverbal signals** can be more important than words—i.e., how you say things more than what you say. This includes body posture, muscle tension, physical gestures, facial expressions, eye contact, vocal tone, etc. Nonverbal cues convey interest or disinterest, trust or mistrust, excitement or apathy, confidence or fear, clarity or confusion, and connection or disconnection. Nonverbal communication requires both conveying what you intend, and reading others' subtle nonverbal signals. To improve it, attend to others rather than planning what to say next, thinking about other things, or daydreaming so as not to miss cues. Make eye contact to gauge others' responses, maintain conversational flow, and convey interest. Attend to nonverbal signals you are sending and receiving—not only face, body, touch, and tone of voice, but also the pace, timing and rhythm of conversation. If what you say does not reflect what you feel, your body will contradict your words.

Being able to **laugh** and make others laugh can relieve stress, improve moods, rebalance nervous systems, lighten mental loads, place things in perspective, and increase EQ. Laughing and playing enable us to take setbacks and difficulties in stride. Gentle humor enables communicating messages that could otherwise offend, anger, or provoke defensiveness in others. Humor also soothes **interpersonal differences**. Communicating playfully both energizes and relaxes, simultaneously alleviating fatigue and dissipating physical tension. It moreover loosens rigid thinking, enabling creativity and new perspectives. To develop playful communication, experts recommend practicing by interacting often with outgoing, playful people; playing with young children, babies, and animals; discovering activities you enjoy that access your playful qualities and loosen you up; and setting aside time regularly for quality playing, joking, and laughing.

Conflict is inevitable, but when constructively managed, it can promote relationship safety, trust, freedom, and creativity. When interpersonal conflicts are not viewed as punitive or threatening but managed positively to build trust, they can strengthen relationships. This skill is informed by the previous four: stress management, emotional awareness, nonverbal communication, and playfulness and humor facilitate skillful handling and defusing of emotionally charged interactions. To develop positive, trust-building **conflict-resolution skills**, focus on the present and acknowledge current reality as an opportunity to resolve old reactions to conflicts, rather than clinging to old resentments and wounds. Regarding arguments, pick your battles: arguing, particularly toward positive resolutions, uses energy and time. Decide whether an issue is worth or not worth arguing over. Forgiveness is also necessary: we must let go of desires for revenge or punishment for others' past hurtful actions to resolve conflicts. Even when a conflict cannot be resolved, continuing it takes two people; although disagreeing, you can end the conflict by disengaging from it.

MENTAL OR EMOTIONAL HEALTH

Mental or emotional health describes an individual's overall **psychological well-being**. This incorporates a person's self-esteem, i.e., the way s/he feels about herself/himself, a person's ability to manage her/his emotions and ability to cope with stress and problems in life, and the quality of an individual's relationships. **Mental and emotional health** are analogous to physical health in the sense that, just as we must make conscious efforts to maintain or build up our physical health, we must equally make conscious efforts to sustain or establish our mental and emotional health. Good mental and emotional health is not simply an absence of anxiety, depression, or other mental health problems. It is moreover the presence of positive attributes. It is not merely the absence of feeling bad, but the presence of feeling good. Some people may not experience any overtly negative feelings, yet it is still necessary for them to do things that afford them positive feelings to attain emotional and mental health.

CHARACTERISTICS ASSOCIATED WITH BEING MENTALLY AND EMOTIONALLY HEALTHY

When people are **healthy**, both emotionally and mentally, they feel and demonstrate **positive personal characteristics**, enabling them to engage in meaningful, productive activities and relationships that promote full participation in life. These include: high self-esteem, i.e., they feel good about themselves. They feel and demonstrate self-confidence in themselves and their abilities. They are able to have fun and laugh, and they experience and display a zest for life. They are able to cope with stress and can bounce back from the impacts of any adverse events they encounter. They feel a sense of contentment. They demonstrate flexibility for adapting to changes and learning new things. They are able to develop and sustain satisfying relationships. In both their relationships and their activities, they experience senses of purpose and meaning. In living their lives from day to day, they achieve a balance between opposites like activity and rest, work and play, waking and sleeping, exercising and eating, physical and mental activity, etc.

RESILIENCE

It is a normal part of life to experience **changes**; disappointments; losses; difficult times; and emotional problems that can provoke anxiety, sadness, and stress. While all people encounter these, some cope better than others. Some people experience a very traumatic event and never recover from it. Some suffer permanent damage, significantly impairing their ability to live normal lives. Others carry on, but with major impingements on their ability to participate in and enjoy life fully. **Resilience** is the ability to bounce back from stress, trauma, and other adverse experiences. People with good emotional and mental health have resilience. One component of resilience is having **personal tools** to keep a positive perspective and cope with difficulties. While some people begin developing these early in life, those who did not can still acquire them later with effort and help. Resilient individuals maintain focus, flexibility, and creativity through good and bad times. Additional components of resilience are stress management and emotional self-regulation skills. Being able to recognize our feelings and appropriately express them prevents becoming lodged in negative emotional states like anxiety or depression. Another component of resilience is a strong **network** of supportive people.

EFFECTS OF PHYSICAL HEALTH ON MENTAL AND EMOTIONAL HEALTH

The body and mind are interdependent and constantly interact. Better **physical health** automatically confers better **mental and emotional health**. For instance, when we exercise, we not only make our hearts and lungs stronger, but the activity also releases endorphins, i.e., neurotransmitters in the brain that relieve pain, elevate mood, energize, and promote euphoria or feelings of well-being. Physical health practices supporting mental and emotional health include adequate **sleep**, about 7-8 hours for most individuals. Learning about and practicing good **nutrition** is also important; it is complex and sometimes not simple to implement, but the more we learn about how what we eat affects mood as well as energy, strength, endurance, etc., the easier it can become to eat for physical and psychological health. **Exercise** not only promotes physical fitness; it powerfully relieves anxiety, depression, and stress. Restricting it to going to a gym is unnecessary: regularly incorporating physical activity into daily life, e.g., taking the stairs, walking more, etc. has enormous benefits. Ten to 15 minutes of sunshine daily improves mood (longer durations require sunscreen to prevent skin damage and cancer). Alcohol, tobacco, and other drugs may produce short-term good feelings, but long-term they impair mood and both mental and emotional health, and so should be avoided.

LIVING STRATEGIES TO SUPPORT MENTAL AND EMOTIONAL HEALTH

Attending to our own emotions and needs is necessary to mental and emotional health by preventing buildup of negative feelings and stress. Striking a balance between duties and enjoyable pursuits is important. **Self-care** enables better coping when encountering challenges. **Endorphins** (brain chemicals promoting well-being) are released not only by physical exercise and activity, but also by the following: helping or positively affecting others, which also enhances self-esteem; practicing self-control and discipline, which counters negative ideas, helplessness, and despair and promotes hope; discovering and learning new things—taking classes, learning languages, attending museums, traveling ("mind candy"); enjoying nature, e.g., walking paths through woods or gardens, sitting by a lake or on a beach, hiking, etc., which research proves not only releases endorphins but also lowers blood pressure and dissipates stress; enjoying art, e.g., art galleries, architecture, etc., which have the same effects; managing stress levels; and consciously avoiding absorption in mental habits like excessive worrying or negative thoughts about the world and/or oneself.

The following practices are strategies recommended to care for ourselves that promote good **mental and emotional health**: do things appealing to the senses, like listening to mood-elevating music; looking at beautiful scenes of nature, art and craft objects, and animals; looking at and smelling flowers; savoring the flavors and temperatures of foods and beverages; massaging one's hands and feet, or giving and receiving these to and from partners; scented baths; petting animals, etc. Adopt a pet. Though they incur responsibilities, caring for pets makes us feel loved and needed; pets give unconditional love, and some promote going outside, exercising, and finding new places and people. Do creative, meaningful work, for pay or not. Building things, playing musical instruments, composing music, drawing, painting, sculpture, pottery, writing, gardening, etc. stimulate creativity, engender feelings of productivity, and result in products we can feel proud of, enjoy, and share. Prioritizing leisure time is not self-indulgent; playing and doing enjoyable things for their own sake, e.g., reading, watching movies, visiting or talking with friends, or enjoying nature are necessary to mental and emotional health. Meditating, praying, reviewing reasons for gratitude, watching sunrises and sunsets, etc. are ways to take time to contemplate and appreciate life.

INFLUENCE OF SUPPORTIVE SOCIAL INTERACTIONS AND RELATIONSHIPS ON MENTAL AND EMOTIONAL HEALTH

Humans are naturally **social**, with emotional needs for connections and relationships with others. Improving mental and emotional health includes social as well as private activities. **Social interactions** provide companionship, intellectual stimulation and exchanges, intimacy, humor and laughter; talking to others about problems and feelings can decrease stress. People who are supportive and listen well without criticizing or judging benefit our psychological health; reciprocally, so do listening well to and supporting others. Some ways to engage in social interactions include: periodically walking away from the screens of our computers, tablets, smartphones, and TV sets for the real world to engage in face-to-face, direct interaction that includes nonverbal communication. Another strategy is to make it a priority to spend face-to-face time with friends, co-workers, neighbors, relatives, and other people that we like and enjoy, and who have positive attitudes and interest in us. When we meet people we like, we can make it a point to ask about them. Volunteering benefits both recipients and ourselves, expanding and enriching our lives. Many organizations rely on volunteers to function. Another way to meet potential friends is joining groups that share our interests and meet regularly.

RISK FACTORS THAT CAN THREATEN MENTAL AND EMOTIONAL HEALTH

Experiences in life, particularly in early childhood, influence mental and emotional health. While genetic and biological influences are involved, these interact with and are affected by **environmental experiences**. Some **risk factors** that can threaten mental and emotional health include: inadequate attachment to one's parent or primary caregiver in infancy or early childhood; feeling unsafe, isolated, lonely, confused, or abused early in life; serious traumas or losses, e.g., parent death, hospitalization, or war, particularly in early childhood; negative experiences whereby an individual develops learned helplessness, i.e., the belief that one has little or no control over the circumstances of one's life; serious illness, particularly disabling illness, chronic illness, or illness that isolates the individual from other people; medication side-effects, which can often become hazardous for older people taking multiple medications that interact unfavorably; and substance abuse. Abusing alcohol and/or other drugs can both exacerbate pre-existing mental health disorders, and cause new mental health or emotional problems.

WARNING SIGNALS THAT PROFESSIONAL HELP FOR EMOTIONAL OR MENTAL HEALTH PROBLEMS IS NEEDED

Some behaviors, feelings, or thoughts to pay attention to as signals to seek **professional help** for emotional or mental health problems include: you are unable to sleep, not just for one night but recurrently. You feel discouraged, sad, helpless, or hopeless a majority of the time. You have trouble concentrating, such that it interferes with work and/or life at home. You are using food, tobacco, alcohol, or other drugs to cope with problematic emotions. You are having negative or self-destructive thoughts or fears you cannot control. You think more often than normal about death and dying. You have thoughts about suicide. Even if you think these are only speculative and you would never act on them, any thoughts of suicide are serious warning signs. If you have consistently worked to improve your mental and emotional health without success, this is reason to pursue professional help. Our natural **human social orientation** makes us amenable to input from caring, knowledgeable professionals. Their knowledge, training, experience, expertise, perspective, techniques, advice, and counsel can help us do things we could not do on our own to help ourselves.

Stress, Depression, and Suicide

CONSERVATION OF RESOURCES THEORY

Conservation of resources (**COR**) theory (Hobfoll, 1988, 1989, 1998, 2001) views the main element in stress as **resource loss**. People lose resource and also use additional resources during stress. Hence throughout the process, they accumulate greater susceptibility to **negative stress impacts**. While many theorists view stress as either environmental/external or psychological/internal, COR is an integrative theory equally incorporating both orientations. Its essential premise is that people endeavor to get, keep, cultivate, and protect things they value. To combat perceived environmental threat, they need a combination of cultural belonging, social attachments, and personal strengths. These attributes are **resources**: energy, condition, personal characteristic, and object resources. They are both cultural products and cross-cultural in nature. When individuals lose resources, resource loss is threatened, or individuals invest significant resources without gaining resources, stress ensues. COR theory principles are: (1) resource loss is disproportionately more impactful than resource gain. (2) To prevent resource loss, recover from loss, and gain resources, people must invest resources. Proactive coping and positive stress outcomes are also aspects considered in COR theory.

Two **conservation of resources (COR) theory principles** are: losing resources has disproportionately more impact than gaining resources; and people have to invest resources to prevent losing them, recover from losing them, and acquire additional resources. There are also four corollaries to these principles. **Corollary 1**: those with more resources are more able to gain and less vulnerable to lose resources; conversely, those with fewer resources are less able to gain and more likely to lose resources. **Corollary 2**: initial loss causes future loss. **Corollary 3**: initial gain causes additional gain. **Corollary 4**: lacking resources engenders defensive responses of conserving what resources one does possess. One example of a **loss spiral** is in research (Lane & Hobfoll, 1992) with people suffering chronic obstructive pulmonary disease (COPD). They experienced a series of increasing resource losses. The more resources they lost, the angrier they became. The angrier they became, the more they alienated possible support givers, increasing their resource loss vulnerability. Another study (Rini et al, 1999) reported lower self-esteem, mastery, and optimism—i.e., personal resources—in lower-income, less-educated Hispanic mothers-to-be, causing greater stress, which caused major infant risk factors of shorter gestation and low birth weights—predicting greater ongoing resource demands and stress.

STRESS MANAGEMENT AND COMMON UNHEALTHY REACTIONS TO LIFE STRESSORS

Stress is inevitable; however, effective **stress management skills and techniques** enable healthy coping. According to the Mayo Clinic, individuals begin stress management by understanding how they currently react to stress, and then adopting new stress management techniques or modifying existing ones to keep life stressors from leading to health issues. There are several unhealthy but common reactions to stress:

- **Pain**: internalized or unresolved stress can trigger headaches, backaches, upset stomachs, shortness of breath, insomnia, and muscular pain from unconsciously tensing the shoulders and neck and/or clenching jaws or fists.
- **Eating and/or activity**: some people skip eating from stress, thereby losing weight; others overeat or eat when not hungry and/or skip exercise, gaining weight.
- **Anger**: some people lose their tempers more easily over minor or unrelated things when stressed.
- **Crying**: some people cry over minor or unrelated things when stressed; experience unexpected, prolonged crying; and/or feel isolated and lonely.

- **Depression and anxiety**: stress can contribute to depressive and anxiety disorders, including problem avoidance, calling in sick, feeling hopeless, or giving up.
- **Negativity**: individuals not coping effectively with stress may exaggerate the negative qualities of undesired circumstances and/or always expect the worst.
- **Smoking and/or substance use**: people may escalate current smoking, drinking, or drug use under stress; those who had previously quit may relapse.

STRESS MANAGEMENT TECHNIQUES

- **Cut back**: when overextended, examine duties and delegate, eliminate, or limit some.
- **Prepare**: set realistic goals for major and minor tasks; improve scheduling; allow time for unexpected events like traffic jams, car trouble, minor medical emergencies, extra work, etc. to prevent stress from accumulating.
- **Reach out**: revisit lapsed relationships; form new ones; volunteer. Surrounding oneself with supportive friends, relatives, colleagues, and spiritual leaders enhances psychological well-being, boosting capacity for coping with stress.
- **Hobbies**: enjoyable activities that do not stimulate competitiveness or anxiety are soothing. These vary individually. Some choices include crafts, music, reading, dance classes, gardening, woodworking and carpentry, electronics, fishing, sailing, etc.
- **Relaxation techniques**: these include meditation, yoga, massage therapy, physical activities, etc. The technique selected is less important than increasing body awareness and refocusing attention onto calmness.
- **Adequate sleep**: lack of sleep exacerbates stress. Insufficient sleep impairs judgment and the immune system. Sleep-deprived individuals are more prone to overreacting to minor irritants. Most of us require eight hours of sleep nightly. Interrupted or irregular sleep impedes REM sleep, dreaming, and deep sleep-enabling physical and neurological repairs.
- **Professional help**: if stress management techniques are insufficient, see a physician before uncontrolled, ongoing stress causes health problems.

LIFE SKILLS TO USE FOR STRESS MANAGEMENT AND STRESSFUL LIFE EVENTS DURING LIFE STAGES

Four major life skills that people can apply to cope with common life stressors are values clarification, decision-making, communication skills, and coping skills. The following are typical life stressors in early childhood, adolescence, middle adulthood, and later adulthood; and coping mechanisms they can apply from the life skill perspective of **values clarification**.

- Early childhood: a pet's death – according to values clarification, reviewing the pet's **positive qualities** (similarly to adults' celebrating the life of the deceased) and considering getting another pet can address stressors.
- Adolescence: unwanted pregnancy – discussing **feasible alternatives** and their ramifications for the teen, unborn baby, family, and society is not only required to make decisions, but also provides positive coping.
- Middle adulthood: divorce – evaluating its **impact** on the couple and their relatives and friends; and the roles played by marital status, social expectations outside home, and religion inform values clarification coping mechanisms.
- Later adulthood: retirement – when people retiring from careers or employment view retirement in terms of their **values**, this can facilitate their ability to choose feasible options for post-retirement living.

Among life skills that enable coping with the stress of common life events are values clarification, decision-making, communication skills, and coping skills. Common stressors in four life stages follow, accompanied by coping mechanisms utilizing the **decision-making** life skill.

- Early childhood: a pet's death – helping the child discuss the **pros and cons** of each alternative for disposing of the pet's remains is a decision-making-oriented way to cope with the loss.
- Adolescence: unwanted pregnancy – careful consideration and evaluation of such **alternatives** as abortion; carrying the baby to term and surrendering it for adoption (and open or closed, public or private adoption, etc.); carrying to term and keeping the baby, etc. are necessary decisions to make and cope proactively with stressors. Decisions about future birth-control methods are also indicated.
- Middle adulthood: divorce – from the decision-making perspective, considering alternatives, risks, and consequences and making **choices** among career options, life roles, and future social relationships have major impacts on post-divorce living.
- Later adulthood: retirement – the decision-making life skill enables the retiree to consider **alternatives** and their advantages and disadvantages, e.g., not retiring, pursuing leisure activities, embarking on a second career, volunteering, realizing a long-deferred dream, etc.

Four major life skills are values clarification, decision-making, communication skills, and coping skills. Examples of common stressors in each life stage, plus ways to cope using **communication skills**, follow.

- Early childhood: a pet's death – when a child feels sadness and anxiety over the loss, encouraging the child to **communicate** his or her feelings and thoughts can mediate psychic distress.
- Adolescence: unwanted pregnancy – teenage mothers need support from various sources including family, friends, counselors, educators, and health professionals. Effectively utilizing communication skills enables them to know how, where, and from whom to **solicit help and advice** to cope with their situation.
- Middle adulthood: divorce – adults undergoing divorces often have to assume various new life roles, including some that their former spouses may always have addressed. As a part of the process of divorce, adults need to apply communication skills to seek out **supportive friends, relatives, and professionals** as they establish and adjust to these new roles and experiences.
- Later adulthood: retirement – when older adults retire, they may lose some of their autonomy. Using communication skills assertively can help them maintain their **independence**.

Four life skills for coping with stressors are values clarification, decision-making, communication skills, and coping skills. Following are stressors common in each of four life stages, and corresponding coping methods associated with the **coping skills** portion of stress management.

- Early childhood: a pet's death – children can emerge from early loss experiences to discover personal abilities and strengths. From the coping skills perspective, they can prevent normal grief becoming depression through **developing aptitudes and interests**.
- Adolescence: unwanted pregnancy – before and after processes of values clarification and decision-making, teen mothers should examine their personal response to pregnancy for its **significance** in the context of their life.

- Middle adulthood: divorce – it is not unusual for adults to experience lowered self-concept and self-esteem during and after divorce. From the coping skills perspective, the individual can cope better with the stressor of divorce through engaging in behaviors that **enhance self-esteem and self-concept**. Personal and/or professional activities that affirm or reaffirm one's skills, talents, abilities, accomplishments, and sense of self facilitate coping.
- Later adulthood: retirement – retirees often encounter changing responsibilities and roles. Physical activity and exercise, hobbies, social activities, traveling, etc. are **positive coping behaviors** to enhance post-retirement life.

Human Sexuality

ADVISING STUDENTS ABOUT WAYS UNPROTECTED SEX CAN CAUSE UNWANTED PREGNANCY, AND PREGNANCY PREVENTION

Some teens may not know how **pregnancy** occurs; others may believe it can only happen when a male ejaculates inside a female's vagina. However, a few drops of pre-ejaculate released before and during sex, which can be almost undetectable, also contains sperm. Though the probability of conception from this small amount is lower, it is still possible. Though less common, conception can also result from semen on the vulva without penetration. Males cannot control pre-ejaculate release; therefore, they should be advised to put on a condom *before*, and wear it continuously during, sex. Though the point is not to encourage sex among immature students, educators can inform those harboring misunderstandings that kissing, body rubbing, masturbating, and oral and anal sex cannot cause pregnancy without vaginal or vulvar contact with sperm; and that abstaining from sex, or using both a condom and birth control continuously during sex, are the ways of preventing pregnancy. Teen couples contemplating sex should discuss birth control with each other and a parent or trusted adult, and see a physician, nurse, or healthcare provider.

INFORMATION TO GIVE STUDENTS ABOUT STIS

Over half of Americans contract an **STI** during their lives. Practicing **safer sex** can include using condoms, having strictly monogamous sex, and engaging in sexual activities that do not transmit STIs. Vaginal and anal intercourse are high-risk activities. Without condoms, they are likely to transmit chancroid, chlamydia, cytomegalovirus (CMV), genital warts, gonorrhea, hepatitis B, herpes, HIV, human papilloma virus (HPV), molluscum contagiosum virus, pelvic inflammatory disease (PID), pubic lice ("crabs"), scabies, syphilis, and trichomoniasis. Unprotected oral sex is high-risk for transmitting CMV, gonorrhea, hepatitis B, herpes, syphilis, and HPV. Skin-to-skin contact without intercourse is risky for transmitting CMV, herpes, HPV, molluscum contagiosum, pubic lice, and scabies. Many STIDs are often asymptomatic.

RAPE

An estimated 80-90 percent of **rapes** go unreported. Recent trends project one-third of American women will be assaulted sexually in life. Typical assailants usually choose women of their race, and at least casually know victims almost half the time from living or working near them. Over one-third of rapes involve alcohol. Over half happen in victims' homes, via break-ins or entry by false pretenses. Expressed via sex, rape is primarily violent, not sexual. Prostitutes and prisoners with reduced credibility, those with limited language or disabilities who cannot call for help, and those facing discrimination are more vulnerable. **Prevention** includes locking doors and windows in homes and cars; checking car backseats before entering; parking in well-lit, open areas; not jogging or walking in isolated or secluded areas at night or when alone; displaying confidence, security, awareness, and strength in surroundings; sitting near drivers or in the front in public transportation; avoiding proximity to young male groups; self-defense training; carrying personal alarms or whistles; screaming loudly or blowing whistles if assaulted; actively resisting attacks and not being passive; and not hitchhiking. PTSD is a common complication. Over half of rape victims have difficulty re-establishing existing relationships or establishing new ones. Victims should avoid urinating, changing clothes, bathing, or douching pre-ER to preserve evidence; should be allowed to interview dressed, not hospital-gowned; and not left alone unless desired. **Treatment** includes examining for and addressing STIs, pregnancy, and physical injury; and providing emotional support.

DEVELOPMENT OF FEMALE REPRODUCTIVE SYSTEM

Because females do not have a Y-chromosome, during embryonic and fetal development they are not affected by **testosterone** to develop male reproductive organs. Without testosterone stimulation, reproductive organs develop into ovaries, a uterus, and other female organs. Most internal female organs are formed by the end of the first trimester. Immature eggs (ova) form in the ovaries in utero; all of a female's eggs are produced before birth. Female infants are born with all **reproductive organs** formed, but immature and not functional. These do not grow much in childhood, but rapidly mature and grow during puberty. Girls typically start **puberty** one or two years before boys; and take around four years to complete, whereas boys take around six years. The primary female sex hormone is **estrogen**. In the brain, the hypothalamus stimulates the pituitary gland to secrete **luteinizing hormone (LH)** and **follicle-stimulating hormone (FSH)**, which stimulate the ovary to produce estrogen. (The same hormones stimulate the testes' testosterone production in males.) Estrogen stimulates uterus and breast growth; pubic hair growth; bone development; the adolescent growth spurt, which begins and ends earlier than in males; and menarche (menstrual cycle onset).

GROWTH AND DEVELOPMENT OF HUMAN MALE REPRODUCTIVE SYSTEM

While a male fetus develops in utero, the **testes** begin to develop. Around two months before birth, the testes begin descending into the scrotal sacs outside of the main body cavity, allowing slightly lower temperatures aiding sperm production. The testes additionally produce hormones enabling development of secondary male sex characteristics. **Puberty** activates an increase in brain hormones, triggering the pituitary gland's increased production and release into the bloodstream of **luteinizing hormone (LH)** and **follicle-stimulating hormone (FSH)**. In the bloodstream, LH stimulates testes cells to produce and release **testosterone**, which enlarges and develops the penis and other sex organs, promotes skeletal and muscular growth, and deepens the voice. Testosterone and FSH stimulate **sperm production** in seminiferous tubules within the testes. Each sperm cell takes 65-75 days to form; about 300 million are produced daily, stored in the epididymis, wherefrom the vas deferens carries sperm through the prostate gland below the bladder to the urethra. The male urethra releases both sperm and urine. The prostate gland and seminal vesicles—accessory sex glands—produce specialized fluids, mixing with sperm during transport, creating **semen** which exits from the urethra through the penis during ejaculation.

INFLUENCE OF MEDIA MESSAGES ON ADOLESCENT SEXUALITY

Researchers find that, although any age group can be influenced by sexual media content, teens can be especially vulnerable to **media messages**. Adolescence is a developmental time when individuals are forming their sexual attitudes, behaviors, and gender roles. Teenagers have recently developed the ability to think abstractly and critically; however, their **cognitive skills** are still not completely developed for critical analysis of media messages and decision-making that takes into account future potential consequences. This places them at higher risk for **media influence**. Researchers have found (Gruber, 2000) that teens viewed an average of 143 instances of sexual behavior on TV weekly during prime time. Activities between unmarried partners were depicted three to four times more often than between spouses. Network and cable TV channels show movies, an estimated 80 percent of which include sexual content. Researchers analysis of music videos estimated that 60 percent included sexual impulses and feelings. Sexual TV messages are found to be nearly always presented in positive terms, with scarce treatment of negative consequences or risks of unprotected sex. High school students have reported substantial access to and viewing of TV and video. Over 80 percent of teens report peer discovery about sex from entertainment media.

RESEARCH FINDINGS ABOUT ADOLESCENT SEXUAL ATTITUDES AND BEHAVIORS

Various studies find teens' sexual attitudes influenced by variables including their parents' attitudes regarding teen sex, religiosity, the media, bonding in school relationships, and adolescents' perceptions of social norms among their peers. According to some experts, such research demonstrates the necessity of considering the wide range of **sexual attitudes** teenagers consider. Warning of **negative consequences** is insufficient; adults must provide **information** enabling teens to weigh positive and negative aspects of both engaging in and abstaining from sex to make their own best decisions as they mature and develop physically, intellectually, emotionally, and socially. While many models of teen risk behaviors emphasize perceptions of possible consequences in decision-making, studies also find positive motivations for having sex. Some investigators found teens valued sexual goals and expectations of intimacy, then social status, then pleasure in that order; but then expected sex to result in pleasure, then intimacy, then social status in that order. Male adolescents valued pleasure more; females valued intimacy more. The National Adolescent and Young Adult Health Information Center (NAHIC, 2007) found almost half of high school students reported having sex. CDC's Youth Risk Behavior Surveillance (YRBS, 2008) found sexual intercourse most prevalent in black, then Hispanic, then white, then Asian teens.

SIGNIFICANT ASPECTS OF THE STAGES OF PREGNANCY

In the **first trimester**, a zygote transforms into an implanted embryo; organs, hair follicles, nail beds, muscles, white blood cells, and vocal cords form; and the baby starts moving around week eight. While pregnancy does not show externally, mothers awash in **pregnancy hormones** feel many symptoms. However, every woman and pregnancy are different; no two necessarily have the same symptoms, but most diminish further into pregnancy (though others develop). During the **second trimester**, babies grow hair; begin sucking and swallowing; and their eyes and ears reposition. They have fingerprints and can hiccup and yawn by week 18. Their limbs are coordinated and their senses develop by week 21. Weight gain, capillary formation, and opening eyes occur by six months. By seven months, fetal weight doubles to two pounds. Babies perceive light and dark, taste what mothers eat, and hear their voices by week 31. Transparent skin becomes opaque by week 32; length may increase an inch during week 33. Weight reaches around six pounds by week 36; waxy vernix and hairy lanugo shed in week 38. By week 40, fetal weight is 6-9 pounds, length 19-22 inches; babies dream, blink, and regulate their body temperatures.

HUMAN LABOR AND CHILDBIRTH

In late pregnancy, symptoms can mask labor signs, or some contractions can be false labor. If contractions persist, become stronger, last longer, and occur closer together, this usually indicates **labor**. The "411" method is one way to judge: contractions 4 minutes apart, lasting 1 minute each, continuing for at least 1 hour. Labor's **first stage** is typically the longest, marked by contractions and gradual cervical dilation. The first stage has three phases: the **early phase**, usually comfortable, with contractions 20 minutes apart progressing to 5 minutes apart. The second, **active phase** generally involves 1-minute contractions every 4-5 minutes. The third, **transition phase** is among the shortest (1-2 hours) but hardest. Contractions are 2-3 minutes apart; some women shake and may vomit. This phase ends with complete dilation. Some women temporarily cease contractions but feel no need to push. Labor's **second stage** involves a need to push. It can last 3+ hours, but often less. Contractions spread out again to around every 4 minutes. This stage culminates in **childbirth**. Then the mother must push out the **placenta**; nursing the newborn aids uterine contractions to expel it. The fourth labor stage is **postpartum**.

CONTRACEPTION METHODS

Some young (or uninformed older) people assume **condoms** worn by males are sufficient for **contraception**. However, condoms can break, leak, or slip off during or following intercourse. Ideally, foam, gel, or other spermicide should accompany condoms. Female contraception includes IUDs, diaphragms, and birth control pills. **IUDs** are typically inserted by physicians and worn continuously. They can periodically require removal and replacement. While effective, they can have undesirable side-effects for some women including irritation, inflammation, cramping, spotting, tissue damage, etc. **Diaphragms** are typically self-inserted by women before intercourse, often with spermicidal gel applied to the surface, and removed afterward. They are also effective, but some women have difficulty inserting them properly and/or cannot tolerate their presence. They can also sometimes shift position, impeding contraception. **Birth control pills** are very effective, though a very small percentage of women using them might still get pregnant. Oral hormones cause some women undesirable side effects like weight gain and symptoms resembling pregnancy. Lower-dose pills have fewer side effects; different dosages affect individual women differently. More extreme measures include **tubal ligation** (reversible but not always) and **hysterectomy** (irreversible) for women, and **vasectomy** (reversible but not always) for men.

HIV/AIDS

The first known case of **human immunodeficiency virus/acquired immunodeficiency syndrome (HIV/AIDS)** occurred in 1951 in the Congo, but the first U.S. case occurred in 1981. Dr. Robert Gallo of the National Cancer Institute identified the cause in 1984. The first cases were in the gay population, resulting in the disease being initially labeled a "gay disease," although it later became clear that it was not limited to gays. AIDS resulted in the deaths of millions of people worldwide before the first Food and Drug Administration (FDA)-approved treatment was available in 1995. By 2002, home testing kits were available. Currently, although males having sex with males are most at risk and African American have the highest rate of racial groups, HIV/AIDS affects all populations, races, and socioeconomic groups with about 50,000 new infections in the United States each year. About 25% of cases are female, and 25% are older than age 50. Modes of transmission include oral, anal, and vaginal sex as well as the sharing of needles and contact with infected blood, semen, vaginal fluids, and breast milk.

PREVENTION AND TREATMENT

Treatment for HIV/AIDS should begin with **diagnosis** and includes medication management, mental health counseling, and supportive and social care as needed. The first step after diagnosis is to undergo a number of **laboratory tests** to determine the viral load and CD4 count (measures the CD4 T lymphocytes to determine the strength of the immune system). Although **antiretroviral therapy (ART)** does not cure HIV/AIDS, it can slow the progression. Six classes of drugs are currently used to treat HIV with initial treatment usually involving three drugs from at least two different drug classes. Several drug regimens are available, depending on the patient's condition, drug resistance, and comorbid diseases. **HIV/AIDS prevention** includes universal testing, needle exchange programs, sex education, consistent and correct use of latex condoms, substance abuse prevention, and treatment programs. Individuals should understand that risk increases with multiple sexual partners, and males having sex with males are particularly at risk.

Conflict Resolution and Violence Avoidance

CONFLICT IN RELATIONSHIPS

Many people try to avoid **conflict** at all costs because they find it unpleasant and feel threatened by **confrontation**. However, conflict is normal and integral to healthy relationships. Its source is differences between and among people, whether major or minor. No two (or more) people can agree about everything 100 percent of the time. Anytime that people disagree, conflict results. Though some disagreements seem unimportant, any conflict that evokes strong emotions indicates some deep personal need at its core—e.g., to be valued or respected, to be closer or more intimate, or to feel safety or security. As one example, young children need to explore and take risks to learn and develop normally, while parents need to protect children's safety, and this can present a child-parent conflict. Conflicts in **personal relationships** can cause discord and even end them when members do not understand each other's different needs. Conflicts in **workplaces** can ruin deals, lower profits, and end jobs. Acknowledging needs that conflict, and a willingness to examine them in understanding, compassionate environments enable team-building and creative problem-solving. Both avoiding and mismanaging conflict can damage relationships, but positive and respectful conflict management can improve them.

CHARACTERISTICS OF CONFLICT PEOPLE NEED TO KNOW IN ORDER TO RESOLVE THEM

According to experts, a **conflict** is not simply a disagreement, but a situation wherein both or either party perceives a real or imagined **threat**. Because such perceived threats are to people's survival and well-being, conflicts continue; ignoring them does not make them go away. **Confronting** and **resolving** conflicts stop them from going on indefinitely, or until the relationship ends. People do not necessarily (or usually) respond to conflicts based on objectively considering the facts, they react to them based on their personal values, beliefs, cultural backgrounds, and life experiences. Hence individual reactions to conflict are according to individual perceptions of the situation. Conflicts naturally provoke strong feelings. Therefore, people who cannot manage their emotions under stress or who are uncomfortable with them will be unable to succeed at resolving conflicts. Another characteristic of conflicts is that they present opportunities for **growth**. When members of a relationship succeed at resolving interpersonal conflict, they build **trust** between themselves. They gain direct experience that their relationship can withstand disagreements and challenges. This proof enables them to feel more secure about their relationship's existence and future.

UNHEALTHY VS. HEALTHY WAYS OF RESPONDING TO, MANAGING, AND RESOLVING CONFLICT

When conflict inevitably arises, one **unhealthy** reaction is being unable to recognize and respond to things that are most important to the other person. A **healthier** response is being able to identify and address things that matter most to another. Emotional reactions that are resentful, angry, explosive, or designed to hurt the other person's feelings are unhealthy. Healthier responses involve staying calm, not becoming defensive, and showing respect for the other person. When one person reacts to conflict by rejecting the other, withdrawing his/her affection, isolating himself/herself, saying or doing things to shame the other, or showing or expressing fears of being abandoned, these are unhealthy reactions. Healthier responses are being willing to forgive the other person; forget undesirable reactions, words and deeds; and progress beyond the conflict without retaining anger or resentment. Being unable to see the other person's viewpoint or make any compromises is unhealthy; being able to compromise instead of punishing the other person is healthier. Fearing and avoiding conflict due to expected negative outcomes is unhealthy; believing in the mutual benefit of confronting conflict head-on is healthier.

EFFECTS OF STRESS

Excessive stress and/or not coping effectively with stress impede the ability to understand other people's nonverbal communications. **Stress** interferes with people's ability to hear what another person is really saying, to be aware of and in touch with their own emotions, and to connect with their deepest personal needs. Moreover, being affected by stress makes a person much less able to **communicate** his or her own needs clearly. These abilities are all required for positively resolving conflict, so when stress interferes with them, it interferes with conflict resolution. Some people become so habituated to stress that they lose recognition of it. Some ways to identify if it is a problem in life are to observe whether conflict preoccupies their attention and time, whether they cannot feel movement in their chests or stomachs while breathing, and/or whether they often feel tightness or tension in certain body parts. Excessive stress limits how many emotions one can attend to, preventing understanding and thus communicating one's needs. Hence stress interferes with **emotional awareness**, which interferes with communicating problems and resolving conflicts.

DOMESTIC VIOLENCE

Domestic violence is domestic or spousal abuse, wherein one relationship partner dominates and controls another, that incorporates physical violence. Some **violent behaviors** include having an unpredictable, bad temper; harming, threatening harm, or threatening to kill the partner; threatening to hurt or take children; threatening suicide if the partner leaves; forcing sex; and destroying the partner's belongings. **Manipulative power tactics** abusers employ include: dominance, humiliation, isolation, threats, intimidation, denial, and blame. The cycle of domestic violence follows a common **pattern**: one partner abuses the other with violent behavior to exhibit dominance. The partner appears guilty, but really fears being caught and punished rather than feeling remorse. The abuser avoids responsibility by making excuses for the violent behavior, rationalizing it, and/or blaming the other partner for it. The abuser, trying to keep the victim in the relationship and regain control, behaves contritely, "normally," or with great affection and/or charm, often fooling the victim into hoping s/he has changed or will change. The abuser fantasizes and plans further abuse to make the victim pay for perceived wrongs. The abuser then places the victim in a situation to justify further abuse, and the cycle repeats all over again.

Safety and Accident Prevention and Emergency Response

MEDICAL EMERGENCIES

Medical emergencies are those in which the person is at severe risk and needs prompt medical attention. For life-threatening **emergencies**, the most appropriate response is to call 9-1-1, but some first-aid procedures may be used if necessary, such as applying pressure to a bleeding wound, while waiting for assistance. In less acute cases (such as severe diarrhea), the person may be transported to an emergency department directly without calling 9-1-1 if he or she appears stable. Medical emergencies include the following:

- Shortness of breath, severe wheezing, difficulty breathing.
- Sudden onset of dizziness and fainting or unexplained weakness.
- Sudden changes in vision.
- Sudden onset of severe pain.
- Chest pain or pressure or pain radiating to neck, shoulders, and arms.
- Severe gastrointestinal problems with vomiting and/or diarrhea.
- Severe uncontrolled hemorrhage.
- Vomiting blood or coughing up blood.
- Difficult speaking or swallowing.
- Threats of suicide.

BASIC FIRST-AID PROCEDURES IN VARIOUS SITUATIONS

The following are first-aid procedures in various situations:

- **Anaphylaxis (allergic shock)** - Immediately call 9-1-1. Administer epinephrine (EpiPen) per autoinjector if the person has one. Begin cardiopulmonary resuscitation (CPR) if in respiratory arrest.
- **Animal bites**
  - *Minor* (if no concern about rabies): Wash with soap and water and apply antibiotic cream/ointment and bandage.
  - *Major*: Apply pressure to stop the bleeding with a dry clean bandage, and transport to the emergency department, or call 9-1-1 if severe.
- **Black eye** - Apply cold compress, avoiding pressure on eye. If blood is noted in the eye itself or if vision is impaired, transport to the emergency department.
- **Chemical burns/eye splashes** - Remove contaminated belongings and flush the burn area with a copious amount of tap water for at least 10 minutes. Transport to the emergency department or call 9-1-1 if burns are severe, the patient feels faint, or the burn is more than three inches in diameter. Flush the eyes for at least 20 minutes, and then transport to the emergency department.
- **Cut/Scrapes** - Apply pressure with a clean bandage to stop the bleeding. Rinse with clear water and wash around the wound with soap and water. Apply antibiotic ointment and dressing. If the wound is deep and requires suturing; transport to the emergency department.
- **Heat cramps, heat exhaustion, heat stroke**
  - *Heat cramps and exhaustion*: Remove the person to the shade, lay flat, and elevate legs; cool by spraying with cold water, and have the person drink cool water.
  - *Heat stroke*: Call 9-1-1. Spray or immerse in cool water and fan; administer CPR if necessary.

- **Hypothermia** - Call 9-1-1. Remove wet clothing, warm gradually with warm compresses to the trunk; give warm drinks. Do not warm too quickly, and do not massage limbs.
- **Insect bites/stings** - Remove stingers, wash with soap and water, and apply a cool compress. Apply cortisone cream to reduce itching. If a severe reaction or bite with a known dangerous insect (such as a scorpion), call 9-1-1. Administer an EpiPen if the person has one for allergies to insects.
- **Bleeding**
  - *Minor*: Apply pressure with a clean bandage to stop the bleeding and apply dry dressing.
  - *Severe*: Call 9-1-1. Remove any large debris from the wound. Apply pressure with a clean bandage to stop the bleeding but not if debris is imbedded in the wound, and don't apply pressure to an eye. In these cases, simply cover with a clean dressing. Lie the person flat and elevate the feet. Apply a tourniquet for bleeding that is life-threatening only if trained to do so.
- **Snakebites (venomous)** - Call 9-1-1. Position the injury below the level of the heart if possible. Cover the wound with a dry dressing. DO NOT apply ice, cut the skin, or apply a tourniquet. Report a description of the snake to first responders.
- **Spider bite** - Cleanse the bite with soap and water, and apply antibiotic ointment and cool compress. Transport to the emergency department if a poisonous spider, such as a black widow or brown recluse, is suspected.
- **Sprains/Fractures/Dislocations**
  - *Sprains*: RICE (rest, ice, compress, elevate). Transport to the emergency department if unable to bear weight or use the joint.
  - *Fractures*: Call 9-1-1 or transport to the emergency department. Apply pressure to stop any bleeding, cover with a dry dressing, immobilize the injured limb, and apply an ice pack.
  - *Dislocation*: Transport to the emergency department. Do not attempt to move the joint. Apply an ice compress to the joint.
- **Shock (any cause)** - Call 9-1-1. Lay the person flat, elevate the legs and feet, and keep still. Loosen clothing. Begin CPR if cardiac or respiratory arrest exist.
- **Stroke** - Call 9-1-1. Keep the head elevated.
- **Nosebleeds** - Sit the person upright and pinch nostrils for 5 to 10 minutes. Transport to the emergency department if bleeding follows an accident or if it persists for more than 20 minutes.

CPR

Hands-only **cardiopulmonary resuscitation** (CPR) is recommended for nonmedical rescuers for unconscious teens or adults who have no pulse or respirations. The rescuer should call 9-1-1 and place the victim supine on a hard surface. To find the correct hand position, run two fingers along the ribs to the center chest, place two fingers over the xiphoid process, and place the palm of the other hand on the sternum directly above the fingers. Then place the other hand on top of the first, fingers linked and elbows locked, to begin **compressions**, which should be done in a rocking movement, using the body to apply pressure. (Note: Use two fingers for infants.) The rate of compressions is at least 100 per minute and at least two inches deep (one-third chest depth for infants and small children). This rate corresponds roughly to the beat of the Bee Gees' song "Staying Alive" (dum, dum, dum, dum, stayin' alive, stayin' alive….). With two trained rescuers, **rescue breathing** may be added at a compression to breathing rate of 30:2.

HEIMLICH MANEUVER

The universal sign of choking is when a person clutches his or her throat and appears to be choking or gasping for breath. If the person can speak ("Can you speak?") or cough, the **Heimlich maneuver** is not usually necessary. The Heimlich maneuver can be done with the victim sitting, standing, or supine. The Heimlich procedure for children (≥1 year) and adults is as follows:

- Wrap arms around the victim's waist from the back if sitting or standing. Make a fist and place the thumb side against the victim's abdomen slightly above the umbilicus. Grasp this hand with the other and thrust sharply upward to force air out of the lungs.
- Repeat as needed and call 9-1-1 if there is no response.
- If the victim loses consciousness, ease him or her into a supine position on the floor, place hands similarly to CPR but over the abdomen while sitting astride the victim's legs. Repeat upward compressions five times. If no ventilation occurs, attempt to sweep the mouth and ventilate the lungs mouth to mouth. Repeat compressions and ventilations until recovery or emergency personnel arrive.

Indications of **choking** in infants younger than one year include lack of breathing, gasping, cyanosis, and inability to cry. Procedures for the **Heimlich chest thrusts** include the following:

- Position the infant in the prone (face-down) position along the forearm with the infant's head lower than the trunk, being sure to support the head so the airway is not blocked.
- Using the heel of the hand, deliver five forceful upward blows between the shoulder blades.
- Sandwich the child between your two arms, turn the infant into the supine position, and drape him or her over your thigh with the head lower than the trunk and the head supported.
- Using two fingers (as in CPR compressions), give up to five thrusts (about 1.5 inches deep) to the lower third of the sternum.
- Only do a finger sweep and remove any foreign object if the object is visible. Repeat five back blows, five chest thrusts, repeating until the foreign body is ejected or until emergency personnel take over.
- If the infant loses consciousness, begin CPR. If a pulse is noted but spontaneous respirations are absent, continue with ventilation only.

HEALTH AND SAFETY OF INDIVIDUALS RESPONDING TO MEDICAL EMERGENCIES

When responding to a medical emergency, it's important to take measures to **prevent self-injury or infection**. Precautions include the following:

- Assess the **safety risks** of the situation before rendering aid (gunshots, gang activity, fire, fallen electrical wires, severe storm conditions), and do not give aid unless the situation is safe.
- Avoid contact with **body fluids** (blood, urine, feces, semen), and use gloves if available; otherwise, attempt to find some type of barrier (plastic bag, towel) to use to prevent direct contact.
- Use a face mask if possible if in danger of **airborne pathogens**, such as when a person has a severe cough.
- **Standard precautions**: Hand hygiene with soap and water or alcohol scrub should be carried out if possible before touching a person, but this is not always possible in an emergent situation. Hands and any contaminated body parts should be washed with soap and water as soon as possible after contact, especially if contaminated by body fluids.

84

AMERICAN RED CROSS CERTIFICATION COURSES IN FIRST AID, CPR, AND AED

The American Red Cross states on its website that knowing what to do in the event of an emergency involving respiratory or cardiac problems, or requiring first aid measures, could help save somebody's life. The Red Cross offers course options among hands-on learning of **first aid**, cardiopulmonary resuscitation (**CPR**), and automated external defibrillator (**AED**) use. These courses are all aligned with the *Best Practices for Workplace First Aid Training Programs* issued by the Occupational Safety and Health Administration (OSHA). They are available in both classroom versions, and blended (i.e., combined classroom and online) formats. Depending on the option chosen, courses last from two to five hours. Upon completing a course successfully, people receive a two-year **certification**. The Red Cross offers refresher courses free of charge for all course options, and short classes for renewing current certification. The first aid course, including a pediatric version, teaches people how to respond to common emergencies including cuts, burns, head injuries, neck injuries, back injuries, and other situations requiring first aid. The CPR and AED courses teach how to respond to breathing and heart emergencies, including using AEDs, for adults, children, and infants.

PRACTICING HEIMLICH MANEUVER AND CPR

For choking, quick response is necessary to prevent unconsciousness, even death. For adults and children (procedures for infants differ), perform the **Heimlich maneuver**: first, remember panicky victims may unintentionally strike out, and protect yourself. Do not perform the Heimlich on someone who is speaking, coughing, or breathing—someone who can do these things is not choking. Stand behind the victim. Wrap your arms around him or her as if hugging. Make a fist with your right hand; put it above the victim's navel. Grasp your right fist with your left hand; thrust in and up forcibly. Repeat thrusting until the victim can breathe. If the victim loses consciousness, begin child **CPR** for children aged 1-8 years, adult CPR above 8 years. Practice universal precautions and use protective equipment if available to avoid contagious or infectious diseases. "Shake and shout" trying to wake the victim. If he or she does not awaken, call 911. If nobody is available, perform CPR for two minutes, then call 911. On children, do two chest compressions per second 30 times; repeat until help arrives. On adults, do chest compressions at least 100 times a minute, 30 times in 18 seconds; repeat until help arrives.

COURSES FOR EMERGENCY RESPONSE AND FIRST AID

The American Red Cross offers a course specifically designed for high school and college students. Students who successfully complete this class receive **certification** in first aid, cardiopulmonary resuscitation (CPR), and using automated external defibrillators (AEDs). The course also provides students with a comprehensive array of skills that prepares them for responding to a varied range of **emergencies** that can occur to adults, children, and infants. By learning these skills and applying them in an emergency situation, students might be able to save a life. This course involves 30 hours of instruction with an emphasis on hands-on learning, and awards a two-year certification to students upon its satisfactory completion. The class includes modules that cover first aid techniques, adult and pediatric CPR and AED use, how to manage various injuries, and how to prevent the transmission of different diseases. The American Red Cross website includes a search engine whereby students can enter their city, state, and ZIP code to find and register for classes available in their areas.

GUIDELINES FOR CALLING 911

Emergencies requiring **911 calls** are defined as any situations that need immediate help from an ambulance, the fire department, or the police. Some examples of such emergencies include medical emergencies needing immediate medical attention, like uncontrollable bleeding, chest pains,

85

allergic reactions, someone not breathing or struggling to breathe, or someone who is unconscious. Automobile accidents, particularly including injuries, are emergencies. Crimes, particularly in progress, are emergencies. Fires are 911 emergencies. Officials recommend if a person is not sure whether a situation is a real emergency or not, he or she should call 911 and let the call-taker help determine this. Callers should be prepared to **answer questions** from the dispatcher like the street address and location of the emergency; the phone number they are calling from; the nature of the emergency; and details, like descriptions of symptoms or injuries in a medical emergency, descriptions of fires in progress, or descriptions of persons who may have committed crimes. Callers should also be prepared to **follow any instructions** given by call-takers, including step-by-step CPR or Heimlich maneuver directions. Callers should not hang up until instructed by the call-taker.

Today **911** can be called using landline and wireless phones. Enabling text messages to 911 is expected in the near future. The National Emergency Number Association (NENA) and 911.gov advise if adults call 911 accidentally, or a child dials 911 with no emergency, callers or parents should briefly explain the mistake, not simply hang up: call-takers may assume there is an emergency and dispatch responders unnecessarily, diverting them from real emergencies. Separate phone numbers exist for non-emergency services. Call-takers can identify emergencies and non-emergencies and direct unsure callers to proper non-emergency numbers. Prank calls to 911 are illegal in most states; local law enforcement agencies address them. Callers should know cross street names, signs, neighboring buildings and other landmarks: 911 centers answering calls may not be those servicing the caller's area. Callers should post their addresses on both mailboxes and houses. Parents should teach young children what 911 is and how to dial from landlines and wireless phones, ensuring they can reach at least one phone in the house. Children must know their name, parents' names, address, and phone number. Parents should teach children to trust 911 call-takers, answer their questions, and not hang up until instructed.

SHI

The Centers for Disease Control and Prevention (CDC) collaborated with school health experts, administrators and staff, parents, and national non-government health and education agencies to develop the *School Health Index: Self-Assessment & Planning Guide 2012* (**SHI**), an online, confidential, and easy-to-use tool available on the CDC website's SHI page—one PDF for elementary schools and another for middle and high schools—that helps schools identify their health and safety policy and program strength and weaknesses; develop student health-enhancing action plans to incorporate into School Improvement Plans (SIPs); and involve students, teachers, parents, and communities in promoting better health and health-enhancing behaviors. The SHI uses the CDC's research-based guidelines for school health programs as its basis. These guidelines identify policies and practices found most effective for **decreasing health risk behaviors** by students. The SHI covers sexual health topics, including teen pregnancy, HIV and other STI prevention; cross-referential health services, mental health services, and family and community involvement modules; and updated nutritional information aligned with Institute of Medicine recommendations and USDA requirements. The SHI can be customized and used interactively online, and/or downloaded and printed.

BEHAVIORAL CHANGE THEORIES APPLICABLE TO HEALTH EDUCATION PROGRAMS FOR PREVENTING AND CONTROLLING INJURY

Behavioral change theories applicable to health education injury prevention and control programs include: community organization theory, diffusion of innovations theory, the ecological/social ecological model, the extended parallel processing model, the health belief model, health promotion models, integrated models, the PRECEDE/PROCEED model, the public health model, social-cognitive theory, the theory of reasoned action/planned behavior, and the stages-of-change or transtheoretical model. **Community organization theory** concentrates on community strengths. Main concepts include community capacity, critical consciousness, empowerment, participation, relevance, and issue selection. The federal Health Start program is an example. **Diffusions of innovation theory** focus on processes whereby new ideas are spread through society. Main concepts include social networks, communication channels, innovations, and time to reach members. Examples include collaboration between the Alzheimer's Association and police to augment Alzheimer's patient safety through a community-based initiative, and Australian public hospital prenatal smoking cessation programs. **Ecological/social ecological models** emphasize multilevel approaches to sociological and environmental influences on individual behavior. Applications include road traffic injury prevention, unintentional injury prevention, world violence and health reporting, and needs assessment for community intervention planning.

The **extended parallel processing model of behavior change** is a theory of fear appeal. It describes how people process messages and respond to them to increase their awareness of personal health risk, and how health education program planners can design methods for overcoming health risks. One application of this model has been to prevent noise-induced hearing loss in Appalachian coal miners (Murray-Johnson et al, 2004). The **health belief model** focuses on perceptions of disease threat and the net benefits of behavior change to ascertain whether and why an individual will change his or her behavior. **Health promotion models** have had actual and proposed applications, including to drinking and driving, preventing violence and injuries, increasing bicycle helmet use, prevention of alcohol-related traffic injuries, and improving fire escape behaviors when responding to smoke alarms. **Integrated models**, including the public health model with the social-ecological model and the PRECEDE framework with the Haddon Matrix, have been applied to injury control and health education, epidemiology and disease prevention, interventions in male violence against females, urban violence, and unintentional injury prevention. The **PRECEDE/PROCEED model** includes epidemiological, ecological, environmental, social, behavioral, educational, policy, and administrative assessments; and evaluations of process, implementation, outcomes, and impacts.

Drugs and their Use, Misuse, Abuse, and Addiction

RISKS OF DRINKING AND DRIVING

According to the National Council on Alcoholism and Drug Dependence, Inc. (NCADD), 32 percent of deadly auto crashes are estimated to involve a driver or pedestrian **intoxicated by alcohol**. The influence of alcohol slows reaction time and impairs attention; judgment; the ability to make quick decisions; reactions to environmental changes; and executing precise, difficult maneuvers while driving. Therefore, **driving** is dangerous and can be deadly under the influence of alcohol and other drugs. Though public awareness has increased, many people still drive under the influence. Almost 13,000 individuals die annually in alcohol-related accidents, and hundreds of thousands are injured. These crashes cost over $100 billion to American taxpayers. Yearly arrests for driving while intoxicated number above 1.4 million, representing below one percent of 159 million self-reported instances of drinking and driving. Of those arrested, 780,000 are convicted; two-thirds of those sentenced to prison are repeat offenders. Most deaths are caused by drivers with at least 0.10 **blood alcohol concentration (BAC)**—the common criterion for intoxication. However, even 0.02 BAC impairs driving ability.

RISKS FROM SMOKING TOBACCO

More than 480,000 Americans, i.e., around one in five, die annually from **smoking cigarettes**. Smoking causes more mortalities than drinking alcohol, using illegal drugs, auto accidents, gunshots, and human immunodeficiency virus (HIV) *combined.* Compared to all war casualties in US history, smoking cigarettes has killed over 10 times as many citizens. More women die annually from **lung cancer** than breast cancer. Of all lung cancer deaths in women and men, 90 percent are caused by smoking. Eighty percent of **chronic obstructive pulmonary disease (COPD)**, including chronic bronchitis and emphysema) deaths are from smoking. Over the past 50 years, risk of death from smoking has risen in American men and women. Smoking raises death risk from all causes. Smokers are at an estimated two to four times the risk for coronary heart disease and stroke; male smokers have 25 times the risk of lung cancer, and female smokers 25.7 times the risk. COPD deaths are 12-13 times more likely in smokers. Fewer than five cigarettes daily can cause cardiovascular disease. Smoking causes bladder, blood, cervical, colorectal, esophageal, kidney, ureter, laryngeal, liver, oropharyngeal, pancreatic, stomach, tracheal, bronchial, and lung cancer. Smoking causes one of every three cancer deaths in the US.

SMOKING CIGARETTES IN ADDITION TO CARDIOVASCULAR DISEASE AND CANCERS

In addition to cardiovascular disease and cancers, smoking cigarettes decreases overall health. Researchers questioning smokers find they self-report **poorer health status**. Smokers are absent from work more often. They require more health care and cost more to themselves, the government, and American taxpayers in healthcare expenses. In addition to the cardiovascular effects of strokes, heart attacks and heart disease—the foremost American killers—plus blood clots, reduced blood flow, blood vessel damage, high blood pressure, multiple cancers, and chronic obstructive lung diseases, smoking can trigger and exacerbate asthma attacks. It damages almost everybody organ. Smoking makes conceiving children more difficult. It also raises risks of miscarriage, premature delivery, stillbirth, low birth weight, sudden infant death syndrome (SIDS), ectopic pregnancy (extrauterine implantation), infant orofacial clefts, and other birth defects. Smoking can lower sperm counts, decreasing fertility. Post-menopausal women smokers have weaker bone density, risking fractures. Smoking damages tooth and gum health and causes tooth loss. Higher risks of eye cataracts and age-related macular degeneration are also associated with smoking. Smoking causes type 2 diabetes, raising risk 30-40 percent, and impedes its treatment. Smoking causes rheumatoid arthritis, other inflammatory conditions, and impairs immune function.

BENEFITS OF SMOKING CESSATION

The Centers for Disease Control and Prevention (CDC) reports smoking has been estimated to raise a person's risk of heart disease, including heart attacks, to between double and quadruple those of a nonsmoker's risk; but also has found that risk drops greatly only one year after **quitting smoking**. A stroke or cerebrovascular accident (CVA) happens when either a blood clot blocks blood flow to a part of the brain (an ischemic stroke), or a blood vessel in or near the brain leaks/bursts (a hemorrhagic stroke). Whereas smoking also increases the risk of stroke to two to four times a nonsmoker's risk; two to five years after quitting smoking, that risk can be similar to that of someone who never smoked. Whereas smoking raises an individual's risks for mouth, throat, esophageal, and bladder cancers, these risks decrease by one-half within five years after quitting smoking. While smoking increases a person's risk for lung cancer by 25 times or more, that risk is cut in half by 10 years after the person has quit smoking. Smoking cessation can extend **life expectancy**.

COCAINE AND CRACK COCAINE

Cocaine is derived from the coca plant and available in powdered form. It is either injected intravenously or snorted nasally. **Crack cocaine** is produced by processing powdered cocaine, altering its chemical composition. It is available in the form of "rocks" which are smoked. One distinction is that, while powdered cocaine is typically quite expensive, crack cocaine is comparatively cheap, making it more accessible and hence more dangerous. Either form of cocaine is in the **stimulant** drug class and is extremely addictive. Using any amount of either incurs physical risks, including: elevated heart rate, respiratory rate, body temperature, and blood pressure; respiratory failure; heart attack; stroke; seizures; reduced capacity to resist and fight infections; hepatitis and/or AIDS from sharing needles for injections; and burn injuries from smoking crack. Psychological risks include: hallucinations, including tactile hallucinations of "coke bugs," i.e., the sensation of insects crawling on the skin; paranoid, erratic, and/or violent behavior; loss of appetite; loss of sexual interest; anxiety; depression; confusion; and "cocaine psychosis," i.e., losing interest in family, friends, hobbies, sports, and all other usual activities; and losing touch with reality.

METHAMPHETAMINE

Methamphetamine is a drug in the **stimulant** class. Chemically it is related to the stimulant amphetamine, but it affects the central nervous system more powerfully. Street names for the drug include speed, crank, and meth. It is available in pills for taking orally, or in powder for injecting or snorting. Through a chemical process ("cooking"), it can be crystallized into an even stronger form, called crystal meth, ice, or glass, which is smoked. **Methamphetamine** use produces physiological and psychological effects including: euphoria; insomnia; elevated blood pressure and heart rate; an increase in physical activity; severe anorexia (lack of appetite); irritability; anxiety; confusion; paranoia; violent behavior; tremors; respiratory difficulties; cardiovascular disruptions, which can be fatal; hypothermia; convulsions; and irreversible damage to blood vessels in the brain, causing strokes. In addition, users who inject methamphetamine and share needles with others have the risk of contracting HIV/AIDS.

ALCOHOL ABUSE AND ALCOHOLISM

According to a publication by the US Department of Health and Human Services' Substance Abuse and Mental Health Services Administration (SAMHSA), citing the National Institute on Drug Abuse (NIDA, 2004), a division of the National Institutes of Health (NIH), as its source, **alcohol abuse** is a problematic drinking pattern that causes social problems, health problems, or both. The term **alcoholism**, or alcohol dependence, however, indicates an illness whose symptoms include abnormal behaviors for the purpose of obtaining alcohol, which causes impairment in an individual's control over his or her drinking. Regular, substantial use of alcohol has short-term effects that include impaired judgment, altered emotions and perceptions, impaired coordination, distorted vision and hearing, halitosis, and hangovers. Heavy use of alcohol has long-term effects that include skin problems; vitamin deficiencies; stomach disorders; loss of appetite; sexual impotence; liver damage; loss of memory; and damage to the central nervous system, heart, and cardiovascular system.

PRESCRIPTION DRUG ABUSE

The most commonly abused **prescription drugs** are opiate and opioid painkillers like Vicodin and Oxycontin; anxiolytic and anti-anxiety and sedative medications like Valium and Xanax; hypnotics like Ambien, prescribed for insomnia and anxiety; and stimulants like Ritalin, prescribed for ADHD and some sleep disorders. These are popular for their consciousness-altering effects. Signs of abuse include asking multiple doctors for prescriptions; repeatedly "losing" prescriptions, requiring replacements; forging, selling, and/or stealing prescriptions; abnormally sedated, energetic, or altered behaviors; extreme mood swings; hostility; decreased or increased sleeping; higher-than-prescribed dosing; and reduced decision-making capacity. **Opiates and opioids** cause symptoms including depression, low blood pressure, constipation, lowered respiration, perspiration, incoordination, and confusion. **Anxiolytics** cause confusion, dizziness, drowsiness, unstable gait, rapid involuntary eye movements, and poor judgment. **Stimulants** cause restlessness, insomnia, irritability, agitation, high blood pressure, heart arrhythmia, weight loss, and impulsivity. Reasons for abuse include to relieve tension or relax; increase alertness; improve concentration, school, or work performance; decrease appetite; get high and feel good; experiment with mental effects; prevent withdrawal once addicted; and/or facilitate socialization and peer acceptance.

Although many patients prescribed pain medications following surgery are afraid they will become addicted to them, this seldom happens when they take them as prescribed. **Addiction** is more likely when potentially addictive drugs are not taken as directed. Some **risk factors** for abusing prescription drugs include: youth, i.e., adolescence or early 20s; some pre-existing psychiatric disorders; current or past addictions to alcohol and other substances; lack of adequate knowledge or information regarding prescription medications; social environments with drug use; peer pressure; and working in healthcare settings or other situations with easier access to prescription drugs. Older adult abuse of prescriptions is an increasing problem: an aging population includes multiple health problems and multiple medications. This creates greater risk for misusing drugs; combining prescriptions with other prescriptions, over-the-counter medications, alcohol, and/or illegal drugs; and addiction. Some serious medical dangers of abusing prescriptions include: memory problems from anxiolytics and sedatives; choking risk; lowered blood pressure; slowed or stopped breathing; coma; and death by overdose from opiates, opioids, anxiolytics, and sedatives. Sudden withdrawal from sedatives and anxiolytics can cause nervous system hyperactivity and seizures. Abusing stimulants can cause paranoia, aggression, tremors, hallucinations, high blood pressure, dangerously high body temperatures, cardiac problems, and seizures.

LEGAL AND SOCIETAL IMPACTS OF SUBSTANCE ABUSE

The National Drug Intelligence Center's National Drug Threat Assessments find millions of people, many aged 18-25, have injected **illegal drugs**. Among adult Americans with AIDS, the CDC reports those contracting it from injecting drugs have lower survival rates than those contracting it from all other forms of transmission. Thousands of Americans die every year from the effects of drug use. **Drug abuse** frequently causes parents to neglect or abuse their children physically and/or emotionally. Children with parents or family members abusing substances are often deprived of shelter, water, food, medical and dental care, and necessary immunizations. Parents manufacturing drugs like methamphetamine pose even higher risks to children for hazardous chemical exposure, neglect, injury, and death. Employee substance abuse causes significant economic impacts on businesses through productivity loss; absenteeism; escalated medical insurance use; workplace accidents; workplace theft; and catastrophic accidents caused by drug impairment in employees like bus drivers, train conductors, air traffic controllers, and airline pilots. Methamphetamine lab operations not only severely strain taxpayer, local, state, and federal government resources, but moreover injure and kill neighbors, police, emergency responders, and children. Meth users seriously increase social services and law enforcement expenses.

Family Relationships

RELATIONSHIP PATTERNS IN MURRAY BOWEN'S FAMILY SYSTEMS THEORY

MARITAL CONFLICT

Bowen's concept of the nuclear family emotional system consists of four basic relationship patterns that determine where family problems develop. Clinical symptoms or problems typically emerge during times of intensified and protracted tension in a family. Stress levels, family adaptations to stress, and family connections with extended family and social support networks determine tension levels. In the **marital conflict pattern**, spouses project their increasing anxiety into the marital relationship. Each partner becomes preoccupied with the other's shortcomings, tries to control him or her, and resists being controlled. For example, a couple with a young child conceives a second child. The wife becomes anxious about meeting two children's needs. The husband questions his wife's ability to cope in order to avoid facing his own anxieties. After the second child's birth, the husband, observing his wife's stress, helps out more at home and is more controlling of her. He starts to feel neglected and disappointed in his wife's inadequate coping. The wife, who used to drink but quit while pregnant, resumes drinking.

DYSFUNCTION IN ONE SPOUSE

In Bowen theory, the relationship pattern of **dysfunction in one spouse** involves one partner pressuring the other to behave in certain ways, and the other acceding to that pressure. While both partners accommodate for maintaining harmony, eventually one does more than the other. Both are comfortable with this interaction for some time; however, if family tensions increase, the subordinate partner gives up enough self-control, yielding to the dominant partner to become significantly more anxious. Combined with other factors, this **anxiety** contributes to a psychiatric, social, or medical problem. For example, a couple with one young child has a second child. In the relationship pattern of marital conflict, the husband projects his own anxiety into criticizing his wife's coping abilities, taking on more household duties, and controlling her while the wife addresses her anxiety by drinking. The husband accuses her of selfishness and lack of effort. She agrees with but resents his criticism, feeling more dependent on him. Feeling increasingly unable to cope and make decisions, she escalates her drinking. He calls her an alcoholic. The wife becomes increasingly under-functional, the husband increasingly over-functional, functioning for her—all in an effort to avoid direct conflict and maintain harmony.

IMPAIRMENT OF ONE OR MORE CHILDREN

In the pattern of impairment of a child or children, parents project their own anxieties onto their child/children. They view the child **unrealistically**—either negatively or idealistically. The child **reciprocates** excessive parental focus by focusing excessively on the parents, overreacting to parental expectations, needs, and attitudes. This undermines the child's differentiation of self from family, increasing his or her susceptibility to either internalizing or acting out family tensions. **Anxiety** can disrupt the child's social relationships, school progress, and health. For example, a couple with one young child has another baby. Anxieties over the added stress of raising another child cause marital conflict and a dysfunctional relationship, developing into greater dysfunction in one spouse or parent. This causes emotional distance between spouses, who focus anxiously on the older child. She reacts by regressing, making immature demands of the parents, especially her mother. The mother externalizes her anxiety onto the child, worrying the new baby will displace her, acceding increasingly to her demands. The father avoids conflict with his wife by supporting her focus on the child, relieving her by giving the child attention when he gets home from work. Parents and child unwittingly conspire in seeing and creating **dysfunction in the child**.

EMOTIONAL DISTANCE

In Bowen's family systems theory, the four basic relationship patterns are marital conflict, spousal dysfunction, child impairment, and emotional distance. Whichever pattern predominates will dictate which family members will manifest familial tensions by developing psychological, social, or medical symptoms. The pattern of **emotional distance** consistently occurs in relation to the other three patterns. When interactions between family members become too intense, they develop emotional distance to decrease intensity. However, the drawbacks of emotional distance are that distanced members can become overly isolated, and can lose intimacy in their relationship. For example, when a couple with one child has another baby, they first project their anxieties onto each other and experience marital conflict. They then withdraw from one another emotionally to reduce the intensity of the conflict. They react to the emotional distance between them by externalizing their anxieties onto the first child, worrying she will feel left out with the new baby. The child reacts to the obsessive parental emotional over-involvement with her, reciprocating their emotional focus and overreacting to real or imagined parental withdrawal—creating impairment of a child. Thus, emotional distance **interacts** with the other patterns.

INFLUENCE OF SOCIOECONOMIC AND HEALTH VARIABLES ON PARENT-ADULT CHILD RELATIONSHIPS

Some sociological researchers investigating relationships of parents in their mid-50s to mid-70s with their adult children found **intergenerational exchanges** were characterized by strong **reciprocity** in both the United States and Great Britain. Contrary to stereotypical views of elderly adults becoming "burdens" on adult children, researchers have seen instead that married parents who gave help and support to at least one adult child were twice as likely to receive support from another adult child as parents who did not provide such support. Investigations showed when researchers controlled for various other parent and child variables, parents who owned homes, had higher incomes, and were married or widowed were more likely to help adult children than divorced parents. Conversely, parents with homes and higher incomes were less likely to receive help from adult children. Parental disability and advanced age **correlated positively** with adult children's responding to parent needs. Investigators inferred socioeconomic variations in support exchange balances between parents and adult children. Researchers predicted in 2005 that demographic trends would likely increase adult children's demands for support from older parents in the future.

TALKING ABOUT PROCREATION WITH CHILDREN

Many parents feel squeamish about "The Talk" or discussing "the birds and bees" with their maturing children. This is not just discomfort over an intimate topic; parents frequently fear that discussing sex with preadolescent and adolescent children is akin to giving them **permission** to engage in it. However, research studies find the opposite is true: teens are more prone to sexual behaviors when their parents have *not* talked about sex with them. When uninformed of possible **consequences**, they are more likely to act, not knowing of any disadvantages; they may experiment to get knowledge their parents have not imparted; and/or sexual behavior may be a reaction against parental avoidance and lack of openness. Communications researchers say sex is a continuing, two-way conversation that starts when very young children see pregnant women and ask questions. They advise parents to use Socratic questions, e.g., "What do you think the right time is for having sex?" and sharing their own thoughts after children do. **Open, receptive attitudes** are critical: if children bring up sex and perceive avoidant or shocked parental reactions, they will stop approaching parents, shutting down this vital conversation.

ROLES AND RESPONSIBILITIES OF EFFECTIVE PARENTING
RESPONSIBILITIES

Effective parenting includes ensuring the safety and well-being of one's children by providing adequate shelter and food as well as the following:

- **Helping the child build self-esteem**: Encouraging the child to become self-sufficient and demonstrate skills.
- **Providing positive reinforcement**: Recognizing and rewarding the child for doing something right rather than focusing on negatives.
- **Setting limits**: Establishing reasonable rules and discipline.
- **Providing consistent discipline**: Following through by providing consequences.
- **Spending quality time with the child**: Engaging one on one with the child. Scheduling activities and time together and being available when the child wants to talk or interact.
- **Providing a good role model**: Modeling the type of behavior that is expected of the child.
- **Communicating with the child**: Being open, honest, and willing to listen and stating expectations directly.
- **Exhibiting flexibility in the parenting role**: Recognizing that children have different needs at different times in their lives and allowing the child to have increasing autonomy with age.
- Providing unconditional love and support: Being nurturing and kind.

DISCIPLINE

Parents use a number of different approaches to discipline adolescents:

Strategy	Parent action
Behavior modification	Uses positive reinforcement to encourage appropriate behavior and ignores inappropriate behavior.
Consequences	Inappropriate behavior results in a consequence, such as losing privileges or a specified punishment.
Corporal punishment	Spanks or otherwise inflicts pain on the adolescent to force appropriate behavior but may have serious negative impacts on self-esteem of adolescent and, in some cases, may cause injury.
Scolding	Uses harsh, often loud, language to express unhappiness with an adolescent's behavior.
Time-out	Uses a specified period of time-out away from activities or time-out from phone, Internet, or other desired activity.
Reasoning	Discusses problem behavior and the reason that it is not appropriate.

PROMOTING GOOD BEHAVIOR

Discipline entails more than punishing or correcting inappropriate behavior. A good parent also uses strategies to **promote good behavior**. Strategies include the following:

- Being realistic about what the adolescent can do and understand, depending on the child's age and maturity level.
- Modeling appropriate behavior.
- Discussing appropriate behavior in new situations, such as before a family event or an outing.
- Attending to inappropriate behavior immediately, including discussion of more appropriate actions.

- Reprimanding the adolescent for bad behavior and not for being a bad person.
- Anticipating circumstances that may encourage inappropriate behavior, such as when the adolescent is stressed or tired.
- Providing reminders to help the adolescent control his/her own behavior.
- Providing rationale for appropriate behavior in accordance to the adolescent's ability to understand.
- Helping the adolescent to understand that different situations require different standards of behavior and language, such as partying with friends as opposed to attending a wedding.

Interpersonal Relationships

BIG FIVE THEORY OF PERSONALITY TRAITS

In a very popular theory developed by a series of researchers (Fiske, 1949; Norman, 1967; Smith, 1967; Goldberg, 1981; McCrae & Costa, 1987; Costa & McCrae, 1994, etc.), the **Big Five universal personality traits** are extraversion, agreeableness, conscientiousness, neuroticism, and openness. **Extraversion** is characterized by sociability, assertiveness, emotional expressivity, talkativeness, and excitability. **Agreeableness** features affection, kindness, trust, altruism, and similar prosocial behaviors. **Conscientiousness** includes organization, detail-orientation, goal-directed behaviors, good impulse control and thoughtfulness. **Neuroticism** includes anxiety, irritability, moodiness, emotional instability, and sadness. **Openness** has characteristics of broad interests, insight, and imagination. Each trait is a continuum, with individuals demonstrating various degrees of each trait between two extremes, e.g., between extreme extraversion and extreme introversion. Some researchers examining the interaction of personality traits with young adult social relationships have found that, while personality traits predict numbers and qualities of peer relationships, relationships do not reciprocally predict personality traits. Also, major relationship changes do not affect personality traits. Extraversion, agreeableness and conscientiousness affected quality and number of social relationships. Longitudinal study found agreeableness influenced later but not initial peer conflict; and conscientiousness influenced later but not initial family contact. Personality traits are more stable than relationship characteristics.

INFLUENCE OF SOCIAL CONTEXT FACTORS ON CHILDREN'S PEER RELATIONSHIPS

In studying the peer interactions of children with **attention deficit hyperactivity disorder (ADHD)**, multiple researchers have found peers dislike children with ADHD within hours of first meeting them, across situations and over time; and ADHD plus peer difficulties cumulatively predict **adolescent psychopathology**. These collected findings indicate serious social problems for ADHD populations. One social context factor is **parental influence**. Though disruptive ADHD behaviors cause conflict in parent-child relationships, one lead investigator (Mikami et al, 2010), questioning whether these parenting problems then also worsened children's peer conflicts, found parents indeed more critical of their ADHD children and less likely than other parents to have strong support networks—even after controlling for disruptive child behaviors. While parental warmth toward children, skilled adult-adult interactions, and modeling and coaching of children's peer interactions normally correlate with children's acceptance by peers, both parental criticism and—unexpectedly—praise predicted ADHD children's *poorer* peer interactions (again, after controlling for disruptive behaviors). Possible influences include parental ADHD; peer observations of parent-child interactions; and effects of parent-child relationships on the accuracy of children's self-perceptions of peer competence.

SOCIAL CONTEXT FACTOR OF TEACHER INFLUENCES OF PEER RELATIONSHIPS AMONG CHILDREN

Children typically develop likes and dislikes among school peers. Some research has revealed children's observations of **teacher responses** contribute to their **social peer preferences**. Some studies found children with ADHD did not gain better peer acceptance even when they improved their behavior because peers continued rejecting them based on their established negative reputations. But others have found teachers can mitigate these bad reputations by directing **positive attention** to children with ADHD. Multiple researchers concur that children's ADHD behaviors cause many teachers difficulty relating to them. Dislike of children with high levels of ADHD symptoms tends to progress over the school year. However, investigators also find teachers who use instructional practices communicating their belief that all children can learn, and who form positive relationships with all students, can change the association of peer difficulties with

ADHD symptoms. Researchers speculate such outcomes may support the possibility that teachers can promote **better peer relationships** through shaping classroom environments. Although studies continue to show peer dislike predicted by children's ADHD symptoms, they also find teacher practices can influence that interaction, making it less invariable.

DISCLOSING UNCOMFORTABLE TOPICS IN INTERPERSONAL COMMUNICATION

Communications experts observe that even in healthy relationships, people avoid bringing up some topics. They often do so strategically. Experts point out that constantly expressing every little criticism and stressor can destroy a relationship. Instead, we protect our personal identities and preserve the peace in our relationships by setting **thresholds of privacy**. Researchers studying motivations for **topic avoidance** identify self-protection or protecting the relationship as potential reasons. For example, bringing up a desire to solidify a relatively new relationship risks the partner's rejection. We may avoid broaching other topics to avoid the other's judgmental response. Researchers find that people avoiding topics for self-protection feel less satisfaction than those who do it to protect their relationship. Experts also note that, in romantic relationships, a delicate balance is necessary between avoidance and direct sharing. For example, sharing about past relationships can inform a new partner's understanding of the person, but only to a point; beyond that, too many details offer no benefit. On the other hand, overly repressing feelings and thoughts is found detrimental to health. Studies find habitually avoiding difficult subjects correlates with exacerbation of **irritable bowel syndrome symptoms**; and when families avoid discussing a member's cancer, patient illnesses become worse.

MAIN GOALS INVOLVED IN INTERPERSONAL CONVERSATIONS

According to communications researchers who have analyzed interpersonal conversations, people frequently strive, consciously or unconsciously, to meet three main goals during serious conversations. (1) **Task goals**. These represent the official purpose or point of the conversation. For example, a conversation with an aging parent may have the purpose of deciding who will make decisions for him/her when s/he is no longer able to make them. (2) **Identity goals**. These are tacit methods of preserving both one's own and another's sense of self. For example, in the preceding example, the family member(s) consider that by bringing up this topic, they are being caring and responsible, and that the aging parent wants to experience continued autonomy despite deteriorating health. (3) **Relationship goals**. These are directed to maintaining interpersonal connections. For example, in the foregoing examples, the parties in the conversation perceive that their open discussion is enabled by their closeness. Conversations with the highest quality entail both (or all) parties' observing these three goals concurrently, which is cognitively very challenging. It requires taking another's perspective, and then composing messages acknowledging that viewpoint while achieving our own goals for the conversation at the same time.

RELATIONSHIP BETWEEN INTERPERSONAL COMMUNICATION AND STRESS

Experts in communications note that research studies show stress is generated by **avoiding discussion** of important subjects, damaging the immune system and personal well-being over time. Conversely, they comment that we are able to achieve some **control** over a problem when we are able to explain it. Therefore, it more often than not benefits us to talk about subjects we find difficult to discuss. Another consideration is that we tend to **expect worse outcomes** of disclosing sensitive information than what really occurs. Research shows that we overestimate how much our negative perceptions coincide with those of our family members or significant others because we project our own beliefs onto them. In reality, it is often both more productive and safer emotionally than we think to bring up a touchy topic. However, another aspect highlighted by communications researchers is that **quality supersedes quantity** in communication. They find when discussing important issues, like serious illness or end-of-life wishes, it can be more harmful to discuss it in the wrong way than not discuss it at all, and that more is not necessarily better. Some research initiatives in healthcare communications have failed by emphasizing the quantity of communication rather than its quality.

EFFECTIVE INTERPERSONAL COMMUNICATION

Among elements making interpersonal conversations effective, experts in communications and clinical psychology include these:

- Ask yourself "**Why**?" Clarify whether you are sharing to benefit the relationship or yourself. Disclosure for the relationship's benefit supersedes self-interest.
- Affirm you **deserve to communicate**. Many people are concerned it is not their place to raise certain issues. However, experts point out a close relationship is not close unless each member speaks up sometimes.
- Use a **less personal approach** first to test another's response. To determine whether to avoid discussing how a topic relates to yourself and/or another, mention a less personal example of it (e.g., "My cousin once had an abortion.").
- Use **natural openings**. To discuss something naturally, be alert to times when another is willing and able to hear it. As a clinical psychologist puts it, waiting for a door to open is better than breaking down the door. Initiating conversation succeeds more when someone is responsive.
- Do not raise touchy subjects when **upset**. This is inconvenient, because this is when we most want to talk about them. But experts advise calming down before resuming difficult conversations.

ELEMENTS RECOMMENDED FOR DIFFICULT SUBJECTS

- **Aim for productive, quality conversations**. A clinical psychologist says hinting at a subject at ten different times is less productive than one productive talk. However, a communications expert also points out that conversation is more typically a process than a single, conclusive discussion. When people reveal information or feelings in one conversation, this frequently requires additional conversations.
- **"I" statements**. It is more useful to say "This is how I feel," than "This is how you are." While this advice is common, psychologists caution people not to use it mechanically as a conversational "trick." They should be authentic acknowledgements of our responsibility: when we are hurt, even when it is not our fault, it is still our hurt and our responsibility to find ways of assuaging it.
- **Take others' points of view**. Empathize to balance honesty; be responsible for your role in a situation. Moreover, be prepared for diverse responses: others can be more sensitive *or* more resilient than we thought.
- **Stick to the subject**. When others introduce distracting issues, defer discussion. Sometimes neutral third parties (e.g., couples or family counselors) can narrow conversational scope.
- **Lighten up**: humor can bring perspective and balance to tense situations and ease expressing resentment, anger, sadness, and frustration.

DISCUSSING SEX IN RELATIONSHIPS

Most people's egos are very sensitive to threats regarding their lovemaking abilities. Conversations about **sex** can be particularly difficult for spouses, because rejection from one's lifelong partner hurts most. Experts advise members of couples not to make the assumption that their partners automatically know they are experiencing dissatisfaction. They discourage saying something like "Lately it seems you are tired a lot of the time," and instead saying something like "Lately I have been feeling like I am being ignored, and I want to find out together how we can make our sex life better." Experts also say that after a couple has such a conversation, they should mutually decide on a specific time in the future when they will talk about the subject again and evaluate what progress they have made. Moreover, they should not bring up the subject again or complain about it until the time they have chosen: if the partner perceives such behaviors as nagging, they become self-fulfilling prophecies. The partner thinks, "S/he thinks I can't change, so why should I try?"

INTERPERSONAL CONVERSATIONS ABOUT DEATH

Most of us understandably do not want people we love to **die**. Moreover, we do not want loved ones to think we welcome this inevitable life passage, and we often fear this is how they will perceive our talking about death with them. Experts suggest taking advantage of **less personal examples** available about third parties to test loved ones' responses and/or bring up the subject. For example, if a news story reports about an individual in a coma, adult children might use that topic to find out what their aging parents think and feel about end-of-life decisions like DNR (do not resuscitate), living wills, using heroic measures to preserve or prolong life, etc. Communications experts point out that rather than introducing the subject of a living will at Christmas dinner, Easter brunch, or similar family celebrations, it is not as threatening to use relevant third-party examples like news stories to initiate the conversation. A general rule for families is not to wait for an "official Big Conversation," but to start **early** and **regularly**, frequently discussing this important topic.

DISCUSSING RELATIONSHIP STATUS

When people are involved in relationships they have established fairly recently, they frequently have not yet determined how they feel about them. They fear bringing up where the relationship is headed too soon could sabotage its future unnecessarily. This is one reason they avoid talking about **relationship status**, especially early. Another reason is gender differences. Researchers find women want more to **evaluate relationship status**; men tend to allow relationships to unfold **passively** without wanting to talk directly about them. Experts in communications say that in new relationships, partners wanting to assess their status should get information through more **indirect means**. For example, if one asks another, "What are you doing this weekend?" and gets an answer like "I'm incredibly busy," one can assume the other is not very interested; both parties can save face without more pointed questions. When relationships have lasted longer, it is normal to want to know whether they are exclusive. Partners should then more explicitly state their own **rules** so they are not broken, their **expectations** so they are not unmet, and their **questions** so they are not unanswered.

SIGNS OF ABUSIVE RELATIONSHIPS AND BELITTLING BEHAVIORS

People who want to determine if they are in an **abusive relationship** should consider whether they think or feel the following: they feel afraid of their partner often, they avoid mentioning certain subjects for fear of making their partner angry, they feel they cannot do anything right with their partner, they believe being mistreated is what they deserve, they wonder whether they are the member of the relationship who is crazy, and they feel helpless and/or emotionally numb. To consider whether their partner engages in **belittling behaviors** toward them, they should consider the following: whether their partner yells at them often; whether the partner says or does things to humiliate them; whether the partner insults them or criticizes them regularly; whether the partner treats them so poorly they find it embarrassing for family, friends, or others to witness it; whether the partner dismisses, disparages, or ignores their successes and/or opinions; whether the partner blames them for the partner's abusive behaviors; and whether the partner views and/or treats them as a sexual object or property instead of a human being.

BEHAVIOR OF ABUSIVE PARTNERS

Victims in abusive relationships should consider whether their partner behaves in an overly possessive and jealous manner toward them; whether the partner controls what they do or where they go; whether the partner prevents them from seeing their family or friends; whether the partner limits their access to the car, the phone, and/or money; and whether their partner is continually checking up on what they are doing and where they are going. These are all behaviors intended to **control** the other person, and are not normal or healthy. Threats of **violence or violent behaviors** to watch for in a partner include: the partner has a bad temper, and is unpredictable about losing his or her temper; the partner threatens to harm or kill them, or actually does harm them; the partner threatens to hurt their children, actually hurts them, or threatens to take them away; the partner threatens that if they leave, the partner will commit suicide; the partner forces them to engage in sex when they do not want to; or the partner takes away or destroys their personal belongings.

DOMESTIC ABUSE

Domestic violence is domestic abuse including physical violence. Physical force that injures or endangers someone is **physical abuse**. Physical battery or assault is a crime: police have the authority and power to protect individuals from physical attacks, whether outside or inside a family or home. **Sexual abuse** is an aggressive, violent act and a type of physical abuse. This includes forced sex, even by a partner with whom one also has consensual sex. Victims of physical and sexual abuse are at greater risk of serious injury and death. Even if incidents seem minor, e.g., being pushed or shoved, they are still abuse, and also can still cause severe injury or death. Even if incidents have only happened once or twice in a relationship, they are still abuse and are likely to continue and escalate. If physical assaults stop when the victim becomes passive, this is not a solution: the victim has given up his/her rights as a partner and a person to independence, self-expression, and decision-making. Even when no physical violence exists, victims may suffer from **verbal and emotional assault and abuse**.

EMOTIONAL AND FINANCIAL DOMESTIC ABUSE

People often associate the idea of domestic abuse with physical battery. However, many partners are victims of **emotional abuse**. Without physical bruises, the victim, abuser, and other people unfortunately overlook or minimize emotional abuse. The intention and result of emotional abuse are to erode the victim's independence, control, and feelings of self-worth. Victims come to feel they have nothing without the abusive partner, or have no way to escape the relationship. Emotional abuse includes **verbal abuse** like blaming, shaming, name-calling, insulting, and yelling. It also includes **controlling behaviors**, **intimidation**, and **isolating** the victim. Threats of punishment, including physical violence, frequently enter into psychological or emotional abuse. Emotional abuse scars are less visible than physical ones, but are equally or more damaging. **Financial or economic abuse** is another way to control the victim. It includes withholding money, checkbooks, credit or debit cards; withholding shelter, food, clothing, medications, or other necessities; making victims account for every cent they spend; rigidly controlling the victim's finances; restricting the victim to an allowance; sabotaging the victim's job by constantly calling there and/or causing the victim to miss work frequently; preventing the victim's working or making career choices; and stealing from or taking the victim's money.

CHOICE AND SELF-CONTROL IN ABUSIVE PARTNERS

Some people observe that abusive individuals lose their tempers; apparently have some psychological disorder; and some also abuse substances (though others do not), and, equating their problems with the illness or disease model of substance abuse, mistakenly assume that abusers cannot **control their behavior**. However, experts point out that abusive behaviors and violence are deliberate **choices** that the abusers make to control their victims. Evidence that they can control their behavior includes that they do not abuse everybody in their lives—only those they claim to love who are closest to them; that they choose carefully where and when to abuse, controlling themselves in public but attacking the victim once they are alone; that they can stop the abusive behavior when it is to their benefit, e.g., when their employer calls or the police arrive; and that they frequently aim physical attacks to parts of the victim's body where they are hidden by clothing, so others cannot see them.

TACTICS EMPLOYED BY DOMESTIC ABUSERS TO EXERT POWER OVER AND MANIPULATE VICTIMS

- **Dominance**: abusers, needing to feel in control of victims and relationships, dominate by making decisions for victims and family, giving them orders, and expecting unquestioning compliance. They often treat victims as children, servants, slaves, or possessions.
- **Humiliation**: to keep victims from leaving, abusers make them feel worthless and that nobody else will want them. To make victims feel inadequate, they insult and shame them publicly and privately, making them feel powerless and destroying their self-esteem.
- **Isolation**: abusive partners make victims dependent on them by cutting off their contact with others. They may stop victims from visiting with friends and relatives, or even going to school or work. Victims may have to ask permission to see anybody, go anywhere, or do anything.
- **Threats**: to frighten victims into dropping charges and/or prevent their leaving, abusers typically threaten to: harm or kill victims, children, other family, or pets; commit suicide; report victims to child services; and file false charges against them.
- **Intimidation**: threatening gestures and looks, property destruction or smashing objects in front of victims, hurting pets, or displaying weapons are tactics signaling violent consequences for noncompliance to frighten victims into submission.
- **Denial and blame**: abusers minimize or deny abuse or blame it on circumstances or, commonly, the victim. "You made/make me do it" is a frequent accusation used by abusers.

WARNING SIGNS OF DOMESTIC ABUSE, PHYSICAL VIOLENCE, AND ISOLATION

Warning signs of **domestic abuse**: the person agrees with everything the partner does and says; frequently checks in with the partner, reporting what they are doing and where they are; often receives harassing phone calls or texts from the partner; appears anxious or afraid to please the partner; and/or mentions the partner's jealousy, possessiveness, or temper. Warning signs of **physical violence**: the person often misses school, work, or social events without explaining; often has injuries, excusing them as "accidents" or "clumsiness"; and/or wears sunglasses indoors, long sleeves in summer, or other means of hiding injuries. Warning signs of **isolation**: the person never or seldom goes out in public without the partner; is unable to see friends and family; and/or has limited access to the car, money, or credit or debit cards. Psychological warning signs of being abused: someone who used to be confident displays significantly lowered self-esteem. An outgoing person becomes withdrawn; or an individual shows other major personality changes. The person appears anxious; depressed; despondent; or suicidal, verbalizing suicidal ideations or displaying suicidal behaviors.

ADVICE FOR PEOPLE WHO SUSPECT SOMEBODY THEY KNOW IS A VICTIM OF DOMESTIC ABUSE

Abusers are experts at **manipulating** and **controlling** victims. Victims are drained, frightened, ashamed, depressed, and confused. They need to escape the situation, but frequently have been isolated from others. Those suspecting abuse should be alert to warning signs, offer support to victims for extricating themselves, getting help, and starting the healing process. Some people may hesitate, thinking they could be mistaken; learn the victim does not want to discuss it or have them interfere; or simply be told that it is none of their business. In these cases, experts advise people to **speak up** regardless: expressing concern not only informs a victim somebody cares, it moreover could save that person's life. They should speak with the person privately, identifying signs they have observed and explaining why they are concerned, reassure the individual they will keep all conversation confidential, that they are there whenever s/he is ready to talk, and will help in any way possible. Regarding dos and don'ts, **do** the following: express concern, ask whether something is wrong, listen, validate the person's communications, offer help, and support the individual's decisions. **Don't**: wait for the person to approach you, blame or judge the individual, give advice, pressure the person, or attach conditions to your support.

CHILD ABUSE

Many things can precipitate child abuse, including stress related to poverty, unemployment, divorce, single parenting, and lack of support. Other causes include parental substance abuse, mental illness, and sociopathic/psychopathic personalities. Child abuse occurs across all socioeconomic levels. **Indications of child abuse** include the following:

- **Physical**: Unexplained bruises and burns, frequent injuries (including fractures), unkempt appearance, and delayed medical treatment. Sexual abuse may result in difficulty sitting or walking, frequent urination, and pain in the genital area.
- **Emotional/Psychological**: Aggressive behavior toward others; shy, withdrawn behavior; fearful of parents and other adults; low self-esteem; poor school performance; marked depression; and anxiety. A child experiencing sexual abuse may refuse to participate in exercises or gym class and may show a precocious interest in sex or sexualized behavior. The child may run away from home, be truant, and show a sudden decline in academic performance. Adolescents who are abused often turn to substance abuse.

PREVENTION OF CHILD ABUSE AND ABDUCTION

Prevention of child abuse and abduction includes a variety of approaches:

- **Parent education**: Includes developmental milestones, positive discipline techniques, age-appropriate behaviors and skills, child safety, and methods to improve parent-child interactions.
- **Support groups**: Parent groups to help members discuss problems and develop coping strategies.
- **Mental health programs**: Support for the child and other family members to help manage symptoms and life challenges.
- **Respite care**: Short-term childcare to allow parents/caregivers to remove themselves from the situation and the stress in order to avoid behaving abusively.
- **Home visiting programs**: Provide guidance for parents/caregivers regarding good health practices, positive parenting, home safety, and community resources.
- **Family resource centers**: Provide education and resources for parents/caregivers, including job training, parenting classes, violence prevention, substance abuse prevention, literacy programs, crisis intervention, respite care, and child care.
- **Law enforcement programs**: Abduction prevention education for parents focusing on how to educate and protect children regarding possible stranger abduction.

AGENCIES AND PROGRAMS DEALING WITH CHILD ABUSE AND ABDUCTION

Agencies and programs that deal with child abuse and abduction include the following:

- **Law enforcement agencies** - They arrest and bring criminal charges against those who abuse and/or abduct children.
- **Government agencies** - State and local child protective services. They investigate charges of child abuse and can remove a child from the home and place in foster care or provide ongoing monitoring of parent(s). They monitor foster children.
- **Children's advocacy centers** - They investigate and collect evidence regarding child abuse and coordinate with law enforcement and child protective services.
- **Nonprofit organizations** - Examples: The International Society for the Prevention of Child Abuse and Neglect, Child Welfare League of America, and National Children's Alliance. These organizations advocate for children, support those working to protect children, and increase public awareness.
- **Professional organizations** - Example: The American Academy of Pediatrics provides guidelines for recognizing, reporting, and dealing with abuse.
- **The National Center for Missing & Exploited Children** - This nonprofit organization established by Congress provides a hotline and tip line, posts pictures and information, raises awareness, and works with law enforcement and families. Serves as a clearinghouse of resources.

SEXUAL HARASSMENT, ABUSE, AND RAPE

Sexual harassment can take many forms, including making unwanted personal comments about appearance or lifestyle, pressing the person to date, promoting offensive material (such as showing pornography or telling off-color jokes), making unwanted physical contact (hugging, kissing, touching, standing very close), and behaving inappropriately (leering, catcalling, whistling, bullying). **Sexual abuse** can include all types of harassment as well as inappropriate and unwanted sexual contact. **Rape** involves coerced or violent sexual contact as well as sexual contact with a person who is impaired and unable to give consent (such as a person who is inebriated or under the influence of drugs). **Prevention** requires education about what constitutes harassment, abuse, and rape; prompt response to reports; having support systems in place; bystander intervention; enlisting others to assist; contacting authorities; avoiding alcohol and drugs; and using distraction. Adolescents and adults should have a clear understanding of date rape and the repercussions for both the perpetrator and the victim and should keep social media sites private and avoid tagging people.

PHYSICAL AND EMOTIONAL/PSYCHOLOGICAL EFFECTS

Sexual harassment, abuse, and rape may result in similar long-term results:

- **Physical**: The victim may experience vaginal or anal tearing that may result in long-term painful intercourse. Chronic urinary infections may occur. STIs may be transmitted, including HIV/AIDS. Some victims may become pregnant and have to make a difficult decision about aborting or carrying the child and then another decision about keeping the child or placing it for adoption.
- **Emotional/Psychological**: The victim often engages in self-blame and may experience deep guilt. Posttraumatic stress disorder is common with flashbacks, especially with violent encounters. The victim often distrusts others and suffers from unexplained bouts of anger and severe depression. The victim may feel powerless and afraid, feeling as though he or she has lost control of life. Some may become very reclusive, afraid to leave their house or apartment, and become unable to work, resulting in increased stress.

AGENCIES, PROGRAMS, AND REGULATIONS

Sexual harassment is covered under **Title VII of the Civil Rights Act** (1964), which prohibits sexual harassment but applies only to employers with 15 or more employees. Complaints are submitted to the Equal Employment Opportunity Commission (EEOC). Employers with fewer employees are covered by various state laws and regulatory agencies. Some nongovernmental agencies have limited programs to assist victims of sexual harassment, including the Legal Advocacy Fund of the American Association of University Women (AAUW). **Sexual abuse and rape** are criminal offenses covered by laws against sexual violence and involve law enforcement agencies, usually the local police, although federal authorities may intervene in sex trafficking and online stalking. Many organizations now have workplace violence prevention programs that include strategies to prevent sexual abuse, stalking, and rape. The National Sexual Assault Hotline refers people to the nearest services. The National Sex Offender Public Website links state, tribal, and territorial sexual offender registries. Numerous organizations provide assistance to victims, including the National Organization for Victim Assistance.

COMMUNICATION SKILLS

ACTIVE LISTENING

Active listening requires more than passively listening to another individual. **Active listening** includes observing the other individual carefully for nonverbal behaviors, such as posture, eye contact, and facial expression, as well as understanding and reflecting on what the person is saying. The listener should observe carefully for inconsistencies in what the individual is saying or comments that require clarification. **Feedback** is critical to active listening because it shows the speaker that one is paying attention and showing interest and respect. Feedback may be as simple as nodding the head in agreement but should also include asking questions or making comments to show full engagement. Listening with **empathy** is especially important because it helps to build a connection with the speaker. The listener should communicate empathy with words: "You feel (emotion) because (experience)" because the speaker may not be sensitive to what the listener is comprehending.

ASSERTIVENESS

Assertive communication occurs when the individual expresses opinions directly and actions correlate with words. **Assertive communicators** are respectful of others and do not bull, but they are firm and honest about their opinions. They frequently use **"I" statements** to make their point: "I would like. . . ." Communication usually includes **cooperative statements**, such as "What do you think?" and distinguishes between fact and opinion. Assertive communicators often engender trust in others because they are consistent, honest, and open in communicating with others. The assertive communicator feels free to express disagreement and anger but does so in a manner that is nonthreatening and respectful of others' feelings. Assertive communication requires a strong sense of self-worth and the belief that personal opinions have value. Assertive communicators tend to have good **listening skills** because they value the opinions of others and feel comfortable collaborating.

"I" MESSAGES AND REFUSAL SKILLS

Using "I" messages is a method of communication in which the speaker focuses on personal feelings rather than characteristics or actions of the listener. For example, if an adolescent stays out late, an **"I" message** would be "I worry that you have been in an accident when you come home late" rather than focusing on the adolescent: "Why are you late?"

Refusal skills are those that help people refuse to participate in activities and to say "no" to situations that are dangerous or unwanted, such as drug taking and sexual contact. The person needs to stand up straight, make eye contact, and say "NO" forcefully and support this statement with the appropriate body language and facial expression. The person should avoid making excuses but remain firm and repeat the same message if necessary. Young people may need to practice these techniques in role-playing activities.

NEGOTIATION SKILLS

Negotiating may be a formal process (such as negotiating with the administration for increased benefits) or an informal process (such as arriving at a team consensus), depending on the purpose and those involved.

- **Competition** - In this approach, one party wins and the other loses, such as when parties state that their positions are nonnegotiable and are unwilling to compromise. To prevail, one party must remain firm, but this can result in conflict.
- **Accommodation** - One party concedes to the other, but the losing side may gain little or nothing, so this approach should be used when there is a clear benefit to one choice.
- **Avoidance** - When both parties dislike conflict, they may put off negotiating and resolve nothing, and the problems remain.
- **Compromise** - Both parties make concessions to reach a consensus, this can result in decisions that suit no one, compromise is not always the solution.
- **Collaboration** - Both parties receive what they want, a win-win solution, often through creative solutions, but collaboration may be ineffective with highly competitive parties.

SELF-ASSESSMENT OF BEHAVIORAL RISK FACTORS

Self-assessment of behavioral risk factors begins with identifying risk factors (drinking, sexual activity, dishonesty, drug abuse) that may be an issue and then assessing the **degree of risk**. Although self-reflection may be helpful, in most cases a **self-assessment tool** is the easiest and most effective way to carry out self-assessment. Examples include the student sexual risks scale and suicide risk screening tools. The National Institute on Drug Abuse provides links to a number of evidence-based screening tools that can be used for the assessment of alcohol and drug use for adolescents and adults. Although the results of self-assessment may be enlightening, they do not necessarily lead to **changes** unless the person is motivated to change. If self-assessment indicates behavioral risk, the person should seek help in making changes, such as through a support group or therapist. The person may also enlist family and friends to help in monitoring and assessing change.

DIFFERENTIATING AMONG SAFE, RISKY, AND HARMFUL BEHAVIORS IN RELATIONSHIPS

A **safe** relationship is one in which the individuals have mutual respect and maintain appropriate boundaries. It can be difficult to differentiate between **risky** and **harmful** behaviors in a relationship because risky behaviors are often a precursor to harmful behaviors. The following behaviors are warning signs that the behaviors are not safe:

Risky behaviors	Harmful behaviors
Critical—Public or private criticism, purposefully humiliating the person.	Aggressive/Abusive—Any type of hitting, shoving, pushing, or physical violence.
Irresponsible/Immature—Constant problems (social, financial) and discord.	Controlling/Possessive—Attempts to control another person's life and to isolate the person from others.
Noncommunicative—Difficulty expressing feelings and being open with others.	Volatility—Unpredictable bouts of anger and rage.
Self-centered—thinks only in terms of personal needs.	Manipulative—Pressuring someone to do something or using guilt or threats to get one's way.

Stress-Related Disorders

CAUSES AND SYMPTOMS OF MENTAL AND EMOTIONAL HEALTH DISORDERS

ANXIETY AND DEPRESSION

Anxiety is characterized by apprehension and worry that is unrealistic and interferes with the quality of life. **Anxiety** may result from substance abuse as well as various types of stress (school, social, financial). Symptoms include irritability, hypervigilance, insomnia, depression, motor tremors and tension, shortness of breath, rapid heart rate, dry mouth, and diarrhea. Anxiety may range from mild to severe, at which point the person has difficulty concentrating. Panic is the most severe reaction, resulting in palpitations, fear of death, and an inability to concentrate.

Depression is a depressed mood in which the individual may experience a constant sense of despair and hopelessness and a loss of interest in activities, friends, and family. Symptoms may vary but can include constant fatigue, insomnia or hypersomnia, weight gain or loss, inability to focus and learn, and suicidal ideation. Family history of depression is a primary risk factor. Depression may also result from hormonal changes that occur during puberty as well as from stressful life situations, such as bullying and abuse.

EATING DISORDERS

Anorexia nervosa: Anorexia nervosa is an eating disorder characterized by the following:

- Refusal to maintain a minimal normal body weight.
- Extreme fear of becoming fat.
- Disturbed perception of body weight or shape.
- Denial of low body weight and a high priority being placed on weight or body shape.

Anorexia nervosa may be restrictive without bingeing and purging, or it may include bingeing and purging. Anorexia nervosa is usually chronic and requires a lifetime of monitoring. Patients with anorexia nervosa exhibit many mental health symptoms and commonly have comorbidity with depression and dysthymia. They may be irritable, have sleep disturbances, lack interest in sex, and withdraw from social interactions. They will be obsessed with the thought of food and may also have other obsessive-compulsive tendencies that may or may not involve food. They are at a high risk for suicide. Characteristic physical findings (emaciation, osteoporosis, hair loss, cardiac dysfunction) result from malnutrition and starvation.

Bulimia Nervosa: Bulimia nervosa is an eating disorder in which the individual eats more than normal within a two-hour period and carries out repetitive behaviors in order to control weight, such as excessive use of laxatives, diuretics, and exercise. Individuals with bulimia often engage in self-induced vomiting. Some may restrict eating and then binge and purge. Weight is often within normal range, but other symptoms include chipped teeth, dental caries, mouth sores, amenorrhea (occurs in about 50%), and heart and gastrointestinal disorders. Some may exhibit Russell's sign (calluses and scarring on the hand from using the hand to induce vomiting). The cause of bulimia nervosa is unclear, although people often have other mental health problems and low self-esteem. Criteria include repetitive cycles of binge eating; use of inappropriate behaviors to prevent weight gain, such as induced vomiting; overuse of laxatives, diuretics, or enemas; excessive exercise or fasting; and binge eating along with inappropriate behaviors to prevent weight gain at least one time per week for at least three months.

SUICIDAL IDEATION

Suicidal ideation occurs frequently in those with mood disorders or depression. Although females are more likely to attempt suicide, males actually commit three times more suicides than do females, primarily because females tend to take overdoses from which they can be revived, whereas males choose more violent means, such as jumping from a high place, shooting, or hanging. Risk factors include psychiatric disorders (schizophrenia, bipolar disorder, posttraumatic stress disorder [PTSD], and substance abuse) and physical disorders (HIV/AIDS, diabetes, traumatic brain injury, and spinal cord injury). **Passive suicidal ideation** involves wishing to be dead or thinking about dying without making plans, whereas **active suicidal ideation** involves making plans. Those with active suicidal ideation are most at risk. Individuals with suicidal ideation often give signals, direct or indirect, to indicate that they are considering suicide because many individuals have some ambivalence and want help. Others may act impulsively or effectively hide their distress.

MANAGING ANXIETY AND GRIEF

The first step in managing anxiety is to get help, such as by seeing a therapist, if the **anxiety** is affecting the quality of life. Other strategies include getting adequate rest, exercising regularly, engaging in activities of personal interest, identifying triggers, reducing stressors as much as possible, and talking about the anxiety with others. People may also practice methods of distraction, such as taking deep breaths, counting to 10 slowly, or thinking about a positive experience. **Managing grief** may require some time, which varies from person to person, but people need to express their feelings of grief and be allowed to grieve in their own ways. People should take care of themselves physically (getting good nutrition and adequate rest and exercise), and many avoid situations that trigger feelings of grief, although there is a danger of becoming reclusive. Grieving people need patient, understanding, and supportive family and friends.

PREVENTING SUICIDE

Strategies for preventing suicide include the following:

- Gain knowledge about the **warning signs** of suicide, such as talking about committing suicide, being preoccupied with death, having self-hatred, being depressed, and withdrawing.
- **Speak up** if someone shows warning signs, show concern, and ask the person about thoughts of and plans for suicide, but avoid arguing, promising confidentiality, or giving advice.
- **Respond quickly** with those at high risk, especially those with a specific lethal plan or means of committing suicide, by asking directly about plans and taking the person at high risk to a crisis center or emergency department. Risk is high any time a person is able to articulate a lethal plan, such as using a gun, taking an overdose, or cutting wrists, even if the person promises not to carry out the plan.
- Help the person to obtain **professional help** and set up a **safety plan**.

MAINTAINING GOOD MENTAL AND EMOTIONAL HEALTH

Strategies for maintaining good mental and emotional health include the following:

- Keep physically active, such as by a regular exercise program.
- Get adequate sleep and nutrition.
- Practice relaxation techniques, such as meditating, to help deal with stress.
- Develop a support system of friends and family members.
- Engage with others, making time to do things with friends, families, and coworkers.

- Develop hobbies or activities of interest, such as photography, painting, sports, or music.
- Get a pet, such as a dog or cat, that requires interaction and attention.
- Avoid excessive use of alcohol (a depressant), and avoid illicit drugs.
- Maintain a healthy work/school/life balance to avoid overwork and burnout.
- Deal with problems when they arise rather than letting them build up.
- Develop strategies for dealing with stress, such as keeping a journal or talking with a friend.
- Engage in volunteer activities in the community.
- Explore spirituality, religion, or belief systems.

Health Literacy, Instruction, and Assessment

Community Health

INFLUENCING PUBLIC POLICY TO IMPROVE COMMUNITY HEALTHCARE

One example of individuals who can **affect public healthcare policy** is nurses, who can draw on hundreds of experiences with patients. Researchers (Maryland and Gonzalez, 2012) find **nurses** can use hands-on patient experience to advocate in their communities regarding healthcare and educational systems and economic issues; and in legislative systems for public healthcare policy. Nurses can use real-life examples they have experienced to illustrate patient needs, and public policy impacts on patient morbidity and mortality, to influence patient access to effective, efficient, appropriate, quality healthcare. In addition to firsthand experience of healthcare system advantages and disadvantages, research (Porter-O'Grady and Malloch, 2011) finds nurses rank highest among the most trusted professions. This respect enables them to advocate for greater immunization access, greater educational funding, etc. by persuading elected officials to make necessary changes in services and care. Nurses need abilities for analyzing their experiences to recommend effective changes, and skills for participating in public policymaking processes. In communities, nurses can advocate, for example, by sharing information with patients about resources for reducing prescription drug costs, relieving the economic burdens of cancer treatment, and informing elected officials of the need to alleviate expenses.

MEDIA STRATEGIES FOR LOCAL HEALTH DEPARTMENTS TO ADVOCATE FOR PUBLIC HEALTH

21st-century **public health issues**—climate change; chronic disease; emerging diseases; healthcare inequities, disparities, and access; and disease control—encourage local health departments to transcend traditional roles as health education and individual service providers, and focus more on environmental, social, political, and physical factors determining individual and community health. They can change the media's typical approach of individual responsibility and behavior to establish wider understanding of environmental and social influences on community health. A **credible source communication strategy** targets individuals, policymakers, and the public. Its spokesperson is a trained program expert. The pace is medium; outcomes are raising awareness and possible behavior changes. **Risk communication** targets individuals, institutions, and the public. A credible, respected official is the spokesperson. Its pace is rapid; outcomes are individual awareness and compliance with health recommendations. Media advocacy targets policymakers and the public. A trained program expert is a spokesperson. The pace is slow; outcomes include norm and policy changes. **Social marketing** targets individuals. A marketing expert is a spokesperson. The pace is slow, the outcome individual behavior change. **Counter advertising** targets policymakers and the public. Spokespersons are a marketing expert and trained program expert. The pace is slow; the outcome is behavior change.

FEDERAL EMPLOYEES AND DEPARTMENTS RESPONSIBLE FOR INFECTIOUS DISEASE CONTROL

The **Secretary of the US Department of Health and Human Services** is legally responsible to prevent introduction, transmission, and spreading of communicable diseases in the US. The **Division of Global Migration and Quarantine** is delegated the authority for meeting this responsibility via activities that include operating quarantine stations at entry ports; establishing standards for medical examinations of people coming to the US; and administering foreign and interstate quarantine regulations of the international and interstate movements of people, animals, and cargo. These activities are legally founded in Titles 8 and 42 of the US Code, and pertinent supporting regulations. The US federal government is authorized for isolation and quarantine through the US Constitution's Commerce Clause. US Code 42, Section 264 – Regulations to control communicable diseases, authorizes the **Surgeon General** to make and enforce regulations including inspection, fumigation, disinfection, sanitation, pest extermination, and destruction of articles or animals contaminated or infected with sources of dangerous infections to humans. Individuals may not be apprehended, detained, conditionally released, or examined under this regulation except for preventing introduction, transmission, and spread of communicable diseases. Amendments include executive orders for public health authority evaluation, and a revised list of quarantinable communicable diseases.

FEDERAL AND STATE REGULATIONS CONCERNING IMMUNIZATIONS

There are no federal-level **immunization laws** in the US; however, certain vaccinations are required for children to enter **public schools** in all 50 states, varying by state. Children are required to be vaccinated for some or all of the following diseases to enter public schools: diphtheria, measles, mumps, pertussis, poliomyelitis, rubella, and tetanus. Because each state has its own requirements, the US Centers for Disease Control and Prevention (CDC) provides a database of state immunization laws, with results from a legislative review of laws in all 50 states requiring vaccination status assessment and vaccine administration for patients, residents, and healthcare workers. The CDC conducted this review in 2005, collecting data on laws for hospitals, individual provider practices, ambulatory care facilities, facilities for the developmentally disabled, and correctional facilities. The CDC also provides data on requirements for school entry by disease and by state. This includes a tool with state vaccination requirements for school and childcare, state exemptions, and links to state websites; a tool listing diseases preventable by vaccines; and state mandates for immunizations required in prenatal, daycare, childcare, kindergarten, elementary, secondary, K-12, college and university, and long-term care facilities.

MEDICAL AND HEALTH MYTHS

For many years, some people believed that drinking milk caused certain individuals' bodies to secrete more mucus. Even some doctors believed this, considering it a type of lactose intolerance that is not necessarily concentrated in the digestive system. Physician authors (Carroll and Vreeman, 2009) report that in a study of over 300 patients, almost two-thirds of them believed in such a relationship between milk and phlegm. However, in an experiment with volunteers who had cold viruses, some drank a lot of milk and were found to have no more nasal secretions, congestion, or coughing than those who did not drink as much milk. Another popular **misconception** is the idea that one can develop arthritis from repeatedly cracking one's knuckles. Scientists find no correlation between cracking the knuckles having arthritis, although one study found it could affect soft tissue around the knuckle joint. It can also decrease hand grip strength and increase hand swelling. However, people who crack their knuckles were not found likelier to develop osteoarthritis.

OCCUPATIONAL POSITIONS IN THE HEALTHCARE FIELD

Physicians diagnose and treat illnesses; perform, order, and interpret diagnostic tests and procedures; prescribe medications; perform surgeries; specialize in specific patient populations and diseases and treatments; and counsel patients. **Physician assistants (PAs)** assist with surgical procedures rather than performing surgeries; counsel patients under physician direction; prescribe medication in most US states; diagnose and treat illnesses; and perform, order, and interpret diagnostic tests and procedures. **Registered nurses (RNs)** treat patients, administer medications, execute physician orders, and advise and educate patients. **Medical assistants** obtain medical histories and vital signs; draw blood; collect laboratory specimens; prepare patients for examination; assist physicians during examinations; and perform administrative duties like filing charts, scheduling appointments, answering phones, and medical coding and billing. **Surgical technologists** prepare patients for surgery, organize operating room instruments and equipment, and assist physicians during surgical operations and procedures. **Pharmacists** fill prescriptions; compound medications; educate patients about medications; advise physicians and other clinical personnel about drug selection and dosages; and conduct drug experiments, tests, and research. **Clinical psychologists** evaluate and treat mental and emotional disorders. There are many more professions.

EDUCATIONAL REQUIREMENTS FOR DIFFERENT HEALTHCARE PROFESSIONS

Physicians must complete undergraduate degrees plus 4 years of medical school, 3-8 years of residency or internship, and pass a national licensure test. **Physician assistants** must complete a 2-4-year PA certification program and pass a national licensure test. **RNs** must complete a bachelor's/associate's degree or diploma and pass a national licensure test. **Medical assistants** must attain a 1-year diploma or certificate or a 2-year associate's degree, and in some US states pass a national certification test. **Surgical technologists** must receive a 9-month diploma/certificate or 2-year associate's degree and pass a national certification test. **Pharmacists** must complete a 6-8-year Doctor of Pharmacy degree and pass a national licensure test. **Clinical psychologists** must complete a doctoral (Ph.D. or Psy.D.) degree and pass a national licensure test. **Audiologists and speech-language therapists** must each complete Master's degrees and pass national licensure tests; in some US states, audiologists must pass an additional licensure test for dispensing hearing aids.

EXAMPLES OF HEALTH ORGANIZATIONS USING COMMUNITY AND SCHOOL EVENTS TO DELIVER HEALTH EDUCATION

Healthcare system leaders recognize the importance of **prevention** and **early detection** to sustaining health and reducing illness. For example, physicians and health teams at the leading nonprofit comprehensive healthcare system **WellStar** demonstrate their belief in prevention and early detection by providing screenings, health fairs, and educational opportunities in a diverse range of settings to help people improve individual and family health and well-being. They produce community events free of charge or low in cost. Throughout communities, health fairs feature medical screenings, community education, and basic preventive medicine through interactive educational events. Some health fairs have particular themes, e.g., weight loss and fitness, diabetes, or heart health. Well*Screen Events offer affordable, convenient screenings for early detection of diabetes, prostate conditions, thyroid disorders, high cholesterol, and other medical issues. Multiple WellStar facilities and other locations like senior centers, religious organizations, and YMCAs host **screening events** throughout the year. WellStar also offers educational events and classes for schools, community groups, local businesses, and religious organizations; and the nationally recognized Safe Sitter babysitter education program for ages 11-13, teaching personal safety, behavior management, injury prevention, first aid, CPR, choking care, and business and ethical aspects of babysitting.

PLANNING SCHOOL HEALTH FAIRS AS A MEANS OF HEALTH EDUCATION ADVOCACY

Fuel Up to Play 60 (© 2013), a program of Play 60, the NFL Movement for an Active Generation supported by the National Dairy Council, offers these tips to educators and parents: work with the school nurse and other health professionals to produce a list of potential **health fair presenters**. Invite community members to set up tables with physical activity and healthy eating information, give presentations, and even just attend to learn more. Guests could include local chefs, health news broadcasters or other local celebrities, and local pediatricians and hospital staff. Plan space and time for an event, including events such as family contests, races, and other fun activities; space for presentations; and healthy picnic foods to eat. Form a team and decide the best place, day, and time with the principal. Indoor and outdoor activities combined enable greater attendee movement to derive the most from the event. Collaborate with **school nutrition professionals** to choose healthy foods, and **physical educators** to choose and organize fun physical activities. Enlist student and parent volunteers to manage activity stations. Contact local organizations and businesses for donations of tables, food, equipment, prizes, etc. Invite the donors.

HEALTH EDUCATORS SERVING AS LIAISONS BETWEEN SCHOOL PERSONNEL, STUDENTS, PARENTS, AND COMMUNITIES

Many health educator activities connect different education stakeholders. For example, when they identify and request resources from school administrators for meeting learning goals and objectives they have developed, they are acting as **liaisons** between students and administrators. When they develop processes to **integrate health education** into other programs across the curriculum, they liaise with school administrators, curriculum coordinators, other school subject teachers, and students. By training others to implement health education, they liaise between trainees and students. When developing and conducting research, they liaise between the school and the research community. They are liaisons between support providers and students when requesting program support; and liaisons among all stakeholders when promoting their collaboration. As resource persons, they are liaisons communicating health information from resources to stakeholders, between existing resources and trainees when providing training, and between other trainers and trainees when they implement training programs and sessions. As consultants, they may liaise between or among different personnel whom they provide consultative assistance. As advocates, they are liaisons between students and parents and families to promote healthy home practices and parental school involvement in health education, and between policymakers and schools and communities when advocating health promotion policies.

SKILLS AND ABILITIES

Health educator skills for assessing community as well as individual needs enable them to **liaison** between the school and the community to **promote school and community health**. Their skills for planning health education programs mean they can interact with other educators, school administrators, curriculum coordinators, etc. Skills for coordinating health education programs naturally require them to liaison among different school personnel, as do skills for managing health education programs and personnel. Coalition-building skills mean they can liaise among the diverse stakeholders they recruit to form coalitions for health promotion, advocacy, and health education advocacy. Skills for making referrals make them liaisons between students and parents and various agencies and service providers to whom they refer them. Skills for developing mass media and social marketing campaigns enable them to liaison between media representatives and the public. Abilities for mobilizing and organizing communities make them liaisons among various community members, and school and community. Abilities to encourage healthy behaviors, and to manage controversial health content and issues, enable them to liaise between parents and students.

GSHS

The **Global School Health-based Student Health Survey** (GSHS), developed in a joint effort by the World Health Organization (WHO), the United Nations organizations UNAIDS, UNESCO, and UNICEF with technical assistance from the Centers for Disease Control and Prevention (CDC), is a school-based survey of **health behaviors and health-protective factors** in students 13-17 years old in over 120 countries. Over 450,000 students had participated through 2013. The data gleaned from this survey is intended to assist world nations in setting priorities, developing programs, and advocating for youth and school health policies and programs; help nations, international agencies, and others compare the prevalence of protective factors and health behaviors across different countries; and determine trends in protective factor and health behavior prevalence according to each nation to utilize for evaluating youth health advocacy and school health. GSHS core questionnaire modules cover hygiene and diet; alcohol, drug, and tobacco use; physical activity; mental health; protective factors; sexual behaviors; unintentional injury; and violence. WHO and CDC offer technical support and continuing capacity-building via training, materials, data analysis, and software. Country reports, data, documentation, bibliography, and fact sheets are available online.

PROMOTING STUDENT PARTICIPATION IN SCHOOL-/COMMUNITY-BASED EFFORTS TO ADDRESS HIGH-RISK BEHAVIORS ASSOCIATED WITH SUBSTANCE ABUSE

Promoting student participation in school-/community-based efforts to address high-risk behaviors associated with substance abuse often begins by recruiting **student leaders** to participate and lead these efforts because students look to their peers for guidance. **Sports coaches** are also often role models and can influence athletes to participate, and athletes often are admired by other students, who may follow their lead. The leaders of school clubs, such as the honor society or chess club, should also be recruited because they can positively influence club members. The school can also include **families** in prevention methods through such programs as Family Matters, in which parents receive booklets and telephone guidance by the health educator. Programs for adolescents that have proven successful include Life Skills Training (focuses on decision making, problem solving, and critical thinking); Lions Quest Skills for Adolescence (focuses on civic responsibility, social skills, and resisting peer pressure); ALERT Plus (Adolescent Learning Experiences Resistance Training), a 9–10th-grade extension of the middle school program; and the Project Toward No Drug Abuse (an interactive classroom project that focuses on motivation, life skills, and decision making).

HEALTH-RELATED CAREERS AND EDUCATIONAL REQUIREMENTS

Health-related careers:

- **Physicians** - Requires a bachelor's degree, four years of medical school, internship, and residency and licensure.
- **Nurses (RNs, LVN, APNs)** - Registered nurses (RNs) require two- to five-year training programs (ASN, BSN) and licensure as well as additional training for advance practice nurses (APNs). Licensed vocational nurses (LVNs) require an 18-month to 2-year training period, licensure, and work under RN supervision.
- **Nutritionists** - Requires bachelor's or master's degree.
- **Certified nurse assistant (aide)** - Requires six to eight weeks of training. Work under the supervision of RNs and LVNs.
- **Physician assistant** - Requires a two-year master degree program. PAs carry out many of the tasks of physicians.
- **Technicians** - Technicians include x-ray technicians, laboratory technicians, ultrasound technicians, dental hygienists, pharmacy technicians, emergency medical technicians, echocardiogram technicians, and phlebotomists. Training varies but is often approximately for two years, whereas those that require one skill, such as phlebotomists, may be trained in a matter of weeks. Some require licensure.
- **Medical assistant** - Programs vary from one to two years and include a certificate and/or associate's degree.

WHO'S WORLD HEALTH SURVEYS

The World Health Organization (WHO) began the **World Health Surveys (WHS)** in 2002-2004, partnering with 70 world nations to gather information about adult health populations and health systems through cross-sectional survey studies. More than 300,000 people aged 18 years and older participated in the studies, yielding a very large sample size. The WHS extended the results of WHO's 2000-2001 Multi-country Survey Study. The purpose of the WHS was to use a valid, reliable survey instrument to reinforce national capacities for monitoring **health systems** and **critical health outcomes**. WHO used statistical probability to select nationally representative samples from countries chosen to represent all of the world's regions. They adjusted the weights of sampling according to population distribution, and corrected for non-response following stratification. The surveys covered household data including household members, health insurance coverage, health expenditures, and permanent wealth or income indicators. On the individual level, the survey information included sociodemographic data, descriptions of health states, valuations of health states, health risk factors, chronic health conditions, healthcare use, mortality, social capital, and responsiveness of healthcare systems.

Health-Related Decision Making

ASPECTS OF DECISION-MAKING TO CONSIDER FOR INSTRUCTING ADOLESCENTS

The life stage of **adolescence** brings greater pressures on teenagers to solve more difficult problems and make harder decisions about matters like risk behaviors, sexuality, school involvement, and career choices. Thus, **decision-making** during adolescence can powerfully affect adult futures. Awareness of the possible impacts of their decisions informs teen motivation to learn effective **decision-making skills**. Such skills incorporate identifying available options and their potential consequences, evaluating the relative desirability or undesirability of each consequence, estimating each consequence's probability, and using a "decision rule" to choose among options. Decision-making models (e.g., Wilson & Kirby, 1984) require the skills of defining a necessary decision, gathering information for self-education and thinking of alternatives, considering options and choosing one, making a plan to execute the decision, and evaluating the decision and its results. Such models enable planned, goal-directed decision-making. Researchers have noted both cognitive elements of decision-making, and other aspects beyond cognition, as important in **adolescent risk-taking**.

RESEARCH-BASED CONCLUSIONS ABOUT HOW ADOLESCENTS MAKE DECISIONS

Various studies have identified variables that determine how prepared each individual adolescent is to make **effective decisions**, including intelligence, age, gender, race or ethnicity, social class, temperament, family dynamics and structure, cultural and social environment, and religiosity. Additionally, adolescent perceptions of and attitudes toward risk, perspectives regarding time, and compliance and conformity relative to parents and peers influence decision making abilities. Both contextual and developmental variables affect how teens ascribe subjective value to consequences, and how they use information, for decision-making. The **teen dilemma** is a need to make critical decisions having lifelong consequences, yet lacking ample life experience to inform those decisions. Studies have found positive results from **intervention programs** to improve adolescent decision-making skills, including decreased antisocial, socially disordered, and self-destructive behavior and increased prosocial, positive behavior; reduced tobacco use; more responsible sexual behavior in parenting and pregnant teens; higher school retention levels; and greater economic self-sufficiency. Some researchers consider decision-making ability to be one component of risk behavior. They emphasize assessing teen decision-making and planning skills for identifying intervention need areas, and teaching future orientation for considering long-term as well as short-term consequences and goals. Transferring acquired cognitive decision-making skills effectively requires opportunities for practicing real-life decision-making.

ASSERTIVENESS

Assertiveness can be defined as expressing our personal rights, feelings, needs and wants honestly, directly, clearly, and appropriately, and insisting that others recognize these, while still always respecting the beliefs, thoughts, and feelings of other people. While not being **assertive** may ultimately be a result of having low self-esteem, **non-assertiveness** may be functionally defined as using **inefficient communication skills**. Assertiveness, in contrast, is viewed as a balanced response in that it is neither aggressive nor passive. Some people confuse assertiveness with aggression. However, aggressiveness is not balanced in that it involves such behaviors as telling people to do things instead of asking them; ignoring others; being inconsiderate of others' feelings; unnecessarily rushing others; verbally insulting, blaming, or attacking others; or being pushy in general. Aggression discourages assertive responses and invites passivity or mutual aggression. Passive responses include saying "yes" when wanting to say "no"; agreeing outwardly when disagreeing inwardly; deferring one's wishes to others'; and not communicating or asserting one's feelings, thoughts, needs, or wants—often motivated by needing to please others and be liked. Passivity avoids and cedes responsibility and decision-making to others.

ASSERTIVE COMMUNICATION

In **empathic assertion**, first acknowledge how the other person feels, then express what you need. For example, "I understand you are having trouble working together, but we need to finish this by Friday. Let's make a plan together." When needs are not met after repeated requests, **escalating assertion** involves increasing firmness, including informing others of consequences for continued noncompliance. Requesting more time is an assertiveness technique to use when caught off-guard, need to compose your thoughts, don't know what you want yet, or are too emotional to respond immediately. Changing verbs can make responses more assertive: substitute "won't" for "can't," "need" for "want," "I choose to" for "I have to," and "could" for "should." Another technique is the "broken record": when someone tries alternately to intimidate, bully, force, wheedle, cajole, beg, or bribe you to do something you cannot, repeat the same "no" message, e.g., "I cannot take on any more work right now." Whether the other person says "I'll pay you for helping me," "This is seriously important," "I'll be in big trouble if you don't help," "Please do a personal favor", etc., repeating the message will eventually make the point clear. This should not be used to manipulate others, but to protect yourself from exploitation.

CHARACTER EDUCATION

Academic underachievement, failure in school, antisocial behaviors, aggressive behaviors, drug use, premature sexual activity, and criminal activities are all social problems among students that researchers have found can be prevented by high-quality, comprehensive **character education programs**. Even though such programs are designed for the purpose of promoting young people's development of good character and their overall positive development, they are also found to be just as effective for preventing specific negative behaviors as other, more specific programs designed specially to prevent those behaviors. Character education not only **reduces youth risk** for engaging in detrimental behaviors, it also has positive effects of helping students develop **proactive attitudes and skills**, personally and socially, that enable their living productive, satisfying lives and participating in society as effective, active citizens. Researchers think this may make effective character education programs more cost-effective in terms of policy to augment learning—as well as promote prosocial behaviors and prevent problems—than implementing numbers of separate specific school-based behavioral prevention programs.

DEFINITIONS OF CHARACTER AND CHARACTER EDUCATION

While some people recognize following rules, avoiding criminal acts, completing school, and becoming productively employed as criteria for having character, experts say these are not enough. They define **character** as encompassing a wider range of attitudes, motivations, skills, and behaviors. These include wanting to do one's best; caring about others' welfare; being committed to contributing to the community and society; critical thinking and moral reasoning skills; emotional intelligence and interpersonal skills enabling effective interactions in various situations; and responsibility, honesty, and confronting injustice by defending moral principles. Experts interpret these qualities to mean character equals a person's realizing positive intellectual, emotional, social, and ethical development to be the best person s/he can be. They also point out that good character is not only personal, but also social, e.g., supporting respect, equality, and justice for all people as part of democratic living. This sometimes includes breaking rules predicated on conscience rather than constant conformation to the status quo. **Character education** is defined as purposefully using all aspects of school—e.g., curriculum content, instructional processes, disciplinary management, co-curricular activity management, relationship quality, and the full learning

117

environment's ethos—to create learning environments enabling all students' optimal character development.

COMPREHENSIVE APPROACH TO CHARACTER EDUCATION

The Character Education Partnership (CEP), has identified the following 11 general principles (Lickona, Schaps, and Lewis, 2003) that serve to articulate **character education** in terms of a comprehensive approach.

- Comprehensively defining character as encompassing thought, emotion, and behavior.
- Applying a proactive, intentional, effective, comprehensive approach.
- Furthering core ethical values as the foundations of good character.
- Establishing caring learning communities in schools.
- Cultivating internal student motivation to be good persons and to learn.
- Giving opportunities for students to act morally.
- Engaging school personnel as professional members of moral learning communities.
- Supplying students with a challenging, relevant curriculum that assists all of them in succeeding.
- Cultivating long-term support for character education and shared moral leadership.
- Engaging students' families and members of the community as partners in character education.
- Informing the endeavor of character education by evaluating the character of the students, employees, and the school itself.

HEALTH-RELATED DECISION-MAKING SKILLS NEEDED TO MAKE POSITIVE HEALTH CHOICES

Individuals need a number of health-related decision-making skills to make positive health choices and to express health information and concepts. Education to improve **health-related decision making** should begin in elementary school so students entering high school have a good base and understand when assistance is needed, what healthy and unhealthy options are, and what outcomes may result from poor choices. The high school student should have the knowledge to understand health information and the skills to identify barriers (such as peer pressure) to good decision making, to understand when to use a problem-solving approach, to justify reaching a decision in collaboration with others or independently, to recognize alternative solutions to health-related problems/issues, to defend the choices they make, and to assess the outcomes of their decisions. Students can participate in role-playing and problem-solving exercises to improve these skills.

INFLUENCES ON HEALTH DECISIONS AND BEHAVIORS

Many factors influence health decisions and behaviors, including the following:

- **Beliefs**: Beliefs about health are often culture-bound and may influence behavior. Some cultures, for example, believe that illness is a punishment or it means that life is out of balance, whereas others believe in karma. Some cultures believe that it is shameful to have a mental disorder and may deny problems or refuse treatment.
- **Knowledge**: People are often better able to make decisions if they are armed with factual knowledge and can use critical thinking skills. Lack of knowledge may lead to confusion about the best health decisions and reliance on anecdotal advice.

- **Attitudes**: Despite knowledge, some people (especially adolescents) may feel that they are invincible and that problems that arise for others, such as from drinking alcohol, will not occur with themselves. Some may have difficulty accepting cause-and-effect relationships, and some may feel resentful of those in authority, such as parents, and purposefully make poor decisions.
- **Peers**: Friends and other peers often have a profound influence on health decisions and behaviors because of the strong desire to be accepted. This influence can be negative or positive, depending on the relationship.
- **Family**: The influence that parents or caregivers have varies according to the relationship. If the relationship is poor, then the influence may be minimal. Older siblings often exert a strong influence, either negative or positive, on younger siblings who look up to the older sibling and try to emulate that person.
- **Role models**: People that adolescents look up to—often sports figures, actors, or singers—may have some influence on behaviors, sometimes in ways that are negative, but positive role models who are actually in the person's life, such as a teacher, can have a more direct positive influence if the adolescent sees the person as a model for success.

SEEKING ADVICE AND GUIDANCE IN MAKING DECISIONS ABOUT PERSONAL HEALTH

Adolescents are often unprepared to make decisions about personal health because of a lack of knowledge and experience. They may be uncertain about decisions or unaware of resources and may need **assistance**. If their relationships with their family members are positive, then those family members can provide valuable **guidance** because they know the individual well and may understand the implications of health decisions. However, they may also be biased toward certain decisions. Healthcare professionals may provide the best advice, especially if the adolescent is concerned about confidentiality. The healthcare professional has the expertise to know what options are available and whether referral is needed, and the adolescent may feel more comfortable asking him or her for help. For example, an adolescent may want to use birth control but is unwilling to or afraid to ask family members.

TEACHING RESPONSIBLE DECISION-MAKING TO STUDENTS

A health educator teaching a responsible decision-making model to middle and high school students can begin with an overhead projection and student worksheets with term definitions. They discuss definitions with students: **empowerment** is feeling control over one's decisions and behavior, resulting in inspiration. Teachers tell students they must take responsibility for their decisions to achieve empowerment; decision-making styles determine responsibility. They explain that teens with **inactive decision-making styles** cannot or do not make choices; they lack control, accountability, and the ensuing self-confidence and empowerment. They explain that teens with **reactive decision-making styles** let others make decisions for them; needing others to like them and being easily influenced by others also impede self-confidence and empowerment. They then identify **proactive decision-making styles** as those involving analyzing a necessary decision, identifying and evaluating potential actions, choosing one action, and taking responsibility for the consequences of taking that action. Teachers can then introduce students to a model for **responsible decision-making** as a guide for making proactive decisions.

A model for responsible decision-making is meant to make sure that student decisions result in actions that show good character; that follow guidelines which parents, guardians or other responsible adults have established for them; that demonstrate self-respect and respect for others;

and that protect safety, obey the laws, and promote health. A health educator can teach students in grades 6-12 the following seven steps included in a **responsible decision-making model**:

1. Describe the situation requiring you to make a decision.
2. List all of the decisions you could potentially make.
3. Share this list of potential decisions with an adult you trust.
4. Evaluate what the consequences of each of the decisions could be.
5. Determine which of the potential decisions you identified is the most appropriate and responsible one.
6. Take action on the decision that you have chosen.
7. Evaluate the outcomes of the decision that you have made.

When instructing middle and high school students, a health educator can help them define **peer pressure** as the influences that individuals exert on others of similar status or age to engage in certain behaviors or decisions. S/he can explain that peer pressure may be positive or negative. The class can then discuss **resistance skills**, defined as skills enabling individuals to leave situations or say no to actions. A model for using resistance skills includes the following steps:

1. The student says "no" in an assertive manner to individual(s) attempting to exert peer pressure.
2. The student tells the other(s) his/her reasons for saying no.
3. The student uses nonverbal communication that matches his/her verbal communication—e.g., eye contact, facial expressions, body postures, and gestures consistent with what s/he is saying.
4. The student avoids getting into situations with peers that will involve pressure from them to make detrimental decisions.
5. The student resists peer pressure to engage in illegal actions.
6. The student works to exert influences on his/her peers to make responsible decisions.

ELEMENTS THAT INFLUENCE ADOLESCENT DECISION-MAKING

Adolescent decision-making is influenced by both **external variables**, like relationships with parents and friends; and **internal variables**, like personal self-concept and locus of control. Teen decision-making is influenced by **motivational variables**, e.g., personal values, beliefs, attitudes, goals, and emotional states. **Developmental variables** including cognitive (intellectual) development, affective (emotional) development, and social development are additional influences. Coping ability also affects decision-making ability. Because critical decisions that teens make occur in changing social contexts, they must develop abilities for evaluating decisions and adjusting and adapting them as needed. Due to society's constraints, teens must learn to identify and cope with options that are relatively more and less available to them. They must learn to apply different decision-making styles to different decision types, like career decisions as opposed to stressful or emotionally sensitive circumstances. Educators can advise teens that any single decision may be viewed as a series of choices rather than a one-time occurrence. Teens do not decide in isolation; decisions are influenced by feedback. Because current decisions influence future ones, decision-making sets precedents. Decision-making is not a linear process but a complex one; as teenagers mature and gain experience, their decision-making skills develop.

RESISTING PRESSURE FROM OTHERS

Children and teens often have more life experience being cared for, controlled, and told what to do, and relatively less experience being on their own, making independent choices, and taking initiative. Adults should tell them that being **pressured** is not good for them and is not right. Many children and teens (and even adults) have difficulty resisting pressure. **Motivations** include because they want to be liked, don't want to alienate friends, are afraid others will reject them, do not want others to make fun of them, do not want to hurt other people's feelings, are afraid others will perceive refusal as rejection, are not sure what they actually want, or do not know how to extricate themselves from the situation. Children and teens must know they have the right to say no, not to give any reason, and to walk away from any situation involving pressure. Some brief tips to support **resisting pressure** and **refusing** include standing up straight, making eye contact with the other person, stating one's feelings clearly, not making excuses, and standing up for oneself.

REFUSAL STRATEGIES FOR CHILDREN AND ADOLESCENTS

Children and teens (and adults as well) can find it hard to **resist pressure** that other people exert on them through their words. It is normal for most of us not to want to hurt other people's feelings or feel responsible for bad feelings in others. However, children and teens especially must be reminded how important it is for them to stand up for themselves in order to prevent others from verbally pressuring them into doing unsafe or unwanted things. Some strategies recommended by experts to help young people refuse to use alcohol, or to do other things that they know are not in their best interests and that they do not wish to do, include the "Dos and Don'ts." **Dos**: do say no assertively. Do abstain from drinking alcohol. Do propose some alternate activity. Do stand up for others being pressured who do not want to drink. Do walk away from the situation. Do look for something else to do with other friends. **Don'ts**: don't go to a party without being prepared to resist alcohol use. Don't be afraid to say "no." Don't mumble. Don't say "no" in an overly aggressive way. Don't behave like a "know-it-all" when refusing.

Health-Related Goal Setting

TEACHING RESPONSIBLE DECISION-MAKING TO STUDENTS

QUESTIONS STUDENTS CAN ASK THEMSELVES IN THE FOURTH STEP FOR EVALUATING THE POTENTIAL CONSEQUENCES

The steps in the **responsible decision-making model** are describing the situation wherein they need to make a decision, listing the decisions they could potentially make, sharing their list with a parent or other responsible adult, evaluating each decision's potential consequences, deciding which decision is the most suitable and responsible, acting on the chosen decision, and evaluating the outcomes of that decision. When evaluating **potential consequences** of each decision, students can ask themselves the following six questions:

- Will making this decision lead to taking actions that are lawful or legal?
- Will making this decision lead to taking actions protecting my and others' safety?
- Will making this decision lead to taking actions that agree with the guidelines and advice that my parents and other responsible adults have given me?
- Will making this decision lead to taking actions that demonstrate my respect for myself and for other people?
- Will making this decision lead to taking actions that are demonstrations of good character?

STEPS RELATED TO THE RESPONSIBLE DECISION-MAKING MODEL IN THE EVENT OF AN INCORRECT OR POOR DECISION

As they learn to make decisions responsibly, students are bound to make mistakes as with all new learning. Teens may experience anxiety over responsibility for poor decisions with unwelcome consequences. Paralyzed by doubt and indecision, they may avoid taking responsibility and action. In the same way that many teens fear being judged, rejected, disliked, or even viewed as different, they also fear **doing the wrong thing**. In addition to peer pressure and desiring acceptance, fear of misusing new responsibilities can motivate inaction to avoid unintentionally doing harm and experiencing guilt. Health educators can offer four steps to take after a bad or otherwise **wrong decision**:

1. Admit it; take responsibility, not trying to hide the mistake, blame others, or make excuses.
2. Immediately consider things done based on the decision; avoid perpetuating actions misguided by a wrong choice.
3. Parents and guardians are responsible for decision-making guidance: inform them of the decision and discuss corrective actions.
4. Apologizing is not always adequate: make restitution for any harm, damage, or loss by paying, replacing something, volunteering time, and/or similar appropriate effort as applies.

STEPS FOR STUDENTS TO TAKE FOR SETTING HEALTH GOALS FOR THEMSELVES

1. Students write long-term and short-term **health goals** in brief sentences starting with "I will..." Educators may suggest potential goals. **Long-term goals** can require a month, year, or even lifetime to attain and may be broken down to more achievable **short-term goals**. For example, a student's long-term goal could be "I will run a mile daily," with the preceding short-term goal being "I will run a quarter-mile daily."
2. Make **action plans**, i.e., detailed descriptions of steps for attaining goals, and have teachers review them for realism. Some teachers and students may establish health behavior contracts as action plans.

3. Identify potential **obstacles** to realizing the action plan. Prioritize these; brainstorm how to address high-priority ones.
4. Establish **timelines** with specific dates for reaching health goals. Consider whether these are realistic in light of other responsibilities.
5. Use a chart, graph, journal, or diary to **track progress**. Keeping records makes goals and progress concrete, supporting accountability.
6. Develop a **support system**. List people to give advice and encouragement, join a support group, form a club, and/or enlist friends. Avoid people who could sabotage health goals.
7. If needed, **revise** timelines and/or action plans, allowing additional time and/or requesting help.
8. Give yourself healthy **rewards** for meeting health goals.

Environmental Health

EPA Source for Reducing, Reusing, and Recycling to Help the Environment

The **US Environmental Protection Agency** (EPA) website offers information on how to reduce, reuse, and donate products to protect the environment and save natural resources and money; how to donate and recycle used electronics; how to compost and reduce wasted food; how to reduce, reuse, and recycle at home, school, work, in the community, and on the go on its wastes website; resources for educators and students including publications, games, and activities; and information on the basics, benefits, and how-to of recycling. **Recycling** reduces waste going to incinerators and landfills; conserves water, wood, minerals and other natural resources; saves energy; reduces greenhouse gas emissions involved in world climate change; sustains the environment for posterity; and creates new, well-paid jobs in American manufacturing and recycling industries. Recycling steps are:

- collection and processing
- manufacturing
- purchasing products made from recycled materials

Recycled product contents include: aluminum cans, car bumpers, carpeting, cereal boxes, comic books, egg cartons, glass containers, laundry detergent bottles, motor oil, nails, newspapers, paper towels, steel products, and garbage bags. EPA also provides instructions on recycling paper, batteries, plastics including plastic ID codes, glass, oil, household hazardous waste, tires, compact fluorescent light bulbs, etc.

Historical and Regulatory Information Regarding Pollution Problems in the United States

Air and water **pollution** and growing hazardous waste disposal problems in America came to government attention in the 1970s. The Environmental Protection Agency (EPA) developed standards, regulations, and enforced laws emphasizing "end-of-pipe" solutions, measurably improving environmental quality. In the 1980s, better detection methods and subtler, diffuser pollution sources raised awareness of the longevity and ubiquity of American waste problems. Realizing global environmental issues and difficulty controlling pollution sources prompted reorientation of America's pollution approach to prevention. The 1990 **Pollution Prevention Act** declares Congress's national policy of preventing and reducing pollution, environmentally safe recycling of non-preventable pollution, treatment of non-preventable and non-recyclable pollution, and environmentally safe disposal and release only as a last resort. It identifies America's annually producing millions of tons of pollution, and spending tens of billions of dollars to control it; industry's significant opportunities for decreasing and preventing pollution at its sources by cost-efficiently changing raw materials use, production, and operations to protect the environment, worker safety and health, and save costs for liability, pollution control, and raw materials; existing laws and industrial resources' emphasizing treatment and disposal, not source reduction; businesses' requiring technical assistance and information to adopt source reduction measures; and the EPA as implementing it.

Conserving Energy for Sustainable Living and Prevention of Severe Global Disruptions from Greenhouse Gas Emissions

In 2009, America produced one-fifth of the world's CO_2 emissions, approximately 6 billion metric tons annually—7 billion projected by 2030. **Buildings** produce the most, 38 percent from private homes, shopping malls, warehouses, and offices, primarily from using electricity; average new American houses are 45 percent larger than 30 years ago. Walmart, maintaining thousands of buildings, has significantly conserved energy by using natural light in shopping areas, radiant floors, high-efficiency refrigeration, evaporative cooling units, etc.; one pilot supercenter consumed 45 percent less power than comparable stores. Oak Ridge National Laboratory researchers say 200 million tons of CO_2 could be reduced annually through smart design and retrofitting, but find this unlikely without financial incentives, appliance standards, and new building codes. For example, commercial building owners are unmotivated because tenants pay power bills. Development increases traveling distance, making **transportation** the second-biggest source. **Industry** is third. Dow saved $7 billion from 1995-2009 by reducing energy intensity, reducing CO_2 emissions 20 percent; DuPont and 3M have also profited through energy-efficiency. Other developed nations surpass America with solar and wind power, bicycling, fuel-efficient cars, and carbon-neutral houses. Experts advocate developing CO_2-burial and elimination technologies, slowing deforestation, and replacing fossil fuels with renewable energy faster to reduce global emissions 80-100 percent by 2050.

CAUSES AND EFFECTS OF ENVIRONMENTAL PROBLEMS
AIR POLLUTION

Air pollution is primarily caused by the use of fossil fuels, such as oil, gas, natural gas, and coal; these fuels release carbon monoxide, hydrocarbons, and other pollutants into the atmosphere when they are burned. **Motor vehicles** are the primary polluters, but industrial emissions from factories and manufacturing plants also are implicated because many depend on fossil fuels as well, and some release various chemicals used in or resulting from the manufacturing process. Air pollution can also result from **agricultural chemicals** (such as crop spraying) and **household chemicals** (such as fumigants). Air pollution can reduce visibility in some cases, but it may also be invisible, so people may be unaware that the air is polluted. Air pollution is considered to be one of the causes of **global warming**. Air pollution can also have a serious impact on **health** by impairing lung function and resulting in an increased incidence of cancer and respiratory diseases, such as asthma and chronic obstructive pulmonary disease.

WATER POLLUTION

Water pollution occurs when pollutants flow into surface water sources, such as rivers, lakes, reservoirs, and oceans. Contamination of **surface water** can result from sewage, oil spills, industrial wastes, and chemical runoffs (fertilizers, weed killers). In areas with air pollution, surface water may become contaminated through atmospheric deposition (rain, snow). **Drinking water**, even from clean water sources, can become contaminated through erosion of lead pipes or lead solder used with other types of pipes that are part of the delivery system. **Groundwater** can also become polluted as pollutants, such as noxious chemicals from fertilizers and weed killers, are leached through the ground and enter underground water. Water pollution not only kills fish and wildlife, but it can harm wetlands and coral reefs. Water pollution has been implicated in waterborne diseases (such as typhoid fever), neurological impairment, and cancer. Children exposed to polluted water may suffer developmental disorders and intellectual disabilities.

HAZARDOUS WASTE

Hazardous waste is waste that poses a threat to the health of individuals or to the environment. The Environmental Protection Agency (EPA) classifies hazardous wastes according to the following characteristics:

- **Ignitable**: Liquids and nonliquids that can ignite and cause fires.
- **Corrosive**: Based on pH or the ability to corrode steel.

- **Reactive**: Wastes that are unstable, may react with water, or result in toxic gases. They may also explode.
- **Toxic**: Wastes that are harmful if ingested or absorbed.

Wastes may also be classified as **listed wastes**. These include wastes from manufacturing and industrial processes. **Hazardous wastes** are often produced in manufacturing, nuclear power plants (nuclear wastes), and healthcare facilities (needles, materials contaminated with body fluids). **Nuclear wastes** are classified as mixed waste because they contain a radioactive component as well as a hazardous component. Hazardous wastes can result in disease (such as from needle punctures), injury (from fire and explosions), and death (from toxic exposure, disease).

NOISE POLLUTION AND OVERCROWDING

Noise pollution is increasingly a problem in the urban environment where individuals are almost constantly surrounded by transportation noises, people, alarms, sirens, dogs barking, and everyday noise from walking, eating, and interacting. Noise is often an issue in the work environment because of the equipment used, especially in manufacturing. **Noise pollution** may also result from inadequate urban planning, social events, and construction. The results of noise pollution can be hearing impairment (especially if exposed to high decibels), stress, fatigue, insomnia, and high blood pressure. Animals exposed to noise pollution may become aggressive, disoriented, or hard of hearing. Wildlife that use mating calls or echolocation may not reproduce or migrate. **Overcrowding,** too many people in a space, is often associated with noise pollution and can occur in individual homes, such as with four or five families sharing one apartment, or in an urban area, such as when a large population is impacted by a severe housing shortage. Overcrowding can result in disease epidemics, mental health problems, and academic problems.

STRATEGIES FOR REDUCING ENVIRONMENTAL HAZARDS AND PROMOTING HEALTH

WATER PURIFICATION AND EMISSION CONTROL

Water purification is the process that removes contaminants, such as biological matter, chemicals, gases, and debris, from water in order to make it safe for drinking or other purposes. Boiling water does not always remove all contaminants—nor does the use of activated charcoal filters. **Drinking water** is typically not made sterile, whereas water for **medical purposes** should be sterile. Steps to purification include pumping the water from the source, screening to remove debris, pH adjustment, coagulation/flocculation, sedimentation, filtering, and disinfection.

Emission control is the system used to reduce emissions that result in air pollution from both mobile sources (such as motor vehicles) and point sources (power plants, manufacturing plants). **Toxic emission pollutants** include carbon monoxide, hydrocarbons, sulfur oxide, organic compounds, nitrogen dioxide, smoke, and soot. Emissions are regulated by the EPA as well as some state regulation agencies. Motor vehicles use catalytic converters to convert carbon monoxide, hydrocarbons, and nitrous oxide to harmless gases.

WASTE MANAGEMENT

Waste management is the process by which waste products are collected, transported, and disposed of or recycled. **Municipal waste management** usually involves weekly collection with separate containers sometimes provided for garden waste, recyclables, and garbage, although garbage is mixed by the consumer and then separated at a facility in some waste management plants. Waste management is regulated by the EPA through the **Resource Conservation and Recovery Act**, which regulates the handling and disposal of hazardous and nonhazardous waste. Because **hazardous waste** can result in disease, injury, or death, special handling is required. Hazardous waste cannot be disposed of with regular trash or in drains or the sewer system. In schools, chemistry labs often have hazardous wastes to dispose of, such as corrosive liquids, heavy-metal solutions, and organic solvents. The art department and the school nurse may also have hazardous wastes, such as used paints, pigments, dyes, needles, and dressings contaminated with body fluids.

IMPROVING COMMUNITY AND ENVIRONMENTAL HEALTH

Individuals can contribute to improving community and environmental health through the following actions:

- **Advocacy**: This include identifying public health problems within the community and/or environment, researching the problems and possible solutions, and taking steps to educate the public and those in positions of power to help reduce or eliminate the problems by influencing political and social policy. A primary goal of advocacy is to increase public awareness in order to generate support for change.
- **Volunteerism**: This involves providing services in the community without financial gain or coercion, such as volunteering to clean up the environment or volunteering in a local hospital or school. Many nonprofit agencies and governmental agencies welcome volunteers or have volunteer programs. Volunteerism is a required part of service learning for students in some areas, but students can often be mobilized to volunteer for causes that interest them, and an educator can provide a good role model through volunteerism.

Health-Related Information

HEALTH EQUITY TERMS AND ISSUES RELATED TO US DEMOGRAPHIC DISPARITIES

The **Healthy People 2020** government initiative informs its focus on eliminating health disparities, attaining health equity, and improving American health with these 2008 US Census Bureau statistics: over 100 million people, approximately 33 percent, belonged to racial or ethnic minorities. Of these, 154 million, i.e., 51 percent, were women. Another 36 million, around 12 percent, not living in nursing homes or other residential care facilities, had disabilities. Yet another 70.5 million, or 23 percent, were estimated to live in rural areas; 233.5 million, or 77 percent, lived in urban areas. HealthyPeople.gov also cites 2002 data that four percent of the American population 18-44 years old was estimated to identify as gay, lesbian, bisexual, or transgender. The initiative defines **health disparity** as a specific health difference associated with environmental, economic, and/or social disadvantages. In the past, endeavors toward health equity and away from disparities mainly concentrated on healthcare services and illnesses or diseases. But current Healthy People 2020 experts point out that good health does not equal absence of illness. They define **individual and population health determinants** as interrelationships among genetics, biology, physical environment, socioeconomic status, individual behavior, literacy levels, discrimination, racism, legislative policies, health, and health services.

FACTORS THAT INFLUENCE AMERICAN HEALTH AND FEDERAL HEALTH INITIATIVES

All American citizens experience numerous **influences on their health status**. These include whether the following **factors** are available, and whether people have access to them: unpolluted air and clean water; safe, adequate housing; reliable, affordable public transportation; nutritious food; high-quality educations; health insurance coverage; and culturally sensitive healthcare providers. The Healthy People federal initiative (www.HealthyPeople.gov) has historically set goals focusing on changing **health disparities** over the past 20 years. In the Healthy People 2000 program, the goal was to decrease health disparities for American citizens. The Healthy People 2010 program augmented its goal to eliminate health disparities rather than just decrease them. The Healthy People 2020 program additionally extended the goal, not only to eliminate health disparities, but also to establish **health equity** and improve all Americans' health. This initiative plans, from 2014-2024, to track the rates of diseases, mortality, chronic conditions, behaviors, and other factors relative to race, ethnicity, gender, sexual identity, sexual orientation, disability status, special healthcare needs, urban and rural geographic locations, and other demographic factors. Through such research, the Healthy People staff members hope to achieve their health equity and improvement goals.

RESOURCES FOR COORDINATED SCHOOL HEALTH APPROACHES

Basic information on **coordinated school health approaches** include: "School Health 101 Packets" from the National School Boards Association; *Guidelines for a Coordinated Approach to School Health: Addressing the Physical, Social, and Emotional Health Needs of the School Community* from the Connecticut State Department of Education; *Guidelines for Coordinating School Health Programs* from the Maine Departments of Education and Health and Human Services; the Comprehensive Health Education Network (CHEN) listserv, a mailing list of national, state, and local school health professionals; a PDF, "Building a Healthier Future through School Health Programs" from the CDC's *Promising Practices in Chronic Disease Prevention and Control;* and an "at a glance" webpage, "School Health Programs: Improving the Health of Our Nation's Youth." All of these are on the CDC website's page of Coordinated School Health Publications and Resources. This page also offers links and PDF documents on the relationship between school and student health and academic achievement. For school health assessment and planning, it includes links to the School Health Index (SHI) Self-

Assessment and Planning Guide, and to Curriculum Analysis Tools for Health Education and Physical Education.

RESOURCES FOR COLLABORATION AND PARTNERSHIP, EVALUATION, AND PARENT AND FAMILY INVOLVEMENT

The Centers for Disease Control and Prevention (CDC) website's page on Coordinated School Health Publications and Resources includes links to PDF documents on **collaboration and partnership**, including a primer for professionals serving children and youth and a guide to community-school health councils, a link to the National Association of Chronic Disease Directors page about how health departments function and how schools can partner with them, and a link to the American Cancer Society's PDF on community-school health councils. Regarding **evaluation** of coordinated school health approaches, the CDC website includes a page, "Evaluations of Innovative Programs," including an overview of its Division of Adolescent and School Health's (DASH) assistance with evaluating programs, a list of links to applied evaluation projects, information on eligibility, characteristics of initiatives subject to applied evaluations, and a contact link for the CDC Evaluation Research Team. Regarding **parent and family involvement**, CDC's web page on Coordinated School Health Publications and Resources offers a PDF, *Parent Engagement: Strategies for Involving Parents in School Health.*

RESOURCES PERTAINING TO POLICY, PROFESSIONAL ASSOCIATIONS, AND PROMISING PRACTICES

Addressing **policy** related to coordinated school health approaches, the Centers for Disease Control and Prevention (CDC) website page of Coordinated School Health Publications and Resources includes download links to PDF documents of an Executive Summary; *A CDC Review of School Laws and Policies Concerning Child and Adolescent Health;* and a link to the National Association of State Boards of Education resource, the State School Health Policy Database, which includes compiled laws and policies from all 50 states covering over 40 school health subjects, e.g., school health councils, school health coordinators, and coordination. This page offers external links to these **professional associations**: American Association for Health Education; Academy of Nutrition and Dietetics; School Nutrition Association; National Association for Sport and Physical Education (NASPE); National Association of School Nurses; American School Counselor Association; National Association of School Psychologists; School Social Work Association of America; and the Health Educator, School Health Coordinators, and Mental Health Professionals Sections of the American School Health Association. Under "**Promising Practices**," this page includes links to National Association of County and City Health Officials, "Building Healthier Schools"; National School Boards Association's database of successful school district health policies and practices; and partnership program and school nutrition success stories.

EFFECTIVE COMMUNICATION WITH STUDENTS, PARENTS, AND THE COMMUNITY

Forming and sustaining partnerships depend on **effective communication** among schools, students, parents, and community. Also, schools are responsible for assisting parents in understanding learning language. School health educators should consider whether and how they communicate student progress to parents in relevant, positive ways; whether and how they clarify what teachers and parents must discuss; whether they have established a language of learning that teachers and parents share for exploring student learning successes, challenges, and development; how schools can collaborate with parents and communities to develop shared educational expectations; how parents with language barriers and/or busy work schedules communicate with the school; and how the school communicates with business and industry partners. Possible **strategies** include: home-school liaisons to teach parents educational language, current classroom characteristics, and how to talk with teachers and children about school experiences. Parent/community and parent-teacher meetings, newsletters, websites, web conferencing, emails, text messages, and assemblies are communication channels and tools to utilize. School-year transition calendars highlighting specific times and activities critical to parent and community engagement can also help. Educators should know and share how to access information in diverse forms and languages. Sharing consistent and ongoing high expectations of students and professional teacher development in communicating with parents are additional strategies.

There are several things that school health educators should consider for open, genuine **consultative communication**. They should encourage honest, open dialogues. To empower parents for effective consulting participation, their schools should offer support and training to build parental leadership capacities. When schools make informal and/or formal decisions, policy reviews and new policies regarding curriculum, assessment, and reporting, they should invite interested community members to consult. They can apply strategies such as flexible consulting with a representative cross-section of students, parents, and community members, rather than only those who are most assertive; make sure they broadly disseminate information in a variety of formats about opportunities to consult; offer opportunities for skill development and/or training to teachers and parents; develop solutions to aid teachers in balancing issues of workloads and time to facilitate their engagement in decision-making consultation; and encourage students to participate in decision-making processes and participate actively in the school council and/or parent and citizen groups.

INDICATIONS OF EFFECTIVE COMMUNICATION

Effective communication achieving strong engagement is indicated when educators acknowledge **parents** as their children's first educators; engage them as partners in children's learning; and encourage their close, sincere interest in the school's work. Educators communicate information to parents about current student learning status, progress over time, and how they can support their further learning. Language used by students, parents, and school personnel in both informal and formal settings reflects caring, respectful relationships. Schools have established continuing, regular methods for determining what parents require for engaging with their children's learning. Parents are able to identify the school's primary expectations for student attendance, homework, and behavior. Teachers and administrators applying diverse communication styles appropriately to parental availability, work conditions, cultural backgrounds, etc., also indicates effective communication, which produces strong engagement. Another indication is that school administrators and teachers connect with every student's parents regularly. Additionally, a school that has mechanisms established for building relationships with pertinent community members indicates effective communication for strong engagement.

FERPA

"FERPA" stands for the **Family Educational Rights and Privacy Act**. According to the US Departments of Health and Human Services and of Education (2008), any educational agency or institution that receives federal funding under any program administered by the Department of Education is subject to FERPA regulations protecting the privacy of **student educational records**. This federal funding specification includes all public school districts and schools, as well as most public and private post-secondary schools, including medical and other professional schools. Elementary and secondary religious and private schools not receiving such funding are not subject to FERPA. "Education records" refers to records directly related to a student, and maintained by an educational institution, agency, or a party acting on its behalf. These include elementary and secondary student health records, immunization records, and records kept by public school nurses. Special education student records kept by public schools, including records of services these students receive under the Individuals with Disabilities Education Act (IDEA), are also included in the FERPA definition of "education records."

HIPAA

HIPAA is the **Health Insurance Portability and Accountability Act** (1996). Among its purposes are to protect the security and privacy of individually identifiable health information and improve the effectiveness and efficiency of the healthcare system by setting national requirements and standards for electronic healthcare transactions. Provisions related to these purposes issued by the US Department of Health and Human Services are called **HIPAA Administrative Simplification Rules**, including a **Privacy Rule**. "Covered entities" subject to these rules include health insurance plans; healthcare clearinghouses; and healthcare providers, e.g., doctors, dentists, other practitioners, hospitals, other medical and health service providers, and any other organizations or persons that provide, are paid for, or bill for healthcare in their normal courses of business, and electronically transmit health information associated with covered transactions. HIPAA's Privacy Rule requires covered entities to protect the privacy of individuals' health records and other information by limiting disclosure without patient permission; and ensures patient rights to examine, get copies, and request corrections of their health records. Schools providing student healthcare with related electronic transactions are "covered entities." However, when school health records are defined as "education records" or "treatment records" under FERPA, they are not subject to the HIPAA Privacy Rule.

MANDATED REPORTING OF CHILD MALTREATMENT

According to the US Department of Health and Human Services Administration on Children, Youth and Families (ACYF) Child Welfare Information Gateway, Children's Bureau (www.childwelfare.gov), as of 2012, 48 states, D.C., American Samoa, Guam, the Northern Mariana Islands, Puerto Rico, and the Virgin Islands designate professions legally required to **report child maltreatment**. These mandated reporters typically are often in contact with children. Such professionals include teachers, principals, administrators, and other school employees; physicians, nurses, and other healthcare employees; social workers; therapists, counselors, psychologists, psychiatrists, and other mental health professionals; child care providers; coroners and medical examiners; and law enforcement officers. Additional professions often mandated to report include clergy in 27 states and Guam; probation and parole officers in 17 states; substance abuse counselors in 14 states; commercial film processors in 12 states, Guam, and Puerto Rico; directors, employees, and volunteers at camps and day camps, youth and recreation centers and other places providing organized activities for children in 11 states; court-appointed special advocates in 10 states; domestic violence workers in seven states and D.C.; humane and animal control officers in seven states and D.C.; and faculty, administrators, other employees and volunteers at public and private colleges, universities, and technical and vocational schools in four states.

Health-Related Products and the Services-Informed Consumer

PREVALENCE OF HEALTH QUACKERY IN ADVERTISING

Advertising has long promised results "too good to be true," such as instant miracle cures for cancer, "smart" drugs ensuring longevity, or things that "magically" make arthritis pain "disappear." **Quackery** is the activity of selling unproven remedies. While quacks have existed for many years, today they have more venues than ever before—in addition to word of mouth, newspapers, magazines, and direct mail, TV and radio have been added, and then the Internet. Not only do websites abound selling a variety of health scams, but most of us are also familiar with seeing ads all over our computer screens as we view our email or surf the web. According to government research, the majority of **healthcare scam** victims are above age 65; fraudsters target vulnerable older people. Unproven remedies not only waste consumers' money, they can also prevent them from getting genuine, effective medical treatment. Some, beyond being useless, can be harmful. They also offer false hope, preying on people's pain and fear. Two of the most common fraudulent remedy categories advertised are for arthritis relief and anti-aging claims.

ACCESS TO HEALTHCARE

Access to quality, comprehensive healthcare is critical to increasing health and life quality for all. **Healthcare access** involves three steps:

- acquiring healthcare system entry
- accessing locations providing needed services
- finding providers that patients can communicate with and trust.

Healthcare access has impacts on overall physical, mental, and social health; disease and disability prevention; health condition identification and treatment; life quality; life expectancy; and preventable deaths. **Impacts** on individuals and society are caused by healthcare access disparities; access limitations impede individuals' abilities to realize their full potentials, diminishing their quality of life. **Service obstacles** include lack of insurance coverage, lack of available services and providers, and expenses; the consequences of these obstacles include lack of preventive services, delayed care, unmet health needs, and hospitalizations which could have been avoided. People without health insurance coverage are less likely to get healthcare, more likely to have poor health status, and more likely to die sooner.

According to the Healthy People 2020 initiative (www.HealthyPeople.gov), an important factor in healthcare access is **primary care providers (PCPs)** as ongoing, regular, usual healthcare sources. PCPs are significant for good patient-provider relationships and communication, higher patient trust, and greater probabilities of receiving needed care. Preventive services include primary prevention, like detecting early symptoms and signs to prevent illness; and secondary prevention, such as identifying illness earlier when more treatable. **Emergency medical services (EMS)** constitute another crucial healthcare area, including basic and advanced life support. In recent years, complicated emergency care system problems have developed. HealthyPeople.gov identifies all citizens' access to pre-hospital, rapid-response EMS as an important population health improvement goal. Time waiting in ERs and provider offices, and time between identification and receipt of tests and treatments, are measures of **healthcare system timeliness**. Delays increase patient attrition, decrease patient satisfaction, and cause clinically significant care delays. More non-emergency patients attending ERs, and fewer total ERs, cause delays. Fewer PCPs and medical students interested in primary care are workforce concerns. Emerging issues include meeting needs for many more newly-insured Americans; measuring and increasing access to safe, quality preventive, emergency, long-term, and palliative services; and decreasing disparities and measuring access for elders and minorities.

ELECTRONIC PERSONAL HEALTH RECORDS

Electronic personal health records eliminate problems with paper records like disorganization, losing and misplacing individual papers, and not having papers available when needed. Unlike hospital, physician practice, or health insurance company electronic medical records, **personal health records** are accessible to **patients**. Though electronic adoption has been slow relative to technological capability, more physician practices, hospitals, and insurance companies are providing records accessible over the Internet via computer, tablet, and smartphone. According to the Mayo Clinic (2014), patients should add information including their PCP name and phone number; drug and other allergies; current medications and dosages; chronic health conditions, e.g., hypertension; major surgeries and their dates; any advance directives or living will; immunization history; and family history. They may also want to include prevention activities, e.g., blood pressure, cholesterol levels, dietary and exercise habits, screening test results; and health goals, e.g., losing weight or smoking cessation. Benefits are not only organization, but emergency life-saving; health assessment and tracking; doctor visit preparation; health management between doctor visits; and timely scheduling of wellness, prevention and screening services, vaccinations, and appointments.

MOBILE HEALTHCARE AND MEDICAL APPLICATIONS

The mobile applications industry estimates that by 2015, 500 million people in the world will be using healthcare apps on their smartphones; and by 2018, half of all smartphone and tablet users, who number over 3.4 billion, will have downloaded **mobile health apps**. Consumers, patients, and healthcare professionals are included among these users. The US Food and Drug Administration (FDA), which oversees safety and effectiveness in medical devices, includes mobile medical apps among those devices, and encourages mobile medical app development that will give consumers and healthcare professionals valuable health information and improve healthcare. Consumers can use mobile apps like **MyFitnessPal** to monitor and manage how many calories they eat and burn to manage their own wellness. The National Institutes of Health provides **LactMed**, an app that gives nursing mothers information about how various medications affect their breast milk and their nursing infants. Healthcare professionals can use apps like **Radiation Emergency Medical Management (REMM)**, which offers guidance for diagnosis and treatment of radiation injuries. Other mobile medical apps can diagnose heart arrhythmias or cancer. And some can serve as command centers for insulin-dependent diabetes patients' glucose meter use and measurements.

STUDENT ACCESS TO VALID HEALTHCARE INFORMATION, PRODUCTS, AND SERVICES

Students should first identify health information, products, and services they need, contacting healthcare providers for information and product recommendations; then find identified information, services, and products. Students researching reports on health topics can find free, reliable **information** from websites including CDC, American Heart Association, American Cancer Society, American Medical Association, and American Association for Health Education; print and online medical journals, public libraries; professional health organization-produced TV programs and videos; school counselors; and healthcare professionals. They can obtain **health products** from healthcare providers, pharmacies, and supermarkets; and parental help accessing prescription and over-the-counter medications. To evaluate information, students should consider source reliability, qualifications of information providers, information's currency, reputable healthcare professional evaluations, whether information's purpose is to inform or sell, whether it educates or only appeals to emotions, how to acquire additional information, and whether claims are realistic. Before paying for products or services, they should consider whether they need them; understand how to use them and what they do; if they are safe, high-quality, and worth their price; consumer agency reviews; and what to do if dissatisfied. The Food and Drug Administration (FDA), Federal Trade Commission (FTC), Consumer Product Safety Commission (CPSC), and US Postal Service for mail-order products and services can help with complaints.

COMMUNITY HEALTH SERVICES OFFERED BY THE AMERICAN RED CROSS

The American Red Cross is a national nonprofit health agency with many local community chapters. It offers **training** in swimming safety for lifeguards, physical education teachers, and others; in first aid techniques, cardiopulmonary resuscitation (CPR), automated external defibrillator (AED) use, how to control bleeding, what to do in the event of seizures, what to do if someone is choking, and other training for dealing with emergencies until medical personnel arrive. Training is also provided to prepare individuals who want to become instructors in American Red Cross first aid, CPR, and AED courses. The Red Cross also offers Babysitter's Training to teach 11-15-year-olds the confidence and skills they need for safely and responsibly caring for infants and children. The training includes caregiving skills like feeding, diapering, playtime, and bedtime routines; and how to address illnesses, household accidents, injuries, and other child emergencies.

COMMUNITY HEALTH CENTERS

The US Department of Health and Human Services (HHS) supports community-based health centers nationwide through its **Health Resources and Services Administration (HRSA)**. These centers are patient-directed organizations designed to serve populations with limited healthcare access. They provide quality, comprehensive, and culturally competent primary healthcare services to vulnerable populations and medically underserved communities. HRSA defines **medically underserved** populations and areas as having insufficient primary care providers, high poverty rates, high infant mortality rates, and/or large elderly populations. It defines **Health Professional Shortage Areas** as geographical (service areas and counties), demographic (low-income populations), or institutional (federally qualified health centers and other public facilities or comprehensive health centers) having shortages of primary medical, dental, or mental health care providers. Health centers serve such high-need communities; are governed by community boards, with 51 percent or more being patients representing the population served; provide comprehensive primary healthcare and support services (translation, transportation, education, etc.) promoting healthcare access; and provide services to all patients, adjusting fees based on ability to pay. Public and private non-profit health centers meeting Medicare and Medicaid criteria are grant-supported, non-grant-supported, identified by HRSA and Medicare and Medicaid-certified, or outpatient health facilities and programs run by tribal organizations under the Indian Self-Determination Act or Indian Health Care Improvement Act.

MASS MEDIA CAMPAIGNS FOR PROMOTING HEALTH MESSAGES

Mass media campaigns can deliver health-promoting messages to large numbers of people. By raising their awareness and communicating educational information through social media, they can enforce positive health behaviors to achieve large-scale **positive health changes**. Messages can be communicated in **print and digital media**. Another avenue is **radio**, found more cost-effective than TV by health organizations because it not only costs less, but moreover it reaches people at work and in cars as well as at home. Also, research in America found radio listeners surprisingly accurate in their memories of broadcast details months later. This retention supports radio's educational potential. In other countries, particularly developing ones, TV and electricity are unavailable in rural villages; however, battery-operated radios are common. Public health, rural development, health education, nutritional education, family planning, and awareness of correct breastfeeding practices have been promoted respectively in Swaziland, India, Nicaragua, the Philippines, and Trinidad and Tobago. **Puppet shows** appeal to younger students and can introduce hygiene, nutrition, and other health topics. Puppetry is an important cultural tradition in Cambodia, and is often used to teach critical health concepts to all ages. UNAIDS advocates mass media TV and radio campaigns for AIDS awareness, education, and destigmatization.

SELECTING APPROPRIATE HEALTHCARE PROVIDERS

The strategy that the individual will use for **selecting appropriate healthcare providers and treatment** may depend on the type of insurance coverage that the individual has. If, for example, the person is covered by Medicaid, then the first concern is whether or not the healthcare provider accepts Medicaid patients. If the individual is in an HMO or PPO, then the individual may need to discuss his or her needs with a primary care physician, who can make referrals. Many specialists require referrals from primary care physicians before they will see a patient, so that's often the best place to begin. Additionally, most individuals aren't adept at diagnosing their own problems and are unsure of what type of healthcare provider to see. The individual can also search online to find out information, such as credentials and experience, about potential healthcare providers, including websites that rank healthcare providers.

OPTIMIZING HEALTH INSURANCE BENEFITS

The first step in optimizing health insurance benefits is to have a clear understanding of the **insurance plan** and what it does and does not cover as well as the **frequency** of which certain procedures, such as laboratory tests, can be done. For example, some tests, such as the Hgb A1c, which monitors diabetes, may be covered only every three months, whereas others may be covered once every 30 days. If the insurance plan provides a network of healthcare providers, it is more cost-effective to seek care from those in the network because the plan will not likely cover the full cost of out-of-network providers. The individual should be aware of preauthorization requirements, such as those for expensive procedures or surgery, and should verify that healthcare providers have received preauthorization before providing care. Once the deductible for the year is met, the individual should plan to see all other necessary healthcare providers before the end of that year so they are covered by the deductible.

PATIENT'S BILL OF RIGHTS

A patient's bill of rights in relation to what should be expected from a healthcare organization is outlined in the standards of The Joint Commission and the National Committee for Quality Assurance. **Rights** include the following:

- Respect for the patient, including personal dignity and psychosocial, spiritual, and cultural considerations.
- Response to needs related to access to pain control.
- Ability to make decisions about care, including informed consent, advance directives, and-end of-life care.
- Procedure for registering complaints or grievances.
- Protection of confidentiality and privacy.
- Freedom from abuse or neglect.
- Protection during research and information related to ethical issues of research.
- Appraisal of outcomes, including unexpected outcomes.
- Information about the organization, services, and practitioners.
- Appeal procedures for decisions regarding benefits and quality of care.
- Organizational code of ethical behavior.
- Procedures for donating and procuring organs/tissue.

COMPARISON SHOPPING SKILLS FOR HEALTHCARE PRODUCTS

The price for healthcare products may vary widely, so the consumer should practice comparison shopping.

- **Telephone**: The individual can make a list of needed healthcare products, including medications, and then call local pharmacies, including big box stores such as Costco and Sam's Club, and ask for prices.
- **Newspapers**: Specials on healthcare products may be printed in weekly flyers for drugstores and other stores.
- **Comparison shop**: The individual may check prices and availability in a variety of stores, including Wal-Mart, Target, and dollar stores, which often carry some healthcare products even if they don't have a pharmacy.
- **Internet**: Online comparison shopping is relatively easy, and the individual can often find products that are less expensive than in local stores. Internet sites that offer free shipping are often a better value because shipping costs can be high, and some states require that items be taxed as well.

INTERPRETATION OF SIGNS AND SYMBOLS

Sign/Symbol	Interpretation
	Flame: Includes flammable materials and gases and those that are self-heating or self-reactive.
	Corrosion: Includes substances that can cause skin burns, metal corrosion, and eye damage.
	Health hazard: Includes carcinogens, toxic substances, and respiratory irritants.
	Poison: Includes materials, gases, or substances that are extremely toxic and may result in death or severe illness.

Sign/Symbol	Interpretation
	Irritant: Includes material, gases, or substances that are irritants to skin, eyes, and/or respiratory tract, acutely toxic, or have a narcotic effect.
	Biohazard: Includes biological substances, such as body fluids, that pose a threat to humans. Appears on sharps containers that hold contaminated needles.

FOOD PRODUCT LABELS

The FDA, under the Federal Food, Drug, and Cosmetic Act, regulates **product labeling**. Labels on food products contain information specific to the product, but the same type of information is contained for all food products:

- **Serving size, servings per container, and calories**: The calories are based on the serving size, so if there are three servings and the calorie count is 150, then the entire product has 450 calories. The calorie count also indicates the number of calories derived from fat.
- **Nutrients**: This includes the amount of fat, carbohydrates, and protein per serving as well as cholesterol, sodium, sugar, and fiber. The amounts are indicated in grams or milligrams but also as a percentage of the daily recommended value. Grams of dietary fiber can be subtracted from the total carbohydrate grams because fiber is carbohydrate that is not digested.
- **Vitamins and minerals**: These are listed as a percentage of daily recommended value per serving.
- **Footnote**: This explains how the percentages displayed are based on a 2,000-calorie diet.

TYPES AND CHARACTERISTICS OF HEALTH INSURANCE

Types and characteristics of health insurance:

- **HMO** - With health maintenance organizations (HMOs), a primary care provider (PCP) coordinates care and referrals to a network of healthcare providers. The individual has little choice and requires a referral from the PCP to see a specialist. Plans may provide preventive care, but they may also require copayments and deductible.
- **PPO** - With a preferred provider organization (PPO), an individual can choose to see any healthcare provider, including specialists, in a network of healthcare providers. The individual is not usually required to select a PCP but may have to pay copayments and a deductible, depending on the plan. Individuals can usually see healthcare providers outside of the network, but reimbursement is typically lower, so the individual may have to pay part of the costs.
- **EPO** - The exclusive provider organization (EPO) is similar to the PPO in that the individual can see any physician within a network except that the individual does not have the option of seeing a healthcare provider outside of the network except in emergency situations.

- **POS** - The point of service plan (POS) is a combined HMO and PPO. The individual has a PCP within a network, and the PCP makes referrals, but the individual can see out-of-network healthcare providers; however, the individual must pay part of the cost for out-of-network providers.
- **HDHP** - The high-deductible health plan (HDHP) may be an HMO, PPO, or EPO, but it is characterized by a high deductible before the insurance begins to reimburse for care. People with low income often select this option to avoid catastrophic costs, but they may end up with large bills for healthcare services.

SOURCES OF HEALTH-RELATED INFORMATION

Source	Characteristics of the source of health-related information
Libraries	Research librarians are available to assist the user to find valid print/electronic information.
Health practitioners	Health practitioners, especially nurses and doctors, are excellent resources for information about disease, treatments, and preventive measures.
Computerized databases	Databases that provide access to valid medical articles in journals and health publications include Cochrane Library, CINAHL Plus (Cumulative Index of Nursing and Allied Health Literature), ClinicalTrials.gov, Drugs@FDA, MedlinePlus, Medline/PubMed, Merck Manual of Diagnosis and Therapy, Online Mendelian Inheritance in Man (OMIM), PDR.net (Physicians' Desk Reference), and PubMed.
Print media	Many magazines and newspapers have health-related information, but the most valid are medical journals, such as the *American Journal of Medicine,* because popular media are often only reporting on articles in these journals or giving anecdotal reports.
Electronic media	Social media, such as Facebook, Twitter, and numerous websites, have health-related information that may or may not be valid because anyone can write anything online whether it is true or not, so this type of information should always be verified with a valid source.

EVALUATING DIFFERENT SOURCES OF HEALTH INFORMATION

Strategies for evaluating different sources of health information include the following:

- **Consider the source**: Medical journals, medical databases, government sources, and medical experts (physicians, nurses) provide the most valid information. Information in the popular press or social media sites, including Wikipedia, should always be verified by searching more valid sources.
- **Check authors' credentials**: It's important to verify authors' expertise by doing an Internet search to confirm the authors' credentials and experience. Researchers and medical experts are often cited numerous times.
- **Do a second search**: Determine if others have written similar information that verifies the findings in the first.

- **Ask a reference librarian**: If unsure about validity, a reference librarian can help to verify whether or not the source is valid.
- **Consider the type of research and the data**: Consider how the authors reached their conclusions and determine whether the conclusions appear to be supported by the data.

ROLES OF GOVERNMENTAL AND NONGOVERNMENTAL AGENCIES IN PROVIDING RELIABLE HEALTH INFORMATION

The National Institutes of Health (NIH) is the primary health-related **U.S. governmental agency** that is involved in health research and health education. The NIH supports numerous individual institutes, including the National Cancer Institute, National Eye Institute, National Institute on Aging, National Institute on Alcohol Abuse and Alcoholism, National Institute on Drug Abuse, and National Institute of Mental Health. The Centers for Disease Control and Prevention (CDC), another governmental agency, provides current information on numerous topics including health conditions, healthy living, travelers' health, and emergency preparedness. The government sponsors numerous prevention centers. **Nongovernmental professional organizations**, such as the American Medical Association, and numerous prevention centers, such as the Child Abuse Prevention Center, carry out or support independent research and publish the results of this research. The Prevention Research Centers are 26 academic research centers in public institutions, such as medical schools, that carry out preventive research and influence public health policy.

STAYING INFORMED ABOUT MEDICAL AND HEALTH-RELATED ADVANCES

Strategies for staying informed about medical and health-related advances include the following:

- Subscribe to free **health-related electronic newsletters**: Johns Hopkins Medicine (Your Health), Cleveland Clinic newsletters (Health Essentials, Children's Health Essentials, Center for Integrative Medicine, Speaking of Women's Health, The Beating Edge, The Competitive Edge), Medpage Today, and Healthbeat (Harvard).
- Subscribe to **print newsletters**: *NIH News in Health* (a PDF version is available), *Global Health Matters* (NIH Fogarty International Center).
- Review newspaper and popular press **health-related articles**: Survey articles for topics of interest including new information about diseases and treatment to research further.
- Use **TV and radio**: Watch or listen to health-related news and shows for current information.
- Use **electronic sources**: Routinely check government sites, such as CDC.gov and NIH.gov, and private organization sites, such as the American Heart Association, for new information. *ScienceDaily* provides summaries of medical research findings, including information about original sources.
- Attend **lectures/presentations**: Local hospitals often provide consumer education about disease and health matters.

EFFECTIVE USE OF TECHNOLOGY IN ACCESSING ACCURATE HEALTH INFORMATION
DATABASES AND BOOLEAN SEARCH

Accessing accurate health information requires comprehensive evaluation of current ($\leq$5 years) and/or historical information. Most literature research begins with an Internet search of **databases**, which provide listings of books, journals, and other materials on specific topics. Databases vary in content, and many contain only a reference listing with or without an abstract, so once the listing is obtained, the researcher must do a further search (publisher, library, etc.) to locate the material. Some databases require a subscription, but access is often available through educational or healthcare institutions. In order to search effectively, the researcher should begin by writing a brief explanation of the research to help identify possible keywords and synonyms to use as **Boolean search** words:

- Truncations: "Finan*" provides all words that begin with those letters, such as "finance," "financial" and "financed."
- Wildcards: "m?n" or "m*n" provides "man" and "men."
- Boolean logic (AND, OR, NOT):
- Wound OR infect* OR ulcer
- Wound OR ulcer AND povidone-iodine
- Wound AND povidone-iodine NOT antibiotic NOT antimicrobial.

NIH HEALTH INFORMATION WEBSITE AND THE HEALTHFINDER WEBSITE

The National Institutes of Health (NIH) maintains the **Health Information website** (nih.gov/health-information) that provides a searchable database and links to other sites with health information. The home page contains links to common topics of interest, such as breast cancer, diabetes, and Zika. Additionally, the site provides a link to health information lines (lists of telephone numbers individuals can call for information about numerous topics, including disease and alcohol and drug abuse). The site also contains information about clinical trials, guides to talking to a doctor, science education, community resources, and an A to Z health search.

Healthfinder (healthfinder.gov, U.S. Department of Health and Human Services) contains a directory of healthcare services (doctors, dentists, other healthcare providers) so individuals can locate a healthcare provider in their community. The site also contains a health topics index (A to Z), free health content that can be loaded onto websites or printed, health news, and information about national health observances and healthcare reform.

MEDPAGE TODAY AND SCIENCEDAILY

MedPage Today is a free daily online newsletter that provides the latest news in the field of medicine with summaries of research articles as well as articles about public health, health policy, and legislation. Additionally, **MedPage Today** provides searches in 30 specialty areas, such as pediatrics and HIV/AIDS. *MedPage Today* also has a video information center.

ScienceDaily is an online source of information about the latest science news, including topics related to health, technology, the environment, society, and quirky (unusual) research. The home page has a list of top science news and the latest science-related headlines and a search option. For example, a search of "high school health education" yielded 20,400 results, but the search results can be organized by relevance or date. The articles are summaries of research articles and contain a citation for the original journal article in case the individual wants to research further.

NES Practice Test

1. Of the following major health behavior theories, which one is another name for the stages of change model?

    a. The behavioral change model
    b. The transtheoretical model
    c. The public health model
    d. The health belief model

2. Which of the following correctly sequences the stages of change in the stages of change model of health behavior?

    a. Precontemplation, contemplation, preparation, action, maintenance
    b. Preparation, precontemplation, contemplation, action, maintenance
    c. Maintenance, preparation, precontemplation, contemplation, action
    d. Preparation, action, maintenance, precontemplation, contemplation

3. In the World Health Organization (WHO) World Health Surveys (WHS), which of the following types of data were obtained on the individual rather than household level?

    a. Indicators of income
    b. Health care expenditures
    c. Health insurance coverage
    d. Health care system responsiveness

4. Of the following research methods for gathering health-related data, which one is most applicable to collecting aggregate information on large population groups?

    a. Questionnaires
    b. Observations
    c. Interviews
    d. Surveys

5. Among the following sources of valid and reliable online databases, which one(s) is/are part of the U.S. Department of Health and Human Services (HHS)?

    a. The National Institutes of Health (NIH)
    b. The U.S. Centers for Disease Control and Prevention (CDC)
    c. Choices (A) and (B) are parts of the HHS, but choice (D) is not
    d. American Alliance for Health, Physical Education, Recreation, and Dance (AAHPERD)

6. Which of the following is correct about the databases provided by the American Medical Association (AMA)?

    a. The AMA began offering access to its Physician Masterfile 10 years ago.
    b. Contractors with database licenses provide access to AMA's databases.
    c. Only practicing physician members have access to the AMA Masterfile.
    d. Physicians cannot request restrictions on their AMA Masterfile records.

7. What is the School Health Index (SHI)?

a. A tool that the Centers for Disease Control (CDC) uses to rate school health policies
b. A tool that the CDC uses for (C) and (D) but not for (A)
c. A tool to help schools in their health self-assessments
d. A tool to help schools create health policies and plans

8. The Global School-based Student Health Survey (GSHS) was developed through collaboration by which of the following organizations?

a. The World Health Organization (WHO) and the Centers for Disease Control (CDC)
b. Joint United Nations Programme on HIV/AIDS (UNAIDS) and United Nations Educational, Scientific and Cultural Organization (UNESCO)
c. United Nations Children's Fund (UNICEF) and UNAIDS
d. All of these groups

9. Which of the following is MOST accurate regarding the components of a coordinated school health program?

a. School health education should be comprehensive.
b. Physical education is separate from such a program.
c. School health services are only for emergency care.
d. Community and family are not part of this program.

10. In a coordinated school health program, which of the following is a factor?

a. Psychological, counseling, and social services are parts of a different program.
b. This program is for promoting the health of students, not of school personnel.
c. Healthy physical, emotional, and social school environments support learning.
d. Coordinated school health programs incorporate physical education but not nutrition services.

11. Which of the following lists some of the vertebrae in the human skeleton in descending order?

a. Atlas, axis, thoracic, lumbar, sacral, coccyx
b. Axis, sacral, coccyx, atlas, lumbar, thoracic
c. Thoracic, sacral, lumbar, axis, coccyx, atlas
d. Coccyx, lumbar, axis, sacral, thoracic, atlas

12. When considering how to communicate health education information to diverse audiences, which of these is true?

a. The best way to address diversity is uniformity in developing materials.
b. Equal numbers of Americans lack basic reading and health literacy skills.
c. More health-literate consumers want challenging, abstract information.
d. The great majority of American adults are lacking in health literacy skills.

13. According to the Centers for Disease Control (CDC), what is a valid guideline for writing clear, relevant health education materials appealing to diverse audiences?

a. Engage the audience by saving the most important information for later.
b. A good rule is to keep the number of main ideas in each document to ten.
c. Use prescriptions rather than proscriptions for giving action instructions.
d. Avoid audience boredom by alternating rapidly among various subjects.

14. Which of these resources for coordinated school health approaches includes information on the connection between school health and academic achievement and on school health assessment and planning?

a. The Centers for Disease Control (CDC) Web site's Coordinated School Health Publications and resources page
b. "School Health 101 Packets" offered by the National School Boards Association
c. School health coordination guidelines from some state education departments
d. The LISTSERV provided by the Comprehensive Health Education Network (CHEN)

15. Of these statements, which is a characteristic of educator communication with parents that is effective in engaging them strongly in their schools?

a. School administration and faculty get parents to identify them as children's first educators.
b. Parents regularly indicate their needs for engaging, so school personnel need not ask them.
c. School administration and faculty apply a universal style of communication with all parents.
d. Parents can identify school expectations of students for homework, attendance, behavior.

16. What is true about the privacy of records protected under Family Educational Rights and Privacy Act (FERPA)?

a. Student health but not immunization records are protected by FERPA.
b. Student health and immunization records are protected under FERPA.
c. Student health but not public school nurses' records are protected under FERPA.
d. Student special education records are protected under Individuals with Disabilities Education Act (IDEA), not FERPA.

17. Which of the following is correct regarding how the Family Educational Rights and Privacy Act (FERPA) and the Health Insurance Portability and Accountability Act (HIPAA) interact with each other?

a. FERPA supersedes the HIPAA Privacy Rule when school health records fit FERPA's definition of "education records" or "treatment records."
b. The HIPAA Privacy Rule supersedes FERPA when schools providing student health care and related electronic transactions are "covered entities."
c. The HIPAA Privacy Rule always supersedes FERPA regardless of their definitions of "covered entities" or "education records" or "treatment records."
d. FERPA always supersedes the HIPAA Privacy rule regardless of their definitions of "covered entities" or "education records" or "treatment records."

18. In the majority of U.S. states and territories, which of these professions are identified as mandated reporters of child maltreatment?

a. Probation or parole officers, substance abuse counselors, and film processors
b. Camps and recreation and youth center employees, directors, and volunteers
c. School, health care, child care, mental health, and law enforcement employees
d. Domestic violence workers, humane or animal control officers, and college faculties

19. From birth to three years, children typically grow to reach _____ of their previous height; during puberty, they typically attain around _____ of their growth in height.

a. 175 percent; 50 percent
b. 300 percent; 75 percent
c. 200 percent; 25 percent
d. 150 percent; 30 percent

20. In professional development (PD) for health educators, which of the following organizations offers a national PD conference for educational support professionals (ESPs)?

a. Society of Health and Physical Educators (ShapeAmerica)
b. The Centers for Disease Control and Prevention (CDC)
c. The American Public Health Association (APHA)
d. The National Education Association (NEA)

21. Which of the following is most accurate regarding historical ideas about disease etiology?

a. In ancient Greece, the idea of airborne sources of disease never occurred to physicians.
b. In ancient Rome, the concept of microorganisms as causes of disease was unknown yet.
c. While others proposed them, Robert Koch first discovered evidence of microorganisms.
d. Sir Austin Bradford-Hill and Richard Doll proved smoking caused cancer during the 1970s.

22. Of the following diseases, which one is NOT caused by the Epstein-Barr virus?

a. Infectious hepatitis
b. Burkitt's lymphoma
c. Infectious mononucleosis
d. Nasopharyngeal carcinoma

23. Exercise can prevent which of these diseases?

a. Stroke
b. Osteoporosis
c. Heart disease
d. All these diseases

24. Of the following, which is accurate regarding modes of human immunodeficiency virus (HIV) transmission?

a. HIV cannot be transmitted by oral sex.
b. HIV cannot be transmitted genetically.
c. HIV cannot be transmitted via nursing.
d. HIV cannot be transmitted perinatally.

25. Which statement is MOST accurate concerning differences between type 1 and type 2 diabetes?

a. Type 1 involves children and teens; type 2 involves onset in adulthood.
b. Type 1 involves more lifestyle factors; type 2 involves genetic elements.
c. Type 1 involves insulin insufficiency; type 2 involves insulin insensitivity.
d. Type 1 involves obesity and inactivity; type 2 involves nutrition deficits.

26. Among the following communicable diseases that most commonly cause death in emergency or disaster conditions, which one does NOT do so equally in all regions of the world?

a. Malaria
b. Measles
c. Diarrhea
d. Acute respiratory infections

27. About 80 percent of all deaths from noncommunicable diseases are caused by four types of disease. Which of these four types causes the majority of these deaths?

    a. Diabetic
    b. Cancerous
    c. Respiratory
    d. Cardiovascular

28. Of the four types of diseases—cancers, cardiovascular diseases, diabetes, and respiratory diseases—that cause the majority of deaths from noncommunicable diseases, which risk factor is not common to all four types?

    a. Unsafe water
    b. Drinking alcohol
    c. Poor diet
    d. Smoking tobacco

29. According to research by the World Health Organization (WHO), the highest future increases in deaths are projected to be in African countries, with which of these as the leading causes?

    a. Communicable diseases
    b. Noncommunicable diseases
    c. Infant mortality from childbirth
    d. Maternal mortality from childbirth

30. According to current research, what is true related to diabetes prevention?

    a. Supplements and foods control blood sugar equally well.
    b. Overall hours of sleep are unrelated to insulin sensitivity.
    c. Research does not connect stress with insulin resistance.
    d. Exercise in cooler temperatures can help glucose control.

31. Among steps health educators can teach students to take after making a poor decision, which statement is MOST representative of one of these steps?

    a. Students should avoid telling others of a poor decision.
    b. Students should tell parents and follow their guidance.
    c. Students should follow through on decision-based acts.
    d. Students should apologize, which always corrects harm.

32. Among eight steps that health educators can teach their students to follow in setting health goals, which of these four should they do first?

    a. Write down their long-term and short-term health goals.
    b. Write down action plans describing steps for goals in detail.
    c. Write down time lines with specific dates to reach the goals.
    d. Write down potential obstacles to realizing the action plans.

33. When health educators teach their students eight steps for establishing and meeting health goals, which of the last four is MOST related to monitoring progress for accountability?

    a. Asking friends to help or forming a club
    b. Using journals, diaries, charts, or graphs
    c. Healthy self-rewards for meeting goals
    d. Making revisions in plans and time lines

34. How is cardiorespiratory endurance best defined?

    a. The ability to perform dynamic exercise using large muscles over long times
    b. The ability to perform dynamic exercises using small muscles for short times
    c. The ability to perform static exercises using all muscles for average durations
    d. The ability to perform any kind of exercising using any muscles for any time

35. Which of these is true about flexibility or range of motion?

    a. Enhancing flexibility is primarily for improving sports performance.
    b. Enhancing flexibility is mainly to facilitate everyday life functioning.
    c. Enhancing flexibility is best for rehabilitating injuries to soft tissue.
    d. Enhancing flexibility is important for realizing a variety of benefits.

36. What does the Frequency, Intensity, Time, and Type (FITT) Principle represent in exercise science?

    a. How physically fit an individual is in general
    b. How often, hard, long, and kind of exercise
    c. How good an individual's aerobic capacity is
    d. How much muscular strength someone has

37. Which of the following foods is classified in two food groups by the U.S. Department of Agriculture (USDA)?

    a. Legumes
    b. Seafood
    c. Cheese
    d. Eggplant

38. We get _____ from _____ in our diet and _____ from _____.

    a. Energy, protein; amino acids, carbohydrates
    b. Energy, vitamins; muscle repair, amino acids
    c. Energy, carbohydrates; amino acids, protein
    d. Energy, minerals; tissue repair, saturated fat

39. For optimal exercising, how should our nutrition be distributed?

    a. One-third each from protein, carbohydrates, and fat
    b. One-half from protein, one-quarter carbohydrates, and one-quarter from fats
    c. Greater than one-half from carbohydrates, less than one-fifth from protein, and less than one-third from fats
    d. Greater than one-half from protein, less than one-quarter from carbohydrates, and greater than one-quarter from fat

40. Of the following, which statement is MOST accurate about common unhealthy reactions to stress?

    a. People under stress are more likely to feel physical pain than to quit smoking, drinking, or drugs.

    b. People under stress are more likely to overeat and gain weight than skip eating and lose weight.

    c. People under stress are more likely to display episodes of anger or temper than episodes of crying.

    d. People under stress are more likely to experience symptoms of anxiety than those of depression.

41. Which statement best reflects expert recommendations of techniques for managing stress?

    a. It does not help to manage stress by cutting back excessive activity.

    b. Being prepared has no impact on unexpected stressors in life.

    c. Relaxation techniques ease body tension, not mental stress.

    d. Adequate sleep is critical for minimizing and managing stress.

42. Among the life skills of values clarification, decision-making, communication, and coping skills, which of the following responses to stressful life events MOST reflects decision-making skills?

    a. Considering positive aspects of the situation

    b. Evaluating the pros and cons of the situation

    c. Expressing your feelings about the situation

    d. Positive behaviors to deal with the situation

43. What is MOST accurate about interventions for decreasing tobacco use to control health risks?

    a. Smokers ignore the graphic health warnings on cigarette and tobacco packs.

    b. Smoke-free public and workplace laws have little impact: People go outside.

    c. Raising tobacco prices and taxes is proven to work and be cost-effective.

    d. Public and private smoking cessation programs often are not affordable.

44. According to research studies, what is true about the impact of physical activity (PA) on health risks?

    a. PA lowers heart disease, stroke, diabetes, and colon and breast cancer risks.

    b. PA reduces risks of heart disease and stroke but not of diabetes or any cancer.

    c. PA reduces risks of all these diseases, but amounts of PA needed for each disease vary greatly.

    d. PA in adequate amounts improves overall well-being but does not lower disease risks.

45. Among the following measures to lower health risks by limiting harmful alcohol use, which has research found effective?

    a. Consumer warning messages and labeling

    b. Fewer stores and times for selling alcohol

    c. Mass media campaigns against alcohol use

    d. Public education and classroom education

46. Which of the following major muscles controls the chewing functions of the jaws?

 a. The orbicularis oris muscle
 b. The zygomaticus muscles
 c. The trapezius muscles
 d. The masseter muscles

47. What is correct about the hormones that stimulate male and female organs to produce male and female sex hormones?

 a. Female organs are stimulated by female hormones and male organs by male hormones.
 b. The same hormones that produce male or female sex characteristics stimulate the organs.
 c. The same hormones stimulate both male and female organs to produce sex hormones.
 d. The hypothalamus stimulates the pituitary gland's secretion of male and female hormones.

48. In which human body system do the white cell blood cells function?

 a. Respiratory
 b. Circulatory
 c. Lymphatic
 d. Endocrine

49. Within personal hygiene, which of these is a fact about oral care?

 a. Gum disease can cause serious disorders of the heart valves.
 b. Unhealthy gums can cause gum infections but not tooth loss.
 c. Brushing one's teeth prevents tooth decay, not gum disease.
 d. Gum disease affects soft tissues rather than the jaw's bones.

50. Which statement is MOST accurate if someone neglects his or her personal hygiene?

 a. Personal hygiene neglect always indicates underlying depression.
 b. Preoccupation with other things never causes neglect of hygiene.
 c. People do not neglect personal hygiene from a lack of awareness.
 d. Depression, preoccupation, or lack of awareness may be reasons.

51. Of the following, which is accurate regarding personal hygiene in adolescence?

 a. The majority of teens experience acne regardless of skin care habits.
 b. Teens should not need to shampoo hair more but do so out of vanity.
 c. The same oral hygiene they used as children should suffice for teens.
 d. Teens who learned good bathing habits as children need not change.

52. What is a common misconception among teenagers that health educators should correct?

 a. That conception cannot occur by body rubbing without vaginal or vulvar sperm contact
 b. That conception will not occur without penetration and ejaculation inside the vagina
 c. That teenage males should put on condoms before sex and wear them continuously
 d. That kissing or oral or anal sex will not cause pregnancy if no sperm touches the vulva or vagina

53. Research shows that how many fatal auto crashes involve alcohol intoxication?

 a. More than one-half
 b. Below one-quarter
 c. Nearly one-third
 d. Exactly one-quarter

148

54. Which of these is included in advice for preventing sexual assault?

a. It is important to park in open, well-lighted areas and check backseats in advance.
b. Confident people need not avoid jogging or walking alone in secluded areas at night.
c. Projecting senses of awareness, confidence, strength, and security does not help.
d. If one is assaulted, it is better to remain passive than actively resisting the attack.

55. How many deaths does smoking cigarettes cause annually in America compared to other causes?

a. More than alcohol and drug use, car accidents, human immunodeficiency virus (HIV), and gunshots together
b. More than alcohol and drug use combined or more than HIV and gunshots
c. More than alcohol and drug use and HIV combined, not including gunshots
d. More than gunshots and HIV combined, but less than alcohol and drug use

56. What is a result of regular and substantial alcohol use?

a. It impairs judgment over the long term but not in the short term.
b. It distorts the perceptions but not the senses of vision or hearing.
c. It damages both the cardiovascular and central nervous systems.
d. It causes liver damage but not impotence or stomach disorders.

57. What is true about guidelines for making emergency 911 calls?

a. Call 911 for uncontrollable bleeding or unconsciousness but not allergic reactions or chest pains.
b. Situations needing immediate help from police, fire departments, or ambulances merit 911 calls.
c. Prank calls to 911 are a great nuisance and interfere with actual emergencies but are not illegal.
d. When a person calls 911 in an emergency, he or she should hang up immediately to free up the lines.

58. According to Bowen Family Systems Theory, when both partners in a couple project their expanding anxieties into their relationship, this reflects which basic relationship pattern identified by Bowen?

a. Emotional distance
b. Impairment of child(ren)
c. Dysfunction in one spouse
d. The pattern of marital conflict

59. In the nuclear family emotional system Dr. Murray Bowen describes in his Family Systems Theory, which basic relationship pattern is represented if a parent shows excessive anxiety about a child, and the child responds by regressing to increased dependence and immature demands on the parent?

a. Dysfunction in one spouse
b. Impairment of a child(ren)
c. Emotional distance pattern
d. The marital conflict pattern

60. Which of the following correctly identifies the big five personality traits?
   a. Introversion, detail-orientation, responsibility, psychoticism, and kindness
   b. Extraversion, agreeableness, conscientiousness, neuroticism, and openness
   c. Oral traits, anal traits, phallic tendencies, latency tendencies, and genital traits
   d. Assertiveness, prosocial behaviors, impulse control, moodiness, and imagination

61. In Hobfoll's Conservation of Resources (COR) Theory of stress processes, which choice accurately represents one of four corollaries to two main principles?
   a. Those having more can lose more and gain less.
   b. Lacking resources causes loss of existing ones.
   c. Initially losing resources causes future losses.
   d. Initially gaining resources causes future loss.

62. What has been found by research into teacher influence on children's peer relationships as a social context factor?
   a. Teachers who believe in and relate positively with attention deficit hyperactivity disorder (ADHD) children can modulate peer dislike of them.
   b. Teachers have difficulty relating to children with ADHD; therefore, they cannot change peers' dislike.
   c. Teachers cannot affect dislike of ADHD children by peers rejecting them despite improved behavior.
   d. Teachers who create classrooms improving peer relationships eliminate all dislike of ADHD children.

63. What has research discovered about the adolescent decision-making process?
   a. Conformity with parental or peer norms is unrelated to teen decision making.
   b. Demographic rather than family or personal variables influence teen decisions.
   c. Adolescents tend to be oriented toward the future regarding long-term goals.
   d. Real-life practice is necessary for teens to transfer cognitive skills to decisions.

64. Decision-making models commonly require adolescents to develop certain skills. Which of these skills do they need to exercise first?
   a. Evaluating the possible consequences of options
   b. Evaluating the decisions they make and their results
   c. Gathering information and generating alternatives
   d. Defining which decisions they will have to make

65. Which statement is MOST accurate regarding the nature of decision-making for teenagers?
   a. The decisions teens make are unlikely to affect their long-term futures.
   b. Social contexts change; hence, teens must evaluate and adjust decisions.
   c. Teens generally have enough life experience to make difficult decisions.
   d. Intervention programs to improve decision-making skills are ineffective.

66. Of the following, which correctly reflects how teenagers make decisions?
   a. Internal, not external, variables influence teen decisions.
   b. Adolescents usually make decisions in isolated conditions.
   c. Feedback influences the decisions that adolescents make.
   d. External, not internal, variables influence teens' decisions.

67. Among emotional intelligence (EQ) skills, which one is most informed by the others?

a. Being able to resolve conflicts positively and confidently
b. Being able to use humor to dissipate interactional stress
c. Being able to use nonverbal communication effectively
d. Being able to reduce stress quickly and manage feelings

68. Regarding emotional intelligence (EQ), what is true?

a. EQ affects physical and mental health, school and work performance, and relationships.
b. EQ affects mental but not physical health and relationships, not school performance.
c. EQ is neither helped nor harmed by a person's abilities in nonverbal communication.
d. EQ is often derailed by humor and undermined by focusing on one's own emotions.

69. Among domains of development throughout life stages, what does Piaget's theory focus MOST on?

a. Emotional development
b. Developing relationships
c. Intellectual development
d. Developing independence

70. According to Piaget's developmental theory, when do children first achieve mental operations?

a. During the sensorimotor stage
b. During the preoperational stage
c. In the concrete operations stage
d. In the formal operations stage

71. Erikson's theory of development focuses MOST on a person's relationship with which other aspect?

a. Self
b. Society
c. Other individuals
d. The parents exclusively

72. In his developmental theory, what did Erikson identify as the positive outcome of successfully resolving the nuclear conflict of basic trust versus mistrust?

a. Will
b. Hope
c. Purpose
d. Competence

73. According to Erikson's theory of psychosocial development, which ability must be achieved during the period of adolescence?

a. Identity
b. Intimacy
c. Industry
d. Autonomy

74. In interpersonal conversations, which main goals entail both the highest cognitive challenge and the highest quality of interaction?

    a. Task goals
    b. Identity goals
    c. Relationship goals
    d. All three of these goals

75. Which of the following accurately represents findings about how stress interacts with interpersonal communications on health care and other important subjects?

    a. We can control a problem better by limiting discussions of it.
    b. Being able to explain a problem affords more control over it.
    c. Sensitive discussions have outcomes worse than we expect.
    d. Quantity supersedes quality for discussing important issues.

76. For discussing difficult subjects with others, which of these reflects expert advice?

    a. "I" statements must be genuine, not automatic.
    b. Honesty is much more important than empathy.
    c. We should broach subjects when they upset us.
    d. Saying something funny is always inappropriate.

77. Of these statements, which correctly represents research findings and expert opinions?

    a. In romantic relationships, there is no such thing as ever sharing too much information.
    b. People always should share every criticism and stressor honestly in their relationships.
    c. Self-protection is a better motive than relationship protection to withhold information.
    d. Research has found that overly repressing communication exacerbates medical conditions.

78. What do experts recommend for adult children to bring up the topic of dying with aging parents?

    a. Family events like Christmas dinner or Easter brunch are good opportunities.
    b. It is better to use less personal springboards such as related TV news stories.
    c. Family members should wait until parents receive terminal status diagnoses.
    d. Adult children should not broach this topic until a parent's death is imminent.

79. When considering conflict management and resolution, what is true?

    a. Conflict in a relationship is a sign the relationship is unhealthy.
    b. Because they find it unpleasant, people should avoid conflict.
    c. Healthy relationships normally and integrally include conflicts.
    d. People should avoid confrontation as they find it threatening.

80. Which of these do experts identify as the most accurate definition of a conflict?

    a. The most accurate definition of a conflict is simply a disagreement.
    b. A conflict is a situation wherein somebody perceives some threat.
    c. One central characteristic of a conflict is that it undermines growth.
    d. A conflict is a temporary upset that will go away if people ignore it.

81. Among the following, which is recommended as a healthy way of approaching conflict?

 a. Seeing mutual benefits in facing conflict directly
 b. Expressing anger emotionally to enable venting
 c. Avoiding conflict to prevent negative outcomes
 d. Standing firm without compromising one's view

82. How is assertiveness primarily characterized?

 a. As passive
 b. As aggressive
 c. As both of these
 d. As neither of these

83. Which statement accurately reflects recommended refusal strategies for children and teens?

 a. Walking away from a pressure situation is avoidant.
 b. Standing up for others being pressured is meddling.
 c. Proposing alternative activities is coping effectively.
 d. To say "no," one often needs to be very aggressive.

84. Listening, reacting, engaging in eye contact, and thoroughly understanding prompts are all useful elements when nurturing a student's ability to develop what broad skill?

 a. Effective interaction
 b. Performance
 c. Rehearsal
 d. Role playing

85. Which of the following statements is true related to gender or sexual identity?

 a. Physiological gender is opposite to gender identity in some individuals.
 b. Sexual or gender identity is necessarily a match with one's physical sex.
 c. People who cross-dress are always either transgender or homosexual.
 d. A person's sexual orientation is the same as his or her sexual expression.

86. Regarding contraception methods, which of the following is correct?

 a. A condom or spermicide is effective enough by itself.
 b. Vasectomy is never reversible; tubal ligation always is.
 c. None of these choices is correct about contraception.
 d. Women insert IUDs, diaphragms, and pills themselves.

87. In abusive relationships, which of these is most commonly the case?

 a. When an abuser apologizes and acts normal, he or she is genuinely sorry and intends to try to change.
 b. When an abuser apologizes and acts normal, he or she is manipulating the victim and will abuse again.
 c. When an abuser apologizes rather than blaming the victim, this is a sign the victim can believe it.
 d. When an abuser apologizes rather than blaming the victim, he or she is unlikely to repeat the abuse.

88. Among tactics typically employed by domestic abusers to control their victims, what is destroying the victim's property an example of?

    a. Isolation
    b. Humiliation
    c. Dominance
    d. Intimidation

89. Among signs of domestic abuse, physical violence, isolation, and psychological symptoms of being abused, which of the following is more specifically a sign of domestic abuse than of the others?

    a. Constantly reporting one's locations and activities to the partner
    b. Often exhibiting or trying to hide injuries, claiming accidents
    c. Marked changes in a person's personality traits or behaviors
    d. Few or no public outings, no car or money use alone, or no visiting with others

90. Which statement is true about factors that influence a person's mood and mental and emotional health?

    a. Smoking cigarettes and drinking alcohol in moderation improve the long-term mood.
    b. Mental and emotional health are psychological; sleeping and eating have no impacts.
    c. Daily exposure to sunshine only causes skin cancer and does not affect mental status.
    d. In addition to promoting physical fitness, exercise improves mood and mental status.

91. What has been found regarding risk factors for mental and emotional health?

    a. Attachment theory has been disproven as causing mental or emotional risks.
    b. Biological and environmental influences interact in mental and emotional risks.
    c. Experiences during early childhood are too remote to create risk for adults.
    d. Substance abuse causes new disorders but does not worsen existing ones.

92. Of the following, which is NOT a sign that an individual may need to get help from a professional for emotional or mental health problems?

    a. Persistent insomnia
    b. Pervasive depression
    c. Difficulty concentrating
    d. Any or all of these are signs

93. Among the following media strategies that local health departments use to communicate with others to advocate for public health, which one targets individuals, policy makers, and the public?

    a. A media advocacy strategy
    b. A social marketing media strategy
    c. A risk communication media strategy
    d. A credible source communication strategy

94. Legally, who in the United States is responsible for preventing communicable diseases from being introduced, transmitted, and spread?

    a. The U.S. Secretary of State
    b. The U.S. Secretary of the Interior
    c. The U.S. Secretary of Homeland Security
    d. The U.S. Secretary of Health and Human Services

95. Which statement is accurate concerning U.S. laws governing immunizations?

a. Federal laws specify immunizations for children to enter public schools.
b. Laws regulating child immunizations for public school vary in each state.
c. Certain states have laws about immunizations for school; others do not.
d. As laws vary by state, there is no central data repository for these laws.

96. What are some of the benefits of recycling?

a. Reducing waste, saving energy, conserving natural resources, reducing greenhouse gases, and creating jobs
b. Reducing waste, saving energy, conserving natural resources, and reducing greenhouse gases
c. Reducing waste and conserving natural resources but not saving energy or reducing emissions
d. Reducing waste, conserving resources, and saving energy but not gas reduction or job creation

97. Which of the following is accurate regarding the history of U.S. regulations addressing pollution?

a. The Environmental Protection Agency (EPA) first developed standards, laws, and regulations in the 1980s.
b. The EPA's focus shifted from the remediation of existing pollution to preventing it during the 2000s.
c. Congress's policy to prevent and reduce pollution is declared in the Pollution Prevention Act of 1990.
d. National policy shifted in the 1990s from reducing pollution sources toward treatment and disposal.

98. In the United States, which source produces the most carbon dioxide (CO2) emissions?

a. Vehicles that burn gasoline
b. Buildings that use electricity
c. Industries that manufacture
d. All these in equal amounts

99. Industry projections are that _____ people worldwide will use health care apps on smartphones by 2015, and ___ of smartphone and tablet users will have downloaded mobile health apps by 2018.

a. 1 million; one fifth
b. 100 million; one-third
c. 500 million; one-half
d. 1 billion; three-quarters

100. Of the following health care professions, which in addition to physician often is able to prescribe medications?

a. Registered nurse
b. Medical assistant
c. Physician assistant
d. Doctor of pharmacy

101. What do the American Red Cross and Planned Parenthood share in common?
   a. Both are providers of training in babysitting to youth.
   b. Both are providers of reproductive health care services.
   c. Both are national nonprofit agencies with local chapters.
   d. Both are providers of training in emergency procedures.

102. The National Health Education Standards (NHES) were developed in response to what?
   a. Standards being developed in hospitals
   b. Standards being developed in education
   c. Standards being developed in public health
   d. Standards being developed in private practice

103. When comparing the federal Healthy People 2000, 2010, and 2020 initiatives, which applies MOST?
   a. The 2000 initiative aimed to decrease health disparities, 2010 to eliminate them, and 2020 to establish health equity.
   b. The 2000 initiative aimed to eliminate health disparities, 2010 to establish health equity, and 2020 to improve health.
   c. The 2000 initiative aimed to improve American health, 2010 to reduce health disparities, and 2020 to eliminate them.
   d. The 2000, 2010, and 2020 Healthy People initiatives all have aimed to improve health for all Americans.

104. For delivering health awareness, education, and advocacy via mass media campaigns, which of these is true about using TV or radio as a medium?
   a. People retain information better from TV than radio.
   b. Radio reaches more people altogether than TV does.
   c. People in rural areas have neither radios nor TV sets.
   d. TV and radio are not as good as print or digital media.

105. Regarding opportunities for health education advocacy, which statement MOST accurately represents some of these venues?
   a. Some schools, but not communities, present health fairs.
   b. School assemblies do not allow any entertaining formats.
   c. Professional meetings and conferences exclude students.
   d. Health fairs are too expensive for most schools to provide.

106. When health educators develop processes for integrating health education across the curriculum, they function as liaisons between or among which of these?
   a. Trainees and students
   b. Administrators and students
   c. The school and the research community
   d. Teachers, administrators, curriculum coordinators, and students

107. Teaching the idea that saturated fat in the diet contributes to heart disease is MOST developmentally appropriate to which stage of Piaget's theory of cognitive development?

a. Sensorimotor
b. Preoperational
c. Formal operations
d. Concrete operations

108. Which of Howard Gardner's multiple intelligence styles would learn best through group instructional activities?

a. Interpersonal
b. Intrapersonal
c. Visual-spatial
d. Mathematical

109. Of the following, which purpose(s) can pretesting accomplish?

a. Determining where to begin the instruction
b. Evaluating the effectiveness of the instruction
c. Formative and summative learning assessments
d. All of these purposes

110. To write learning objectives in planning health instruction, which of the following verbs represents a measurable student action?

a. Learn
b. Explain
c. Understand
d. Any of these

111. Which of the following arranges four categories of effective lesson plans in their correct sequence?

a. Preparing students for learning; instruction; monitoring for comprehension; independent practice
b. Instruction; independent practice; monitoring for comprehension; preparing students for learning
c. Independent practice; preparing students for learning; instruction; monitoring for comprehension
d. Monitoring for comprehension; independent practice; preparing students for learning; Instruction

112. What is true about statutory curriculum policies regarding health and physical education for schools in the United States?

a. All U.S. states require both health education and physical education.
b. All U.S. states require physical education, but not all states require health education.
c. All U.S. states require health, but not all require physical education.
d. All U.S. states vary in requirements of health and physical education.

113. What is a valid claim when comparing Rosenshine and Stevens' model of direct instruction with the Direct Instruction method of Engelmann and colleagues?

    a. Both are teacher directed, but only one is skills oriented.
    b. Both are face-to-face, but only one uses small groups.
    c. Both use task analysis, but only one is sequenced.
    d. Both teach explicitly, but only one is generic.

114. Among competitive, individualistic, and cooperative learning models, which one(s) use criterion-referenced assessments rather than norm-referenced assessments?

    a. Cooperative and individualistic learning models
    b. Individualistic and competitive learning models
    c. Competitive and individualistic learning models
    d. All three

115. Among the following instructional techniques, which is equally amenable to individual or multiple student work and also to student work with or without the teacher's active involvement?

    a. Role-playing
    b. Brainstorming
    c. Guided discovery
    d. Cooperative learning

116. In the reflective process of teaching, which tools would MOST help a teacher to self-analyze his or her own body language and movement within the classroom and adjust these to be more effective?

    a. Journals and diaries
    b. Video recordings
    c. Audio recordings
    d. Peer observation

117. Which of the following are used as formative assessments?

    a. Student final class projects
    b. Tests given at the ends of units
    c. Curriculum-based measurement
    d. Standardized state examinations

118. Of the following, which can be used as a formative or summative assessment?

    a. Course grades
    b. Portfolio assessments
    c. Large-scale standardized tests
    d. Teachers' observational checklists

119. When should teachers and students primarily apply a rubric?

    a. After learning
    b. During learning
    c. Before learning
    d. During all these times

120. Which of the following is recommended for teachers to deal with an individual student who is always misbehaving in class?

    a.   Speaking with the student in private
    b.   Disciplining the student during class
    c.   Differentiating behavior versus the student
    d.   (A) and (C) but not (B) unless necessary

Answer Key and Explanations

1. B: The transtheoretical model is another term for the stages of change model of health behavior. The behavioral change model (A) encompasses multiple theories, including the public health model (C); a planning model containing four steps (defining the problem, identifying the risk, developing and testing prevention methods, and communicating which interventions were effective); and the health belief model (D), which ascertains whether and why an individual will change his or her behavior by evaluating the perception of threat from disease and the net benefits of behavioral change.

2. A: In precontemplation, individuals have no plans to act anytime soon. This can be caused by lack of information, lack of motivation, and resistance. In contemplation, individuals plan to make changes within roughly six months but are not ready to act immediately. They have acquired awareness of both the costs and benefits of change, causing ambivalence that fuels procrastination. In preparation, individuals usually have made some significant action in the last year; plan to act within a month; and have developed some plan of action. In action, people have accomplished obvious lifestyle changes in the last six months, sufficient to reduce disease risk according to professional and scientific criteria, for example, quitting smoking. In maintenance, people devote more effort to preventing relapse than initiating change processes, which they have already largely done. This stage can last six months to five years.

3. D: In the World Health Surveys (WHS), income indicators (A), health care expenditures (B), health insurance coverage (C), and household members were data collected on the household level. Data collected on the individual level included sociodemographic information, health state descriptions, health state valuations, health risk factors, chronic health conditions, health care use, mortality, social capital, and the responsiveness of health care systems (D).

4. D: While questionnaires (A) can be sent to large groups of people, they also can be used to collect data on an individual and small group basis equally well or better (i.e., not all recipients return mailed questionnaires, whereas individuals and small groups, when given these directly in clinical, public health, or other settings, are obligated to complete them). Observations (B) are most useful for gathering data about individuals or small groups as they require researchers to watch their actions and interactions directly (overtly or covertly). Interviews (C) typically require one-to-one question-and-answer interactions between researchers and respondents. The survey (D) method enables researchers to collect large-scale data on entire population groups, often through a combination of these other methods, by obtaining the same information from a much greater number of respondents.

5. C: The National Institutes of Health (NIH) (A), which offers valid and reliable health-related data via a selection of public databases that users can access online, is part of the U.S. Department of Health and Human Services (HHS). The Centers for Disease Control (CDC) (B), which provides interactive online database systems on a wide variety of health topics, is also a part of HHS. However, American Alliance for Health, Physical Education, Recreation, and Dance (AAHPERD) (D), also called ShapeAmerica—SHAPE is an acronym for Society of Health and Physical Educators—is a professional membership organization and not a part of the HHS or any other department of the federal government.

6. B: The American Medical Association (AMA) has been offering access to its Physician Masterfile to members of the health care community for more than 60 years, not 10 (A). Today, contractors

160

with database licenses act as intermediaries to provide access to the AMA's various health-related research and marketing activity databases (B). Not only practicing physicians who are AMA members (C) but also consultants, hospitals, medical schools, pharmaceutical manufacturers, insurance companies, medical supply and equipment companies, market research companies, and commercial organizations are allowed access to the AMA Masterfile. Physicians can request restrictions on their AMA Masterfile records (D), including restricting their prescription information from pharmaceutical sales representatives and restricting contact and release of their Masterfile records.

7. B: The School Health Index (SHI) was developed jointly by the Centers for Disease Control (CDC) and national health and education nongovernmental organizations (NGOs), school staffs, school health experts, and parents as a self-assessment (C) and planning (D) guide. Schools use it to help conduct needs assessments to identify the strengths and weaknesses of their health and safety policies and programs, develop action plans for enhancing health to include in their School Improvement Plans (SIPs), and engage students, teachers, parents, and communities in health-promoting, health-enhancing behaviors.

8. D: The World Health Organization (WHO) (A) collaborated with Joint United Nations Programme on HIV/AIDS (UNAIDS), United Nations Educational, Scientific and Cultural Organization (UNESCO) (B), and United Nations Children's Fund (UNICEF) (C), with technical assistance from the U.S. Centers for Disease Control and prevention (CDC) (A) to develop the GHSH, a school-based survey of protective health factors and health behaviors in more than 450,000 students age 13 to 17 years in more than 120 world nations.

9. A: A coordinated school health program includes comprehensive school health education addressing physical, cognitive, affective, and social health domains, differentiated for every developmental and age level to promote health knowledge, skills, and attitudes, decrease health risk behaviors, and enhance student health. Physical education is not separate (B) but is an essential component of a coordinated school health program. So are school health services, which include not only emergency care (C) but also prevention, education, referral, and acute and chronic health condition management. Another essential component of a coordinated school health program is family and community involvement (D).

10. C: Components of a coordinated school health program include psychological, counseling, and social services (A); health promotion for school personnel as well as for students (B); healthy school environments that support learning through physical, emotional, and social safety and health (C); and school nutrition services as well as physical education (D).

11. A: From highest to lowest: the atlas is cervical vertebra 1, supporting the skull; the axis is cervical vertebra 2; next come cervical vertebrae 3 through 7, the bones in the back of the neck, which are omitted in all choices; then the 12 thoracic vertebrae are the upper back bones; below these are the 5 lumbar vertebrae in the lower back; the 5 sacral vertebrae (together, the sacrum) are the pelvic and hip-level back bones; and the coccyx or tailbone at the bottom of the spine contains 3-5 small bones, which are often fused together.

12. D: The U.S. Department of Education's National Assessment of Adult Literacy (NAAL) found that approximately 88 percent of consumers lack health literacy skills proficiency. This assessment found that approximately 33 percent of Americans lack basic reading skills; hence, these numbers are not equal (B). The Centers for Disease Control (CDC) has observed that diversity prohibits a uniform approach in developing materials (A) for health education. Even consumers with superior health literacy do not want challenging, abstract information (C) but rather easily understood and applied, personally relevant information.

13. C: The Centers for Disease Control (CDC) advises health educators that it is more effective to give positive than negative instructions, for example, "Wear helmets when riding bicycles" rather than "Do not ride bicycles without wearing helmets." They also recommend engaging the audience immediately by stating the most important information first (A); keeping the number of ideas in each document or section to three or four (B); and instead of confusing audiences by alternating among subjects (D), fully developing one idea at a time before proceeding to another one.

14. A: The Coordinated School Health Publications and Resources page on the Centers for Disease Control's (CDC's) Web site includes information on the connection between school health and academic achievement and on school health assessment and planning. The National School Boards Association's "School Health 101 Packets" (B); the school health coordination guidelines published by state education departments (C), for example, the Connecticut State Department of Education and the Maine Departments of Education and Health and Human Services; and the Comprehensive Health Education Network's (CHEN's) LISTSERV, which publishes an online mailing list for national, state, and local school health professionals all provide basic information on coordinated school health approaches.

15. D: When parents can identify the school's primary expectations of students for doing homework, attending school, and behavior in school, this is one sign educators are communicating effectively with parents to engage them in their children's learning and schools. Another sign is that school administrators and teachers acknowledge parents as their children's first educators and support parents' own recognition of this (A). Another is that school personnel have methods for regularly finding out on an ongoing basis what parents need to engage with their children's learning (B). An additional characteristic is that school personnel vary their communication styles according to parental diversity (C).

16. B: Student health records in educational institutions and agencies receiving federal Department of Education funding are protected under the Family Educational Rights and Privacy Act (FERPA); immunization records are not excluded (A). Neither are records kept by public school nurses (C) on students, whose privacy is also protected under FERPA. Student special education records, including records of services they receive under the Individuals with Disabilities Education Act (IDEA), also are defined as "education records" by FERPA; hence, their privacy is also protected by FERPA (D).

17. A: The HIPAA Privacy Rule mandates that "covered entities," including schools that provide students with health care and transmit related information electronically, must protect the privacy of these records by limiting disclosure without patient permission and comply with patient rights to look at, procure copies of, and request corrections of their records. However, when school health records also fit FERPA's definition of "education records" or "treatment records," FERPA supersedes the HIPAA Privacy rule, and the records are not subject to this rule.

18. C: As of 2014, 48 U.S. states, the District of Columbia, plus Puerto Rico, the Virgin Islands, Guam, American Samoa, and the Northern Mariana Islands school, health care, child care, mental health, social services, and law enforcement employees are all mandated reporters of child maltreatment. Probation or parole officers are mandated reporters in 17 states; substance abuse counselors are in 14 states; and commercial film processors are in 12 states, Guam, and Puerto Rico (A). Employees, directors, and volunteers of camps and recreation and youth centers (B) are mandated reporters in 11 states. Domestic violence workers and humane or animal control officers are mandated reporters in 7 states and Washington, D.C.; college and university, technical and vocational school faculties, administrators, and other employees and volunteers (D) are mandated reporters in 4 states. Clergy are mandated reporters in 27 states and Guam.

19. C: Milestones of physical growth and development include that, from birth to three years, children typically grow to twice their previous height and that, during puberty, they typically attain around 25 percent of their growth in height.

20. D: The National Education Association (NEA) offers a national professional development (PD) conference for educational support professionals (ESPs), its Leaders for Tomorrow program, and various other PD trainings. ShapeAmerica (aka American Association of Health, Physical Education, Recreation, and Dance [AAHPERD]) (A) offers a PD webinar series on various topics, a Researcher's Toolkit, a Distinguished Lecture Series, and workshops. The Centers for Disease Control (CDC) (B) has a Division of Scientific Education and Professional Development (DSEPD), its Learning Connection containing thousands of public health learning products and continuing education (CE) courses through CDC TRAIN, online resources, Quick-Learn lessons for mobile devices, and Facebook and Twitter links to public health topics. The American Public Health Association (APHA) (C) has a Center for PD, Public Health Systems, and Partnerships.

21. C: Robert Koch (1843–1910), the German physician considered the founder of modern bacteriology, was first to discover scientific proof that microorganisms caused anthrax, cholera, and tuberculosis. In ancient Greece, though they did not have the technology to prove it, the physicians Galen and Hippocrates did consider that disease could be caused by unknown airborne particles (A). In ancient Rome, the scholar Marcus Terentius Varro suggested that diseases could be caused by microorganisms (B) in the first century BC. A series of studies by Hill and Doll established the connection between smoking tobacco and lung cancer during the 1950s, not the 1970s (D).

22. A: Infectious hepatitis is caused by different viruses depending on which type it is: three separate viruses cause hepatitis A, B, and C. Burkett's lymphoma (B), infectious mononucleosis (C), and nasopharyngeal carcinoma (D) all can be caused by the Epstein-Barr virus under different conditions.

23. D: All these diseases can be prevented by regular exercise. Aerobic exercise can prevent stroke by lowering blood pressure, strengthening arteries, and decreasing arterial plaque. Weight-bearing exercise can prevent osteoporosis (B) by strengthening the bones. Aerobic exercise can prevent heart disease (C) by strengthening the heart, lowering cholesterol, and lowering blood pressure.

24. B: It is impossible for parents to pass the human immunodeficiency virus (HIV) genetically to their children as it is not a genetic disease. However, HIV can be transmitted by oral sex (A) as well as genital and anal sex. Infected nursing mothers can transmit HIV to their babies (C) in breast milk. Infected mothers also can transmit HIV perinatally (D) to their unborn children.

25. C: Whereas historically, type 1 diabetes involved children and teens more and type 2 involved onset in adulthood, today this is not true (A): More and more children and adolescents are developing type 2 diabetes due to lifestyle factors. Both types of diabetes are influenced by genetic and lifestyle factors; however, genetic elements contribute more to type 1, while lifestyle behaviors contribute more to type 2 (B). In type 1, the pancreas fails to produce insulin; in type 2, the pancreas produces insulin, but the body loses its sensitivity (C) and fails to respond to it. Obesity, inactivity, and poor nutrition all contribute to type 2 diabetes (D).

26. A: The communicable diseases listed are the most common world causes of death in emergency or disaster conditions. However, malaria (A) is only one of the most common causes in certain regions of the world. Measles (B), diarrhea (C), and acute respiratory infections (RIs) (D) are the communicable diseases that most commonly cause death in emergency or disaster conditions equally in all areas of the world, according to the World Health Organization (WHO).

27. D: Cardiovascular diseases like strokes and heart attacks were found in 2013 by the World Health Organization (WHO) to cause 17.3 million deaths yearly. Diabetes (A) was found to cause 1.3 million deaths yearly. Cancers (B) were found to cause 7.6 million deaths annually. Respiratory (C) diseases like asthma and chronic obstructive pulmonary diseases (COPD) were found to cause 4.2 million deaths a year. Thus (D), (B), (C), and (A) is the order of most to least causes of mortality, with (D) far exceeding all the others.

28. A: Unsafe water is a risk factor for many diseases, but not for all four types of diseases listed. Drinking alcohol, poor nutrition, and smoking tobacco are all risk factors shared in common by all four types of illnesses that cause the majority of deaths from noncommunicable diseases.

29. B: The World Health Organization (WHO) projects that, by 2030, noncommunicable diseases will cause more deaths in African countries than communicable diseases (A), nutritional diseases, infant mortality from childbirth (C), and maternal mortality from childbirth (D) combined.

30. D: Current (2014) research finds that exercising in temperatures up to 62 to 65 degrees Fahrenheit maximum increases the odds of producing and activating healthy brown fat, which promotes building lean muscle tissue and burning more calories and keeps the internal organs warm. New research suggests brown fat may enhance glucose control and decrease insulin resistance. Studies find whole foods effective as opposed to supplements (A) for controlling blood sugar and weight because vegetables and fruits contain enzymes that activate antioxidants the body needs for controlling blood sugar and weight (as well as preventing cancers). Supplements lack these enzymes. A meta-analysis of multiple studies recently found people 28 percent more apt to develop diabetes when sleeping below 5 to 6 hours nightly, compared to those sleeping 6 to 8 hours. Insulin sensitivity also improved greatly in people who slept 6 hours on weeknights but caught up by sleeping 10 hours on weekend nights (B). Studies also show stress raises levels of the hormone cortisol and of inflammatory cytokines, which both cause insulin resistance (C).

31. B: Health educators can teach students to take four basic steps following poor decisions: (1) They should admit their mistakes rather than hiding them (A). (2) They should avoid continuing actions based on the poor decision (C). (3) They should tell their parents of the poor decision and follow their guidance for correcting it (B) because parents are ultimately responsible for guiding children in making better decisions. (4) Apologizing is not always enough to correct the harm done (D) by a poor decision. Students also may need to redress losses or damages caused by their decision, for example, volunteering their time or effort, replacing something, or paying for something.

32. A: The first step that health educators can teach their students to take for setting their health goals is to write down their long-term and short-term health goals. Educators can help students who do not know their health goals by suggesting possibilities. The second step they can teach students is to create and write down action plans, which describe in detail what steps they will take to achieve their health goals (B). Educators can review plans and advise students whether they are realistic. The third step is to identify potential obstacles to realizing these action plans (D). Educators should instruct students to prioritize these obstacles and help them brainstorm ways to address those with the highest priority. The fourth step is to have students write down time lines with specific dates when they aim to achieve their health goals (C) and help them evaluate how realistic these are.

33. B: Students can use journals, diaries, charts, or graphs to keep track of their progress toward their health goals and ensure accountability. Asking friends to help or forming a club (A) is related to developing a support system for meeting health goals. When students give themselves healthy rewards for meeting their goals (C), this is related to positive reinforcement. Revising their action plans or time lines (D) is related to ensuring success in meeting health goals by adjusting the means or time by which they need to achieve them.

34. A: Cardiorespiratory endurance is best defined as the ability to perform dynamic, that is, movement, exercise rather than static (C) or passive exercise using the large, that is, limb and trunk muscles, not small (B) muscles like those in the hands and feet, or both large and small, that is, all muscles (C), or any muscles (D) for extended time periods. Cardiorespiratory means involving the heart and breathing. Endurance requires long, not short (B), average (C), or any (D) durations.

35. D: Enhancing flexibility provides a variety of benefits. It not only improves sports performance (A), but it also prevents sports injuries; makes functioning in everyday life easier (B); rehabilitates soft tissue injuries (C); prevents stiffness and soreness after exercising; relieves both general and specific muscular tightness, muscle spasms, and lower-back pain; decreases future problems; and relieves headaches caused by muscle tension.

36. B: FITT is an acronym for frequency, that is, how often one exercises; intensity, that is, how hard one exercises; time, that is, how long one exercises; and type, that is, what kind of exercise one does. It does not refer to general physical fitness (A) but rather these specific dimensions of exercising. It encompasses not only aerobic capacity (C) but also muscular strength (D), body fat percentage, and weight, which change for the better when one applies sufficient and appropriate variables of frequency, intensity, time, and type for one's individual physiology, body composition, fitness level, skill levels, mental disposition, and preferences.

37. A: Legumes, that is, beans, split peas, and lentils, are classified in both the vegetables and the proteins food groups by the U.S. Department of Agriculture (cf. ChooseMyPlate.gov) because they have much higher protein content than other vegetables. Seafood (B) is in the protein food group only. Cheese (C) is in the dairy food group only. Eggplant (D) is in the vegetable food group only.

38. C: Carbohydrates in our diet (e.g., from fruits, vegetables, and grains) are sources whereby our bodies make glucose, which supplies energy. Our bodies get amino acids, which they use to repair cells, muscle and other tissue, and organs by breaking down protein in our diet (e.g., from meats, poultry, seafood, dairy, and beans). Our bodily functions require 20 to 35 percent of our diet from fats but not saturated fat (D). Unsaturated fats are healthier for the heart, blood vessels, body composition, weight, and organs.

39. C: For optimal exercising, experts recommend that our nutrition should be 55 percent from carbohydrates, 15 percent from protein, and 30 percent from fat. One-third from each category (A) would not provide enough carbohydrates for sufficient energy; would have too much protein to allow optimal movement by diverting too much energy and blood flow toward digestion; and slightly more fat than is optimal for energy to move. Choice (B) would also provide too much protein, too few carbs, and slightly less than optimal fat for exercise. Choice (D) would provide adequate fat but too much protein and too few carbs for exercising.

40. A: One common unhealthy reaction to stress is pain, for example, headaches, backaches, stomach aches, muscular aches from unconsciously tensing or clenching muscles, and other physical symptoms. People are far more likely to being or resume using substances than quit using them in reaction to stress. Changes in eating are also common reactions to stress: Some individuals overeat and gain weight, while others skip eating and lose weight (B). Anger and crying are also equally common reactions (C). Symptoms of anxiety, depression, or both are also common unhealthy reactions to stress (D).

41. D: Not getting a sufficient quantity or quality of sleep impairs physiological and neurological repair, dreaming, the immune system, and normal judgment. It also makes stress worse and causes people to overreact to minor problems. Thus, adequate sleep is necessary for reducing and managing stress. Cutting back activity when one is overextended does help to manage stress (A). Being prepared by setting realistic goals, scheduling better, and allowing time for unexpected life events is also recommended for stress management (B). Relaxation techniques like physical activity, progressive muscle relaxation, massage therapy, yoga, meditation, and so on not only relieve body tension; they also alleviate mental stress (C).

42. B: Carefully weighing and evaluating the pros and cons of a stressful life situation facilitates making decisions that aid coping with stress and most reflects the decision-making life skill. Considering the positive aspects of the situation (A) most reflects the life skill of values clarification. Expressing feelings about the situation (C) most reflects the life skill of communication skills. Engaging in positive behaviors that raise self-esteem or develop interests to enable dealing with the situation (D) most reflects the life skill of coping skills.

43. C: The World Health Organization (WHO) finds raising prices and taxes for tobacco does encourage quitting smoking and discourage starting, particularly by the poor and young, and is cost-effective. WHO also finds the graphic warnings on cigarette and tobacco packages do dissuade people from smoking (A), as do creative media campaigns (in spite of limited health resources and powerful tobacco company opposition). These measures are also cost-effective. So are enforced smoke-free laws in public places and policies in workplaces: Rather than going outside for smoke breaks (B), more smokers comply with these rules and quit, and fewer youth start. When public and private health care providers offer smoking cessation therapy, these are affordable (D) and effective. So are public information and education. These methods have been provided to the minority of the world, yet WHO research finds all global nations can afford them.

44. A: Multiple research studies repeatedly demonstrate that cardiovascular diseases, diabetes, and colon and breast cancer risks are lowered by regular physical activity (PA). Researchers recommend 30 to 60 minutes a day of PA to reduce the risks of breast and colon cancer significantly, and 150 minutes a week to decrease risks of cardiovascular diseases and diabetes. Thirty minutes a day for five days a week equals 150 minutes a week; therefore, the amounts needed are similar to lower the risks of these diseases. (Sixty minutes is double this and may afford some people greater cancer risk reduction.) Hence, risks for all these diseases are lowered, not some. The amounts necessary to reduce risk do not vary greatly among these diseases. Regular PA in adequate amounts does lower disease risk.

45. B: World Health Organization (WHO) research finds restricting the community concentrations of stores selling alcohol and the amounts of time when it is sold effective in decreasing harmful alcohol use. WHO also recommends the following as effective: government regulation of alcohol availability and minimum legal ages for purchasing it; where possible, government monopoly of retail alcohol sales; comprehensive bans on advertising alcohol; marketing regulations restricting exposure to alcohol advertising and sales; lower limits on blood alcohol concentrations for drivers; zero tolerance or lowered limits for younger drivers; random breathalyzer tests; sobriety checkpoints; brief interventions against harmful or dangerous drinking; and alcohol use disorder treatments. However, research has not found (A), (C), or (D) similarly effective. Researchers do say, though, that informational and educational campaigns supporting the more effective methods can encourage the public to accept them.

46. D: The masseter muscles in the sides of the face connect the jaws and control their chewing functions. The temporalis muscles in the side of the head also are involved in chewing. The orbicularis oris muscle (A) encircles the mouth and is used to make facial expressions, open and close the mouth and pucker the lips to kiss, and blow trumpets and other musical horns, but not to chew. The zygomaticus major and minor muscles (B) are in the cheekbones, running between the cheek below the eye and the corners of the mouth; they control smiling, not chewing. The trapezius muscles (C) are large, triangular muscles extending from the neck, across each shoulder, and down the upper back and thus not in the jaws or face.

47. C: In both females and males, the brain's hypothalamus stimulates the pituitary gland to secrete luteinizing hormone (LH) and follicle-stimulating hormone (FSH). In females, these two hormones stimulate the ovaries to produce estrogen; in males, they stimulate the testes to produce testosterone. Hence, female and male organs are stimulated by the same hormones, not by separate hormones for each (A). LH and FSH, the hormones that stimulate the male and female sexual organs, are not the same as estrogen and testosterone, which respectively stimulate the male and female organs to produce these sex hormones (B). The pituitary gland does not secrete these (D); it secretes LH and FSH.

48. C: White blood cells are known as lymphocytes, a clue to the fact that they function in the lymphatic system to produce antibodies and destroy virally affected or foreign cells. While they are also found within the circulatory (B) system, that is, in the bloodstream, they do not function there but are only in transit from the bone marrow to the lymphatic system. The endocrine (D) system includes the pancreas, male testes, female ovaries and uterus, and all of the body's glands, which secrete hormones regulating bodily function, metabolism, and growth.

49. A: Gum disease can develop when oral bacteria build up due to poor oral hygiene and can cause serious heart valve disorders when the bacteria travel from the gums directly to the heart. Unhealthy gums cannot only lead to periodontal (gum) infections; they also can cause loosening and loss of teeth (B). While flossing and gum massage are important for preventing gum disease, brushing the teeth also prevents both tooth decay and gum disease (C). Gum disease not only affects the soft tissues of the gums but also causes irreversible bone loss in the jaw (D).

50. D: One reason a person may neglect personal hygiene is from underlying depression. This is particularly applicable if the neglect is unaccustomed for the individual. However, some people are not depressed and may neglect their personal hygiene out of preoccupation with other things (B). Other people may neglect their personal hygiene out of a lack of awareness (C), particularly if their neglect is habitual rather than a new development.

51. A: At least 80 percent of adolescents develop acne. This is not due to inadequate or incorrect facial skin care but to hormonal changes. Health educators should inform teen students how to treat and not treat acne. Hormonal changes in puberty also frequently make teens' hair oilier, so they are likely to need to shampoo it more often (B). Many teenagers have to wear braces, which makes oral hygiene more complicated and challenging; additionally, fresh breath becomes more important to them in adolescence. Therefore, the same oral hygiene they practiced in childhood usually will not suffice (C). Hormonal changes also cause increased perspiration, so adolescents need to bathe more often than in childhood (D).

52. B: A common misconception among teenagers is that only vaginal penetration and ejaculation will cause pregnancy. Health educators should inform them that small drops of pre-ejaculate they may not detect can be released before as well as during sex. Pre-ejaculate also contains sperm; males cannot control its release; and vulvar contact alone can cause conception. Thus, there is a smaller but real chance of impregnating a girl without penetrating or ejaculating inside her vagina [a reason to do (C)]. Choices (A), (C), and (D) are all facts, not misconceptions, of which health educators can inform teens.

53. C: The National Council on Alcoholism and Drug Dependence, Inc. (NCADD) estimates that 32 percent of fatal auto crashes involve a driver's or pedestrian's alcohol intoxication; that is, nearly one-third, not over 50 percent (A) but considerably more than 25 percent (B), (D). This causes almost 13,000 annual deaths, hundreds of thousands more injuries, and costs taxpayers over $100 billion.

54. A: Advice for preventing sexual assault includes parking in open, well-lighted areas and checking backseats before getting into parked vehicles, even if they were locked. Even confident individuals are advised to avoid jogging or walking alone in secluded areas at night (B), which raises assault risk and decreases chances of getting help. It does help to project senses of awareness, confidence, strength, and security (C) in surroundings where other people may be. Experts also advice assault victims not to remain passive but to resist the attack actively (D), including loudly screaming or blowing a rape whistle.

55. A: The seriousness of health risks from smoking cigarettes is driven home by the statistic that it causes more deaths in America every year than alcohol use, drug use, car accidents, human immunodeficiency virus (HIV), and gunshots combined—that is, around one in five people, exceeding 480,000. Another statistic to put smoking deaths in perspective is that they equal more than ten times the number of all casualties of war in American history. Moreover, one of every three deaths from cancer in America is caused by smoking.

56. C: The short-term effects of regular, substantial alcohol use include impaired judgment (A); distortion of perceptions, vision and hearing (B), and emotions; impaired coordination; bad breath; and hangovers. The long-term effects of heavy alcohol use include liver damage, sexual impotence, stomach disorders (D), vitamin deficiencies, skin problems, loss of appetite, loss of memory, damage to the heart and entire cardiovascular system, and damage to the central nervous system (C).

57. B: Emergencies that warrant 911 calls are identified as any situations needing immediate help from the police, a fire department, or an ambulance. People should call 911 not only for uncontrollable bleeding or unconsciousness but also for allergic reactions, which can be fatal; for chest pains (A), which can indicate heart attacks; and if someone is not breathing or having trouble breathing. Prank calls to 911 are not only nuisances and interfere with actual emergencies; they are also illegal (C) in most U.S. states and subject to law enforcement. When a person calls 911 in an emergency, he or she should not hang up until instructed to do so by the call taker, who will first need to get information from or give instructions to the caller.

58. D: As described by Dr. Murray Bowen in his Family Systems Theory, the pattern of marital conflict involves both spouses' projecting their escalating anxieties into their relationship. The pattern of emotional distance (A) occurs in relation to the other three patterns, as family members seek to escape the excessive intensity of their interactions by withdrawing emotionally. The pattern of impairment of one or more children (B) involves the parents' projecting their anxiety by focusing excessively on the child(ren). Dysfunction in one spouse (C) results when one partner becomes overly dominant and hyperfunctional, while the other becomes overly dependent and dysfunctional in response. This pattern can emerge out of the pattern of marital conflict.

59. B: This scenario describes the relationship pattern involving impairment of one or more children. The parent projecting anxiety onto the child becomes overly concerned that something is wrong with the child; this becomes a self-fulfilling prophecy as the child comes to believe something is indeed wrong with him or her and behaves accordingly. The dysfunction in one spouse (A) pattern involves one spouse overcompensating for, criticizing, and dominating the other, who becomes more dependent and dysfunctional in response. The emotional distance pattern (C) involves emotional withdrawal or isolation by one or more family members when their interactions with others become too intense for comfort. The marital conflict pattern (D) involves projection of their unmanageable personal anxiety by both partners into their marital relationship.

60. B: The big five personality traits are extraversion, agreeableness, conscientiousness, neuroticism, and openness. All people are said to possess some greater or lesser degree of each along a continuum; for example, very introverted (A) people are low in extraversion; very irresponsible people are low in conscientiousness; very emotionally stable individuals are low in neuroticism, and so on. Detail-orientation (A) is a characteristic of conscientiousness. Kindness (A) is a characteristic of agreeableness. Assertiveness (D) is a characteristic of extraversion. Prosocial behaviors (D) are characteristic of agreeableness. Good impulse control (D) is characteristic of conscientiousness. Moodiness (D) is characteristic of neuroticism. Imagination (D) is characteristic of openness. Oral, anal, phallic, latency, and genital traits or tendencies (C) are concepts from Freud's psychosexual theory of personality, not the big five trait theory of personality.

61. C: Two main principles of Hobfoll's Conservation of Resources (COR) Theory are (1) that losing resources has proportionately more impact than gaining resources and (2) that people must invest resources to gain resources, prevent losing them, or recover from losing them. Corollary 1 is that people with more resources are more able to gain more and less likely to lose resources, contradicting (A) and that people with fewer resources are conversely less able to gain and more likely to lose resources. Corollary 2 is that initial loss causes future loss (C). Corollary 3 is that initial gain causes future gain, contradicting (D). Corollary 4 is that lacking resources causes defensive conservation of existing ones, contradicting (B).

62. A: Research has found that, although teachers do have difficulty relating to children with attention deficit hyperactivity disorder (ADHD), this does not mean they cannot change peer dislike of these children (B). Peers do tend to continue rejecting ADHD children based on their existing negative reputations, even after those children improve their behavior, but this also does not mean teachers cannot affect this (C). Teachers who create classroom environments that promote better peer relationships do not eliminate all dislike of ADHD children (D), which classmates continue to display; however, they do influence peer interactions to enable more variation and less consistent dislike.

63. D: According to research findings, adolescents must have practice with making decisions in real life to transfer the cognitive skills they have acquired for decision making to reality. Studies identify that variables influencing teen decision-making skills include their levels of conformity with parental or peer norms (A); demographic characteristics like age, race, ethnicity, gender, social class; and family dynamics, family structure, and personal characteristics like intelligence and temperance as well (B). Research also shows that adolescents tend to be more oriented to the present and short-term consequences and goals and need to be taught future orientation, long-term goals (C), and planning.

64. D: According to most decision-making models, the first skill adolescents must apply is to define the decision that they will need to make. Next they must educate themselves by gathering information and generate potential alternatives (C). Then they must evaluate the possible consequences of each option (A) and estimate how desirable or undesirable and how likely each consequence is. Next they must choose an option from those they have considered, make a plan for the decision they have chosen, and execute that plan. Finally, they must evaluate the decision they made and the results (B) it produced.

65. B: Because the social contexts in which teenagers make decisions are subject frequent change, they must learn to evaluate and adjust those decisions in response to such changes. A challenging paradox for teens is that the decisions they make are frequently critical, with long-term consequences affecting their futures (A); yet they commonly lack enough life experience to inform these decisions (C). Research has found intervention programs to improve teen decision-making skills effective (D) in enhancing positive, responsible, prosocial, constructive and self-sufficient behaviors and decreasing negative, irresponsible, antisocial, destructive and self-destructive behaviors.

66. C: Teenagers' decisions are influenced by both internal variables (A), like self-concept and locus of control, and external variables (D), like their relationships with their parents and friends. They do not make decisions in isolated conditions (B); rather, their decision-making is influenced by the feedback they receive (C).

67. A: The ability to apply humor and playfulness to alleviate stress during interactions (B); the ability to apply nonverbal communication effectively (C) for interacting positively with others by both conveying one's intentions and reading others' signals; the ability to control or decrease stress quickly during interactions; and the ability to recognize and manage one's own feelings (D) all inform the ability to manage conflicts with positivity and confidence (A).

68. A: Emotional intelligence (EQ) affects physical as well as mental health and school or work performance as well as relationships (B). Abilities to use nonverbal communication enable a person to relate to others emotionally, helping to develop EQ (C). Humor enables a person to sustain interpersonal relations despite challenges, supporting rather than derailing EQ and recognizing one's own emotions and not becoming overwhelmed by them (D).

69. C: Piaget's theory identifies progressive stages of cognitive development; hence, it focuses most on intellectual development. While cognitive development interacts with and affects emotional development (A), relationship development (B), and the development of independence (D), and Piaget does explain how it does, his primary concern is how the intellect develops from birth to adulthood.

70. A: During the latest part of the sensorimotor stage, from around 18 to 24 months of age, Piaget said children develop early representational thought when they begin using symbols to represent other things, like playing make-believe by pretending to be adults or fictional characters and using objects to represent other things or beings, for example, pretending a broom is a horse, a block is a phone, and so on. This is the first instance of mental operations. In the preoperational stage (B), children display more intuitive than logical thinking. Though capable of basic mental operations, they do not perform logical ones. In concrete operations (C), they begin performing logical mental operations but only concerning concrete objects or events. In formal operations (D), they begin performing mental operations that are abstract as well as logical.

71. B: Erikson's is a theory of psychosocial development, and his most famous book is titled *Childhood and Society*. His developmental theory focuses most on an individual's relationship with society, not with self (A) or other individuals (C). Erikson did not focus as primarily on the child–parent relationship as Freud did. While he used the child's relationship with parents in earlier stages of development as a basis for the individual's subsequent relationship with society, he did not focus on the relationship with parents exclusively (D) but on the developing individual's increasing relationship to society.

72. B: Erikson described the nuclear conflict of infancy as basic trust versus mistrust: A baby whose needs are met fully and consistently develops trust in the world, while a baby whose needs are inadequately or inconsistently met develops mistrust. Erikson found that the positive outcome of this stage was hope. He identified will (A) as the positive outcome of successfully resolving the nuclear conflict of autonomy versus shame and self-doubt during toddlerhood. He identified purpose (C) as the positive outcome of successfully resolving the nuclear conflict of initiative versus guilt during the preschool years. He identified competence (D) as the positive outcome of successfully resolving the nuclear conflict of industry versus Inferiority during the elementary school years.

73. A: Erikson identified a nuclear conflict to be resolved in each stage of psychosocial development. Babies confront basic trust versus mistrust, toddlers autonomy (D) versus shame and self-doubt, preschoolers initiative versus guilt, school-aged children industry (C) versus inferiority, adolescents identity (A) versus role confusion, young adults intimacy (B) versus isolation, middle adults generativity versus stagnation, and older adults integrity versus despair.

74. D: Task goals (A) involve the official purpose of a conversation, for example, discussing who will be responsible for making decisions on behalf of an aging parent when the parent is no longer capable of doing so. Identity goals (B) involve protecting the identities of both or all parties in the conversation; for example, when family members feel caring and responsible for bringing up the aforementioned subject, while the parent feels able to have continuing autonomy in spite of failing health. Relationship goals (C) involve maintaining interpersonal connections; for example, the closeness of family members in the example given enables their open discussion of a challenging subject. Conversations that present both the greatest cognitive challenge and the highest quality (by combining seeing others' perspectives and accomplishing their own goals) incorporate all three of these goals (D) at the same time.

75. B: Researchers find that, over time, avoiding discussion of important issues causes stress, damaging health and well-being, rather than affording more control over them (A). Instead, they find we attain more control over problems when we can explain them (B). Studies also find we overestimate the outcomes of sensitive discussions, which are emotionally safer and have more productive outcomes than we expect (C). Investigators also find quality supersedes quantity of discussion (D); that is, more is not better. They also find discussing important issues in the wrong way (e.g., by emphasizing quantity over quality) can cause more harm than not discussing them at all.

76. A: Because most of us are very familiar with the advice to use "I" statements during difficult interpersonal discussions, psychologists warn us not to do this automatically but authentically as a reflection of genuinely taking responsibility for having, expressing, and resolving hurt feelings even when they are not our fault. Experts also note the importance of empathy for others to balance honesty (B) during difficult discussions. They warn us not to bring up sensitive subjects while we are upset about them (C), despite our inclination to do so. We can communicate more effectively when we are calmer and have more perspective. Gaining perspective is also often aided by injecting some humor, which is not always inappropriate (D).

77. D: Studies have shown that, when people repress their emotions and thoughts too much, their medical conditions become worse. For example, people with irritable bowel syndrome experienced exacerbated symptoms when they habitually avoided talking about difficult subjects, and people's cancer became worse when their families avoided discussing it. Experts advise that, in romantic relationships, although people should share information to understand one another, there is definitely such a thing as too much information (A) to be beneficial. They also observe that relationships can be ruined when people constantly share every single criticism and stressor (B) that occurs to them. Research shows people withholding information for self-protection feel less satisfied than those doing so to protect their relationships (C).

78. B: Experts recommend that it is less threatening to use a less personal instance of the topic of dying, like a TV news story about a coma patient or a living will, as a springboard for discussing an aging parent's feelings about end-of-life decisions rather than bringing up such a subject at a family celebration like Christmas dinner, Easter brunch (A), birthday parties, and so on. Experts also advise families not to wait until an aging parent is diagnosed with terminal illness (C) or about to die (D) but rather to start discussing these matters well in advance and continue talking about them regularly and frequently.

79. C: People cannot possibly agree about everything all the time. Therefore, in any relationship between or among people, conflict is inevitable, and it is normal and integral to a healthy relationship rather than a sign that the relationship is not healthy (A). Although people tend to find conflict unpleasant, this is not a good reason to avoid it (B). People also should not avoid confrontation just because they feel threatened by it (D). Conflicts provoking strong feelings are signs of deep personal needs that must be addressed. When people are willing to acknowledge their conflicting needs, examine them with compassion, and solve problems creatively, they can improve their relationships through managing conflict positively and respectfully, whereas avoiding conflict is more likely to damage relationships.

80. B: Whether it is real or imagined, when a threat is perceived by one or more persons in a situation, this defines a conflict, which experts say is not simply a disagreement (A). An additional characteristic of conflicts is that they present opportunities for the people involved to experience growth (C) when they succeed in resolving them, which builds interpersonal trust. Conflicts will not go away if people ignore them (D) because the threats people perceive that trigger conflicts are to their survival and welfare. Hence, they will continue indefinitely or until the relationship ends if they are ignored.

81. A: In responding to inevitable conflicts, experts find it healthier to see the reciprocal benefits of directly confronting them than to avoid conflicts for fear of negative outcomes (C). They find people who remain calm, show respect for others, and avoid defensiveness manage conflict more healthily than those who react emotionally by exploding, venting anger (B), expressing resentment, or intentionally hurting others' feelings. Being able and willing to compromise is a healthier response to conflict than refusing to see others' viewpoints (D).

82. D: Assertiveness is characterized as neither passive (A) nor aggressive (B) in nature and also as not being a combination of the two (C). Instead, it entails responding in a balanced way that both respects the needs of others and clearly and appropriately expresses one's own needs. Passive responses avoid responsibility, allowing others to control one; aggressive responses are pushy, controlling others. Assertive responses do neither but acknowledge mutual rights, responsibilities, beliefs, and feelings.

83. C: Experts advise children and teens particularly to use refusal strategies when others try to pressure them, including walking away from the situation (A); standing up for others who are being pressured (B); proposing alternatives to whatever unwanted activity others are pressuring them to engage in (C); and not being overly aggressive when saying "no" (D).

84. A: Learning how to effectively interact with others is extremely important to a child's understanding of theatre. In order to fully grasp effective interaction, one must develop certain skills, such as listening, reacting, engaging in meaningful eye contact, and taking note of prompts from other performers. Performance, rehearsal, and role playing are great methods for honing interaction skills, but a student must understand the basic fundamentals of effective interaction before they can perform these activities.

85. A: Some individuals who are transgender psychologically identify with the gender opposite to their physiological gender throughout their lives. Thus, sexual or gender identity does not necessarily match physical sex (B). People who cross-dress are not necessarily transgender or homosexual (C); many people who are comfortable with their physiological genders engage in cross-dressing. A person's sexual orientation, for example, heterosexual, homosexual, lesbian, or bisexual, is not the same as the person's sexual expression (D), which consists of external behaviors and characteristics that variable cultural and social norms define as feminine or masculine.

86. C: None of these is correct. Neither a condom nor a spermicide by itself is effective enough (A); the two should be used in combination. Vasectomy is often reversible, but not every time; tubal ligation is often reversible, but not in every case (B). While some women may ask a physician to insert a diaphragm for them, at least initially, they usually insert diaphragms themselves prior to intercourse once they have learned how. However, intrauterine devices (IUDs) are inserted for long-term use by physicians and removed by physicians as needed. Women swallow birth control pills orally rather than inserting them (D).

87. B: In abusive relationships, when an abuser apologizes and acts normal, he or she is not genuinely sorry and does not intend to change (A). Rather, he or she is manipulating the victim to get him or her to stay in the relationship and to regain control of the victim so he or she can abuse him or her again (B). Abusers may blame the victim for causing the abuse, or they may apologize, which is not a sign the victim can believe him or her (C). In spite of apologies, the abuser is likely to repeat the abuse (D).

88. D: Destroying the victim's property is an example of domestic abusers' typical tactics of intimidation, which they use to frighten victims into submission by indicating the violent consequences they will suffer if they do not comply with the abuser. Examples of isolation (A) include cutting their victims off from contact with family and friends to make the victims dependent on the abusers. Examples of humiliation (B) include making victims feel worthless, undermining their self-esteem by shaming them both in private and public. Examples of dominance (C) include giving their victims orders, treating them like children, servants, slaves, or even possessions and expecting them to comply unquestioningly.

89. A: Constantly reporting one's locations and activities to the partner is a sign of being domestically abused as well as appearing desperate to please the partner; agreeing with all the partner's words and actions; often receiving harassing partner contacts; and mentioning partner possessiveness, jealousy, or temper. Often exhibiting or trying to hide injuries or excusing them as accidents (B) or clumsiness is a sign of being physically abused. Marked personality and behavioral changes (C) are psychological symptoms of being abused. Making few or no public outings, use of the car or money, or visits with friends and family (D) are signs of being isolated by an abuser.

90. D: Exercise not only promotes physical fitness; it is also powerful for relieving stress, depression, and anxiety and elevating the mood. Smoking cigarettes and drinking alcohol may improve the mood in the short term, but in the long term, they impair mood and mental and emotional health (A). Getting the adequate quantity and quality of sleep and nutrition for individual needs has significant positive impacts on mental and emotional health; the lack thereof has significant negative impacts (B). While prolonged sun exposure without sunscreen can cause skin cancer, daily exposure to 10 to 15 minutes of sunshine is enough to improve mood and not long enough to cause significant skin damage or cancer (C).

91. B: It has been found that people have biological predispositions to some mental and emotional health risks and also that environmental influences interact with these to create risk factors. Attachment theory has been supported, not disproven, as a risk factor in mental and emotional health (A): Having insecure attachment to parents or caregivers in infancy or early childhood constitutes a mental and emotional health risk factor. Early childhood experiences are found to be among the most influential as risk factors in adulthood (C). Substance abuse both causes new mental and emotional health disorders and also exacerbates existing disorders (D).

92. D: If an individual has insomnia, not just occasionally but persistently (A); feels sad, depressed, discouraged, or hopeless more of the time than not (B); or has enough difficulty concentrating to impede home or work functioning (C), these are signs that the person should probably consult a mental health professional. Uncontrollable fears, negative thinking, or self-destructive thoughts are additional signs. Preoccupation with death and suicidal ideations are also warning signals to seek professional help. Qualified professionals can help when self-help measures cannot.

93. D: A credible source communication strategy targets individuals, policy makers, and the public in its communications to increase awareness and potentially change behavior. A media advocacy strategy (A) targets policy makers and the public, but not individuals, to change norms and policies. A social marketing strategy (B) targets individuals, but not policy makers or the public, to change people's personal behaviors. A risk communication strategy (C) targets individuals, institutions, and the public, but not policy makers, to raise individual awareness and health recommendation compliance.

94. D: Legally, the U.S. Secretary of the Department of Health and Human Services is responsible for preventing communicable diseases from being introduced, transmitted, and spread in the country. The authority for fulfilling the secretary's responsibility is delegated to the U.S. Division of Global Migration and Quarantine by establishing medical examination standards for people coming to America, administering foreign and interstate quarantine regulations, and operating quarantine stations at ports of entry to the United States.

95. B: There are no federal laws in the United States concerning immunizations required for children to enter public schools (A). These laws vary from state to state (B). However, all 50 U.S. states do have such laws (C). Because the laws vary by state, the U.S. Centers for Disease Control and Prevention (CDC) does offer a database of all state immunization laws (D) for schools, hospitals, health care facilities, provider practices, child care providers, long-term care facilities, facilities for the developmentally disabled, and correctional facilities.

96. A: Recycling manufactured products reduces waste sent to incinerators and landfills; saves energy used in manufacturing, transportation, and incineration; reduces emissions of greenhouse gases that contribute to climate change; conserves natural resources by not depleting as many of them to manufacture new products; and creates new jobs in a country's manufacturing and recycling industries.

97. C: The Environmental Protection Agency (EPA) first developed standards, laws, and regulations to address environmental pollution during the 1970s, not the 1980s (A). Its focus shifted from remediation in the 1970s toward prevention in the 1980s and 1990s, not the 2000s (B). In 1990, Congress's national policy to prevent and reduce pollution was declared in the Pollution Prevention Act (C). This law called for the national policy to shift away from emphasizing treatment and disposal and toward emphasizing source reduction, not vice versa (D).

98. B: Buildings that use electricity, including private homes, offices, warehouses, and shopping malls, produce the most carbon dioxide (CO_2) emissions in the United States. Transportation by vehicles that burn gasoline (A) is the second-largest producer of CO_2 emissions. Manufacturing industries (C) are the third largest. Therefore, (D) is incorrect.

99. C: The mobile applications industry projects that 500 million people in the world will use health care apps on smartphones by 2015, and half of all smartphone and tablet users will have downloaded health apps by 2018. (A) and (B) have far smaller estimates than these; (D) has larger ones.

100. C: In many U.S. states, physician assistants (PAs) can prescribe medications as physicians can. However, PAs can assist with surgical procedures but do not perform surgery as MD surgeons do. Registered nurses (A) and medical assistants do not prescribe medications. Pharmacists, who have a doctor of pharmacy (D) degree, fill prescriptions but do not write them.

101. C: Both the American Red Cross and Planned Parenthood are national nonprofit agencies with local chapters or centers. The American Red Cross provides babysitter's training to 11- to 15-year-olds (A). Planned Parenthood provides reproductive health care services (B) like family planning, birth control, gynecological care, cancer screenings, sexually transmitted disease (STD) testing and treatment, medical and surgical abortions, midlife services, pregnancy testing and education and information, education, and advocacy about responsible human sexuality and voluntary reproductive health care. The American Red Cross provides training in emergency procedures (D) like first aid techniques, cardiopulmonary resuscitation (CPR), automated external defibrillator (AED) use, bleeding control; what to do in the event of seizures, choking, and other medical emergencies until emergency medical technicians (EMTs) arrive; and course instructor training. The American Red Cross also offers swimming safety training.

102. B: The original impetus for the National Health Education Standards (NHES) was that health education, physical education, public health, and school health authorities observed standards being developed for other subject-area content in education (B) and decided that the subject area of health education needed similar standards developed. Health educators were not influenced by standards developed in hospitals (A), public health (C) agencies, or private medical practice (D).

103. A: The federal Healthy People 2000 initiative had as its main goal to decrease health disparities in America. The Healthy People 2010 initiative made its main goal to eliminate those disparities rather than just decrease them. The Healthy People 2020 initiative established goals not only to eliminate health disparities but moreover to establish health equity and improve health for all Americans.

104. B: Health organizations find radio more cost-effective than TV for mass media campaigns, not only because it costs less but also because people can listen to radio but not watch TV at work and while driving as well as at home. Also, people in rural areas without electricity typically do not have TV sets but commonly do have battery-operated radios (C). Moreover, research studies find that, even months after listening to radio broadcasts, Americans have surprisingly accurate retention of the information they heard, thus they do not necessarily retain information better from TV than radio (A). Print and digital media are also ways of disseminating mass health information and education, but they have not been found superior to radio or TV (D) as even illiterate people who cannot read printed messages on paper or computer screens can still absorb information by listening to radio or watching TV.

105. C: Professional meetings and conferences are excellent settings for health education advocacy but are more for educators and other professionals as target audiences because they typically exclude students, other than graduate students pursuing education credentials and student teachers. Primary and secondary school students typically are not invited to these events. Health fairs are ideal venues for health education advocacy in both schools and communities (A) due to their formats, which include indoor and outdoor activities; healthy picnic foods; information tables; interactive displays; presentations from local chefs, celebrities, medical personnel, broadcasters, and so on; contests; and family attendance. Health fairs need not be cost prohibitive for schools (D): Educators and parents can solicit donations of tables, equipment, materials, food, prizes, and so on from local organizations and businesses. School assemblies can include entertaining formats (B); for example, Jill Jayne's *Jump with Jill*, an interactive instructional program using original rock-and-roll music, professional sound and lighting, costumes appealing to youngsters, and student audience participation, has received high marks from educators and students alike for both entertaining and educating students, faculty, and parents.

106. D: When developing processes to integrate health education across the curriculum of school subjects, health educators function as liaisons among teachers of other subjects, school administrators, curriculum coordinators, and students. They function as liaisons between trainees and students (A) when they train others to implement health education. They function as liaisons between administrators and students (B) when, for example, they request resources from administrators to help them meet learning goals and objectives for students. They function as liaisons between the school and the research community (C) when they develop and conduct research.

107. C: The idea that saturated fat in the diet contributes to heart disease is an abstract concept. This would be most appropriate to teach to students in Piaget's stage of formal operations (typically preadolescent and adolescent ages), who can understand abstract concepts. Babies in Piaget's sensorimotor (A) stage and toddlers in Piaget's preoperational (B) stage cannot grasp abstract concepts. Preschoolers are best taught using single, simple subjects one at a time and intuitive or animistic ideas. Middle childhood students in Piaget's concrete operations (D) stage can think logically and perform mental operations but only related to concrete objects and events; they still have not developed the facility for comprehending completely abstract ideas that emerge during the formal operations stage. They are best taught using concrete illustrations of food groups, digestion and energy processes, the food chain cycle, weight gain and loss, and so on rather than future nutritional benefits or abstract relationships.

108. A: Students high in Gardner's interpersonal intelligence style learn best through social interactions with others. Those high in intrapersonal (B) intelligence prefer to be alone and would not learn best through group activities. Those high in visual-spatial (C) intelligence learn best through visual instructional activities and materials, for example, looking at, using, and making drawings, charts, graphs, photos, images, models, videos, multimedia, illustrations, and jigsaw puzzles and using videoconferencing and TV. Those high in logical-mathematical (D) intelligence learn best through solving mysteries and puzzles, conducting experiments, learning and formulating concepts, learning and applying logic, identifying and exploring patterns and relationships, and performing calculations.

109. D: Pretesting establishes a baseline of student knowledge before instruction. This enables teachers to determine where their instruction should begin (A) without teaching what students already know or skipping over things they have not learned yet. Teachers also can use student baseline information to compare with later student knowledge, which enables them to evaluate the effectiveness of their instruction (B). Additionally, they can use this information to monitor student progress during instruction (formative assessment) and assess student learning following instruction (summative assessment) (C).

110. B: *Explain* is an observable behavior that others can see and hear a student do; hence, it is also measurable. *Learn* (A) and *understand* (C) are verbs that refer to internal states, which others cannot observe students doing and which are also open to variable interpretations. The SMART acronym lists the characteristics of ideal learning objectives: specific, measurable, attainable, relevant or results oriented, and targeted (to learner and learning level). *Identify, define, describe, compare, contrast, analyze, classify, list,* and so on are some additional examples of measurable verbs. Therefore, (D) is incorrect.

111. A: Before delivering instruction, teachers must prepare students for learning by reviewing; getting them interested using a hook; focusing their attention using an anticipatory set; relating the new information they are about to teach to existing student knowledge; and informing students of the learning objective. Next, teachers deliver instruction by providing input and modeling or demonstrations. Then, teachers monitor for student comprehension by checking with students to see whether they understand the material, giving them guided practice and feedback on their practice without grading it. Finally, teachers give students an assignment that enables them to practice what they have learned independently and grade their completed assignments.

112. D: Every U.S. state has its own curriculum policy regarding health and physical education. Some require a minimum amount of credit in either health education (HE) or physical education (PE) or in both to graduate but do not require these courses otherwise in their curricula. Others require HE but not PE; others require PE but not HE; still others require both. Some states simply require these classes with no specifications; others require comprehensive courses. Some states specify course content areas, amounts of instruction, and grades; others specify some but not all of these.

113. D: The model described and named *direct instruction* (lower-case) by Rosenshine and Stevens in 1986 is a generic instructional model; the Direct Instruction (capitalized) model pioneered in the 1960s by Siegfried Engelmann and his colleagues is a specific instructional model. However, both share in common the characteristics of teacher-directed, skills-oriented (A), face-to-face, small-group (B) instruction that uses task analysis, deliberate sequencing (C), and explicit teaching (D).

114. A: Cooperative learning models and individualistic learning models both use criterion-referenced assessments to test student learning based on preestablished criteria. Competitive learning models, (B) and (C), use norm-referenced assessments to test student performance in comparison to that of other students. A major difference between cooperative and individualistic learning, even though they use the same type of assessment, is that students work separately in individualistic learning, whereas they work together in cooperative learning. Therefore, (D) is incorrect.

115. B: Brainstorming can be done alone by individual students, or together by more than one student, and with or without the teacher's active involvement. Role-playing (A) can be done with or without the teacher's active involvement but requires more than one student. Guided discovery (C) can be done by individual or multiple students but requires the teacher's active involvement to guide students. Cooperative learning (D) may be done with or without active teacher involvement but requires more than one student. (Note: For all techniques that can be done without active teacher involvement, it is assumed that the teacher has previously instructed the students in the procedures involved when necessary, e.g., if students were not already familiar with them.)

116. B: For teachers to self-analyze and adjust their own body language and movements within the classroom, video recordings would enable them to observe where they were positioned in the classroom; whether and how they moved around; and their posture, body language, and so on and make changes accordingly. Journals or diaries (A) help teachers reflect on what took place during class, their own reactions and feelings, student reactions they observed, and related questions that occur to them. Teachers may or may not recall their physical positions and movements, but they cannot view them as they can in videos. Audio recordings (C) give teachers a record of what was said but no visual recording. Peer observation (D) allows teachers to hear observations from colleagues about their physical positions and movements but not to observe and analyze these themselves.

117. C: Curriculum-based measurement (CBM) is a standardized measure that is used as a formative assessment to evaluate student progress during instruction. Final projects (A), end-of-unit tests (B), and standardized state examinations (D) are used as summative assessments to evaluate student learning after instruction.

118. B: Portfolio assessments are collections of student work products over time. They can be reviewed periodically during instructional units, school terms, or school years to evaluate progress during instruction as formative assessments, and as parts of comprehensive evaluations, they can be used as evidence of fulfilling learning objectives as summative assessments. Course grades (A) are typical examples of summative assessments. So are large-scale standardized tests (C), which assess learning after the fact. Teachers' observational checklists (D) are commonly used as formative assessments to inform teachers and students of student progress during instruction.

119. D: A rubric should be used before learning (C), when teachers go over all parts of the rubric with the students to explain how it defines what they are expected to learn, that is, their learning objectives. Then teachers should instruct students to use the rubric during learning (B) to guide their learning experiences, activities, and products according to the learning objectives specified in the rubric. Finally, teachers apply the rubric after learning (A) to assess whether the students have fulfilled the learning objectives it specifies.

120. D: It is recommended that the teacher speak with the student in private (A) if at all possible rather than discipline the student in front of the whole class (B). This can backfire in two ways: (1) Humiliating the student in front of the entire class can have a negative impact on the student's attitude, making the misbehavior worse, or (2) making the student the center of attention can reinforce the misbehavior if it is motivated by attention seeking. It is also important for the teacher to make clear to the student that it is the behavior, not the student him- or herself, which the teacher finds unacceptable.

How to Overcome Test Anxiety

Just the thought of taking a test is enough to make most people a little nervous. A test is an important event that can have a long-term impact on your future, so it's important to take it seriously and it's natural to feel anxious about performing well. But just because anxiety is normal, that doesn't mean that it's helpful in test taking, or that you should simply accept it as part of your life. Anxiety can have a variety of effects. These effects can be mild, like making you feel slightly nervous, or severe, like blocking your ability to focus or remember even a simple detail.

If you experience test anxiety—whether severe or mild—it's important to know how to beat it. To discover this, first you need to understand what causes test anxiety.

Causes of Test Anxiety

While we often think of anxiety as an uncontrollable emotional state, it can actually be caused by simple, practical things. One of the most common causes of test anxiety is that a person does not feel adequately prepared for their test. This feeling can be the result of many different issues such as poor study habits or lack of organization, but the most common culprit is time management. Starting to study too late, failing to organize your study time to cover all of the material, or being distracted while you study will mean that you're not well prepared for the test. This may lead to cramming the night before, which will cause you to be physically and mentally exhausted for the test. Poor time management also contributes to feelings of stress, fear, and hopelessness as you realize you are not well prepared but don't know what to do about it.

Other times, test anxiety is not related to your preparation for the test but comes from unresolved fear. This may be a past failure on a test, or poor performance on tests in general. It may come from comparing yourself to others who seem to be performing better or from the stress of living up to expectations. Anxiety may be driven by fears of the future—how failure on this test would affect your educational and career goals. These fears are often completely irrational, but they can still negatively impact your test performance.

Elements of Test Anxiety

As mentioned earlier, test anxiety is considered to be an emotional state, but it has physical and mental components as well. Sometimes you may not even realize that you are suffering from test anxiety until you notice the physical symptoms. These can include trembling hands, rapid heartbeat, sweating, nausea, and tense muscles. Extreme anxiety may lead to fainting or vomiting. Obviously, any of these symptoms can have a negative impact on testing. It is important to recognize them as soon as they begin to occur so that you can address the problem before it damages your performance.

The mental components of test anxiety include trouble focusing and inability to remember learned information. During a test, your mind is on high alert, which can help you recall information and stay focused for an extended period of time. However, anxiety interferes with your mind's natural processes, causing you to blank out, even on the questions you know well. The strain of testing during anxiety makes it difficult to stay focused, especially on a test that may take several hours. Extreme anxiety can take a huge mental toll, making it difficult not only to recall test information but even to understand the test questions or pull your thoughts together.

Effects of Test Anxiety

Test anxiety is like a disease—if left untreated, it will get progressively worse. Anxiety leads to poor performance, and this reinforces the feelings of fear and failure, which in turn lead to poor performances on subsequent tests. It can grow from a mild nervousness to a crippling condition. If allowed to progress, test anxiety can have a big impact on your schooling, and consequently on your future.

Test anxiety can spread to other parts of your life. Anxiety on tests can become anxiety in any stressful situation, and blanking on a test can turn into panicking in a job situation. But fortunately, you don't have to let anxiety rule your testing and determine your grades. There are a number of relatively simple steps you can take to move past anxiety and function normally on a test and in the rest of life.

Physical Steps for Beating Test Anxiety

While test anxiety is a serious problem, the good news is that it can be overcome. It doesn't have to control your ability to think and remember information. While it may take time, you can begin taking steps today to beat anxiety.

Just as your first hint that you may be struggling with anxiety comes from the physical symptoms, the first step to treating it is also physical. Rest is crucial for having a clear, strong mind. If you are tired, it is much easier to give in to anxiety. But if you establish good sleep habits, your body and mind will be ready to perform optimally, without the strain of exhaustion. Additionally, sleeping well helps you to retain information better, so you're more likely to recall the answers when you see the test questions.

Getting good sleep means more than going to bed on time. It's important to allow your brain time to relax. Take study breaks from time to time so it doesn't get overworked, and don't study right before bed. Take time to rest your mind before trying to rest your body, or you may find it difficult to fall asleep.

Along with sleep, other aspects of physical health are important in preparing for a test. Good nutrition is vital for good brain function. Sugary foods and drinks may give a burst of energy but this burst is followed by a crash, both physically and emotionally. Instead, fuel your body with protein and vitamin-rich foods.

Also, drink plenty of water. Dehydration can lead to headaches and exhaustion, especially if your brain is already under stress from the rigors of the test. Particularly if your test is a long one, drink water during the breaks. And if possible, take an energy-boosting snack to eat between sections.

Along with sleep and diet, a third important part of physical health is exercise. Maintaining a steady workout schedule is helpful, but even taking 5-minute study breaks to walk can help get your blood pumping faster and clear your head. Exercise also releases endorphins, which contribute to a positive feeling and can help combat test anxiety.

When you nurture your physical health, you are also contributing to your mental health. If your body is healthy, your mind is much more likely to be healthy as well. So take time to rest, nourish your body with healthy food and water, and get moving as much as possible. Taking these physical steps will make you stronger and more able to take the mental steps necessary to overcome test anxiety.

Mental Steps for Beating Test Anxiety

Working on the mental side of test anxiety can be more challenging, but as with the physical side, there are clear steps you can take to overcome it. As mentioned earlier, test anxiety often stems from lack of preparation, so the obvious solution is to prepare for the test. Effective studying may be the most important weapon you have for beating test anxiety, but you can and should employ several other mental tools to combat fear.

First, boost your confidence by reminding yourself of past success—tests or projects that you aced. If you're putting as much effort into preparing for this test as you did for those, there's no reason you should expect to fail here. Work hard to prepare; then trust your preparation.

Second, surround yourself with encouraging people. It can be helpful to find a study group, but be sure that the people you're around will encourage a positive attitude. If you spend time with others who are anxious or cynical, this will only contribute to your own anxiety. Look for others who are motivated to study hard from a desire to succeed, not from a fear of failure.

Third, reward yourself. A test is physically and mentally tiring, even without anxiety, and it can be helpful to have something to look forward to. Plan an activity following the test, regardless of the outcome, such as going to a movie or getting ice cream.

When you are taking the test, if you find yourself beginning to feel anxious, remind yourself that you know the material. Visualize successfully completing the test. Then take a few deep, relaxing breaths and return to it. Work through the questions carefully but with confidence, knowing that you are capable of succeeding.

Developing a healthy mental approach to test taking will also aid in other areas of life. Test anxiety affects more than just the actual test—it can be damaging to your mental health and even contribute to depression. It's important to beat test anxiety before it becomes a problem for more than testing.

Study Strategy

Being prepared for the test is necessary to combat anxiety, but what does being prepared look like? You may study for hours on end and still not feel prepared. What you need is a strategy for test prep. The next few pages outline our recommended steps to help you plan out and conquer the challenge of preparation.

STEP 1: SCOPE OUT THE TEST

Learn everything you can about the format (multiple choice, essay, etc.) and what will be on the test. Gather any study materials, course outlines, or sample exams that may be available. Not only will this help you to prepare, but knowing what to expect can help to alleviate test anxiety.

STEP 2: MAP OUT THE MATERIAL

Look through the textbook or study guide and make note of how many chapters or sections it has. Then divide these over the time you have. For example, if a book has 15 chapters and you have five days to study, you need to cover three chapters each day. Even better, if you have the time, leave an extra day at the end for overall review after you have gone through the material in depth.

If time is limited, you may need to prioritize the material. Look through it and make note of which sections you think you already have a good grasp on, and which need review. While you are studying, skim quickly through the familiar sections and take more time on the challenging parts.

Write out your plan so you don't get lost as you go. Having a written plan also helps you feel more in control of the study, so anxiety is less likely to arise from feeling overwhelmed at the amount to cover.

STEP 3: GATHER YOUR TOOLS

Decide what study method works best for you. Do you prefer to highlight in the book as you study and then go back over the highlighted portions? Or do you type out notes of the important information? Or is it helpful to make flashcards that you can carry with you? Assemble the pens, index cards, highlighters, post-it notes, and any other materials you may need so you won't be distracted by getting up to find things while you study.

If you're having a hard time retaining the information or organizing your notes, experiment with different methods. For example, try color-coding by subject with colored pens, highlighters, or post-it notes. If you learn better by hearing, try recording yourself reading your notes so you can listen while in the car, working out, or simply sitting at your desk. Ask a friend to quiz you from your flashcards, or try teaching someone the material to solidify it in your mind.

STEP 4: CREATE YOUR ENVIRONMENT

It's important to avoid distractions while you study. This includes both the obvious distractions like visitors and the subtle distractions like an uncomfortable chair (or a too-comfortable couch that makes you want to fall asleep). Set up the best study environment possible: good lighting and a comfortable work area. If background music helps you focus, you may want to turn it on, but otherwise keep the room quiet. If you are using a computer to take notes, be sure you don't have any other windows open, especially applications like social media, games, or anything else that could distract you. Silence your phone and turn off notifications. Be sure to keep water close by so you stay hydrated while you study (but avoid unhealthy drinks and snacks).

Also, take into account the best time of day to study. Are you freshest first thing in the morning? Try to set aside some time then to work through the material. Is your mind clearer in the afternoon or evening? Schedule your study session then. Another method is to study at the same time of day that you will take the test, so that your brain gets used to working on the material at that time and will be ready to focus at test time.

STEP 5: STUDY!

Once you have done all the study preparation, it's time to settle into the actual studying. Sit down, take a few moments to settle your mind so you can focus, and begin to follow your study plan. Don't give in to distractions or let yourself procrastinate. This is your time to prepare so you'll be ready to fearlessly approach the test. Make the most of the time and stay focused.

Of course, you don't want to burn out. If you study too long you may find that you're not retaining the information very well. Take regular study breaks. For example, taking five minutes out of every hour to walk briskly, breathing deeply and swinging your arms, can help your mind stay fresh.

As you get to the end of each chapter or section, it's a good idea to do a quick review. Remind yourself of what you learned and work on any difficult parts. When you feel that you've mastered the material, move on to the next part. At the end of your study session, briefly skim through your notes again.

But while review is helpful, cramming last minute is NOT. If at all possible, work ahead so that you won't need to fit all your study into the last day. Cramming overloads your brain with more information than it can process and retain, and your tired mind may struggle to recall even previously learned information when it is overwhelmed with last-minute study. Also, the urgent nature of cramming and the stress placed on your brain contribute to anxiety. You'll be more likely to go to the test feeling unprepared and having trouble thinking clearly.

So don't cram, and don't stay up late before the test, even just to review your notes at a leisurely pace. Your brain needs rest more than it needs to go over the information again. In fact, plan to finish your studies by noon or early afternoon the day before the test. Give your brain the rest of the day to relax or focus on other things, and get a good night's sleep. Then you will be fresh for the test and better able to recall what you've studied.

STEP 6: TAKE A PRACTICE TEST

Many courses offer sample tests, either online or in the study materials. This is an excellent resource to check whether you have mastered the material, as well as to prepare for the test format and environment.

Check the test format ahead of time: the number of questions, the type (multiple choice, free response, etc.), and the time limit. Then create a plan for working through them. For example, if you have 30 minutes to take a 60-question test, your limit is 30 seconds per question. Spend less time on the questions you know well so that you can take more time on the difficult ones.

If you have time to take several practice tests, take the first one open book, with no time limit. Work through the questions at your own pace and make sure you fully understand them. Gradually work up to taking a test under test conditions: sit at a desk with all study materials put away and set a timer. Pace yourself to make sure you finish the test with time to spare and go back to check your answers if you have time.

After each test, check your answers. On the questions you missed, be sure you understand why you missed them. Did you misread the question (tests can use tricky wording)? Did you forget the information? Or was it something you hadn't learned? Go back and study any shaky areas that the practice tests reveal.

Taking these tests not only helps with your grade, but also aids in combating test anxiety. If you're already used to the test conditions, you're less likely to worry about it, and working through tests until you're scoring well gives you a confidence boost. Go through the practice tests until you feel comfortable, and then you can go into the test knowing that you're ready for it.

Test Tips

On test day, you should be confident, knowing that you've prepared well and are ready to answer the questions. But aside from preparation, there are several test day strategies you can employ to maximize your performance.

First, as stated before, get a good night's sleep the night before the test (and for several nights before that, if possible). Go into the test with a fresh, alert mind rather than staying up late to study.

Try not to change too much about your normal routine on the day of the test. It's important to eat a nutritious breakfast, but if you normally don't eat breakfast at all, consider eating just a protein bar. If you're a coffee drinker, go ahead and have your normal coffee. Just make sure you time it so that the caffeine doesn't wear off right in the middle of your test. Avoid sugary beverages, and drink enough water to stay hydrated but not so much that you need a restroom break 10 minutes into the test. If your test isn't first thing in the morning, consider going for a walk or doing a light workout before the test to get your blood flowing.

Allow yourself enough time to get ready, and leave for the test with plenty of time to spare so you won't have the anxiety of scrambling to arrive in time. Another reason to be early is to select a good seat. It's helpful to sit away from doors and windows, which can be distracting. Find a good seat, get out your supplies, and settle your mind before the test begins.

When the test begins, start by going over the instructions carefully, even if you already know what to expect. Make sure you avoid any careless mistakes by following the directions.

Then begin working through the questions, pacing yourself as you've practiced. If you're not sure on an answer, don't spend too much time on it, and don't let it shake your confidence. Either skip it and come back later, or eliminate as many wrong answers as possible and guess among the remaining ones. Don't dwell on these questions as you continue—put them out of your mind and focus on what lies ahead.

Be sure to read all of the answer choices, even if you're sure the first one is the right answer. Sometimes you'll find a better one if you keep reading. But don't second-guess yourself if you do immediately know the answer. Your gut instinct is usually right. Don't let test anxiety rob you of the information you know.

If you have time at the end of the test (and if the test format allows), go back and review your answers. Be cautious about changing any, since your first instinct tends to be correct, but make sure you didn't misread any of the questions or accidentally mark the wrong answer choice. Look over any you skipped and make an educated guess.

At the end, leave the test feeling confident. You've done your best, so don't waste time worrying about your performance or wishing you could change anything. Instead, celebrate the successful completion of this test. And finally, use this test to learn how to deal with anxiety even better next time.

> **Review Video: Test Anxiety**
> Visit mometrix.com/academy and enter code: 100340

Important Qualification

Not all anxiety is created equal. If your test anxiety is causing major issues in your life beyond the classroom or testing center, or if you are experiencing troubling physical symptoms related to your anxiety, it may be a sign of a serious physiological or psychological condition. If this sounds like your situation, we strongly encourage you to seek professional help.

Thank You

We at Mometrix would like to extend our heartfelt thanks to you, our friend and patron, for allowing us to play a part in your journey. It is a privilege to serve people from all walks of life who are unified in their commitment to building the best future they can for themselves.

The preparation you devote to these important testing milestones may be the most valuable educational opportunity you have for making a real difference in your life. We encourage you to put your heart into it—that feeling of succeeding, overcoming, and yes, conquering will be well worth the hours you've invested.

We want to hear your story, your struggles and your successes, and if you see any opportunities for us to improve our materials so we can help others even more effectively in the future, please share that with us as well. **The team at Mometrix would be absolutely thrilled to hear from you!** So please, send us an email (support@mometrix.com) and let's stay in touch.

> **If you'd like some additional help, check out these other resources we offer for your exam:**
> **http://MometrixFlashcards.com/NESINC**

Additional Bonus Material

Due to our efforts to try to keep this book to a manageable length, we've created a link that will give you access to all of your additional bonus material:

mometrix.com/bonus948/nesinchealth